Latin Numbers

Latin Numbers

Playing Latino in Twentieth-Century
U.S. Popular Performance

BRIAN EUGENIO HERRERA

University of Michigan Press
Ann Arbor

Published in the United States of America by the
University of Michigan Press
Manufactured in the United States of America
⊗ Printed on acid-free paper

2018 2017   2016   2015   4   3   2   1

A CIP catalog record for this book is available from the British Library.
ISBN 978-0-472-07264-4 (hardcover : alk. paper)
ISBN 978-0-472-05264-6 (paperback : alk. paper)
ISBN 978-0-472-12106-9 (e-book)

In Loving Memory
Richard L. S. Herrera
(1942–2006)

Acknowledgments

———— ∾ ————

I wrote most of this book during a period of extraordinary transition, as I moved between two academic appointments, relocating from the Department of Theatre and Dance at the University of New Mexico to the Program in Theater in the Lewis Center of the Arts at Princeton University. The intellectual communities at each of these institutions incubated this book in essential ways as it was being written.

During my years at the University of New Mexico, I benefitted from the sustaining collegiality of a host of extraordinary artists and scholars in a broad array of departments and programs. Within UNM's Department of Theatre and Dance, Kristen Loree, Elaine Avila, and Susan Pearson greeted me as a fellow artist and enthusiastically embraced my scholarship as a work of creative investigation. James Linnell and Mary Anne Santos Newhall were fellow advocates of the value of historical inquiry within the art-making process. Beyond my home department at UNM, the intellectual companionship of Alex Lubin, Alyosha Goldstein, Amy Brandzel, Tey Diana Rebolledo, Elizabeth Q. Hutchison, Eva Hayward, Holly Barnet-Sanchez, Jesse Alemán, Monica Cyrino, and Rebecca Schreiber made the university an extraordinary place in which to develop this book.

Since arriving at Princeton, I have benefitted immeasurably from the generous, stimulating, and challenging mentorship provided by my Program in Theater colleagues Jill Dolan, Michael Cadden, Robert Sandberg, Tim Vasen, and Stacy Wolf, as well as the hospitality of the staff

and the affiliated faculty at Princeton's Lewis Center for the Arts, at the
Center for African American Studies, and in the programs in American
Studies, Latino Studies, and Gender and Sexuality Studies. At Princeton my work on this book was fortified by clarifying conversations with
Daphne Brooks, Wallace D. Best, Anne Cheng, Valerie Smith, Elizabeth
Armstrong, Tey Meadow, Gayle Salamon, Joseph Fonseca, and Alexandra Vazquez. For the invitation to share my work in conversation with
diverse segments of Princeton's intellectual community, I am especially
indebted to Patricia Fernandez-Kelly, Judith Weisenfeld, Edward Telles,
Marta Tienda, Alison Isenberg, Marni Sandweiss, Dirk Hartog, and Wen-
dy Belcher. I gratefully acknowledge my many colleagues at both UNM
and Princeton for their contributions to this book's completion.

Three particular intellectual communities sustained me at critical
junctures in this project's development. First, my earliest articulations
of this project's guiding premise happened at what we, as graduate students at Yale University, simply called "quilting." My "quilting" cohort—
as led by the expertise and vision of Heather A. Williams—included
Qiana Whitted, Françoise Hamlin, Leigh Raiford, Lisa McGill, Tanya
Hart, Catherine Whalen, Andrea Becksvoort, Victorine Shepard, Elaine
Lewinnek, Kari Main, Aaron Wong, and Robin Bernstein (our resident
whittler), among others. This ad hoc convening of crafty geniuses gathered to piece, stitch, and configure extraordinary visions from mere
scraps. Along the way, we also modeled a practice of reciprocal mentorship that inspires and guides me still. It was at quilting that I first gained
the confidence that, at its core, this project was one worth pursuing.

Next, it was the friends of StinkyLulu who brought me back to this
project at my moment of deepest doubt and most paralyzing writer's
block. "StinkyLulu" is the *nom de blog* under which I wrote thousands
upon thousands of words of online film and cultural commentary, all
when I should have been writing my dissertation. It was through my StinkyLulu blog that I began to truly appreciate the pleasure and privilege of
writing for an inspiring, discerning, and unsparing audience, especially
one that knew me only through the words I wrote. My years of work as
StinkyLulu tutored me in the rigors of writerly discipline and introduced
me to an inspiring blogging cohort of fellow cinephiles, some of whom—
Gabriel Shanks, Nick Davis, Nathaniel Davis, Michael W. Phillips, Jeffrey
Middents, Bobby Rivers, Manuel Betancourt, Manuel Muñoz, and Aaron
C. Thomas, among others—also became valued colleagues "in real life."
Writing as StinkyLulu taught me many things, but more than anything,
crafting pieces for StinkyLulu's readers eased me out of my crippling

writer's block and convinced me that I could write words worth reading. I am enduringly grateful to StinkyLulu's dedicated readership for that simple gift.

Finally, I am grateful to the hundreds of students at the University of New Mexico, especially the many who showed up each term, under the duress of degree requirements, to take one or the other of my two-semester world theatre history survey course. My UNM students configured the audience that most helped me to discover and trust my own authorial voice. As I sought to balance the big theoretical questions with the minutiae of historical detail, all in the context of brisk surveys of culturally complicated performance, my UNM students reminded me, time and again, that the most intricate ideas came through most vividly when I chose to speak with my own voice, perhaps adding a dash of humor. My learning curve as a teacher of large lecture courses was at times quite steep, and so I remain grateful for the presence and perspective of those graduate students (including Casey Mraz, Erin Phillips Mraz, Kevin R. Elder, and Riti Sachdeva) charged with the task of assisting me along the way. Being part of each of these communities—quilting, writing as StinkyLulu, and teaching the many extraordinary students at UNM—are among the happiest privileges of my personal and professional life, and I am proud to carry some of what I learned from each of these communities forward with this book.

Funding, programmatic, and institutional support from a variety of sources proved essential to this manuscript's development. Research and Career Development grants from the dean of the College of Fine Arts at UNM, along with a grant for Researchers with Heavy Teaching Loads from the American Society for Theatre Research, enabled my participation in crucial conferences and symposia. A Dissertation Fellowship from the Ford Foundation underwrote a pivotal year in this project's earliest development. My interlocutors at a broad array of campus presentations both challenged and inspired me to refine the clarity of my work. Alex Lubin and Rebecca Schreiber's invitation to present an early iteration of what became this book's first chapter as part of UNM's "Transnational Americas" lecture series helpfully directed the manuscript's route of revision. A well-timed grant from UNM's Feminist Research Institute prompted my return to the materials comprising this book's fifth chapter. Invitations from the National Association of Latino Arts and Cultures to offer the keynote address at the Regional Arts Training Workshops in both Albuquerque and the Bronx enabled me to refine what became the book's prologue. An unexpected grant of teaching leave awarded by the

Provost of UNM, together with a partial teaching release during my first semester at Princeton, afforded me the necessary time to continue my writing, even amid the interruption of a cross-country move. At Princeton the opportunity to teach a course called "Playing Latino" amplified the book's focus in unexpected ways. Thanks are due to the students in that course, especially Jenesis Fonseca, for reminding me why I sought to undertake this project in the first place.

I developed this book's many components in conversation with a great many brilliant minds. I have been fortunate to count among my interlocutors Shannon Steen, Shafali Lal, Sandy Zipp, Philip Nel, Penny Farfan, Patrick C. Snee, Patricia Ybarra, Patricia Herrera, Michael Wolfe, Michael Cohen, Meredith Raimondo, Mark Krasovic, Lyneise Williams, Lawrence La Fountain-Stokes, Kirsten Pullen, Kimberly Ramírez, Julia Foulkes, Joseph Entin, Jonathan Kidd, Jennifer Greeson, Jason Ramírez, Jason Shaffer, Irma Mayorga, Ferentz LaFargue, Eric-Christopher Garcia, Emily Meixner, Dorian Warren, Deb Paredez, David Ebershoff, Christine Evans, Christian McMillan, Cheryl Finley, Ben Caldwell, Ashley Lucas, Amy Reading, and Aaron Sachs. Formal and informal conversations at meetings of the American Society for Theatre Research, the American Studies Association, the Comparative Drama Conference, and the Latino Focus Group of the Association for Theatre in Higher Education afforded invaluable opportunities to rehearse the ideas animating this book. Long before the contours of this project came into focus, the academic mentorship of Jane Caputi, Gerald L. Davis, and Dorothy Chansky was invaluable. I remain indebted to Beth Bailey, under whose careful scrutiny the beginnings of this book's fifth chapter first found shape. Foundational conversations about this project with Glenda Gilmore, Nancy Cott, Laura Wexler, Alicia Schmidt-Camacho, Stephen Pitti, and Jean-Christophe Agnew offered generous, exacting early guidance. Throughout, Joseph Roach's example—melding adventurous intellect with impassioned pedagogy to forge discipline-defying scholarship— continues to inspire my work as a performance scholar. As I first began to think about the particulars of this project, the publication of three field-defining books on performance by three out gay Latino scholars— Alberto Sandoval-Sánchez, David Román, and José Esteban Muñoz— proved both inspiring and intimidating, and I am grateful to this queer trinity for their fierce generosity in breaking this path and for being so welcoming when I invited myself along.

Writing an original, interdisciplinary work of scholarly nonfiction can take a while, and the experience often feels like a cruel test of endurance, wherein the presumptive finish line keeps being pushed farther down the track. Thus, the presence of cheerleaders along that long path to publication can make all the difference. This book is better for the generous attention to it (and me) offered by three very different writing groups comprised of, respectively, Kip Kosek, Robin Bernstein, and Tavia Nyong'o; Betsy Erbaugh and Kate Lehman; and Chris Eboch, Kimberley Griffiths Little, Lois Bradley, and Caroline Starr Rose. In each of these groups, I felt like a writer among writers, which eases the isolated work of writing in all kinds of ways. Cary Tennis and Lynn C. Miller also shared their writerly tools, expertise, and wisdom with prodding generosity. Although they might not have known it at the time, simple gestures of intellectual friendship from Stacy Wolf, David Román, and Jorge Huerta, as well as invitations to collaborate from Henry Bial and Nick Salvato, boosted my morale at critical moments. Ramón Rivera-Servera's gentle but steady queries about the book's progress kept me honest; Jon D. Rossini's stealthy advance promotion of the book's potential contribution to the field kept me on task; and Davíd Hernandez's infectious enthusiasm for my work never failed to fill the sails of my confidence. Early on, Robin Bernstein became one of this work's most steadfast champions. I would have almost certainly consigned this project to the digital limbo of unrevised dissertations were it not for Robin's persistent encouragement; I am grateful for her astute colleagueship. This project's staunchest advocate, though, has always been Matthew Frye Jacobson, whose long-standing, tenacious support of my work and me kept me going, especially when the going got really, really tough.

LeAnn Fields of the University of Michigan Press had her eye trained on this project for a good while, and I am grateful both for her patience and for her expertise in bringing it to press. Thanks, too, to Alexa Ducsay, Christopher Dreyer, and Marcia LaBrenz, and to the manuscript's anonymous readers for their invaluable guidance. A modified version of chapter 5 appeared as "Toying with Desire" in *TDR: The Drama Review* 58, no. 4 (Winter 2014) and excerpts from chapter 3 appeared in "Compiling *West Side Story*'s Parahistories, 1949–2009," in *Theatre Journal* 64, no. 2 (May 2012). Thanks to the publishers for their permission to use this material in the present work. Financial support from Princeton's University Committee in the Humanities and Social Sciences assisted with the manuscript's preparation and acquisition of image permissions. Collaborating with artist Chad Sell on the cover illustration proved to be an unexpectedly clarifying delight, as did working with Daniel Gundlach on the book's index. Throughout, the extraordinarily keen yet exceptionally kind editorial acumen of Roxanne Willis guided me through the painstaking work of final revision and kept me on track, on task, and on time.

It might seem odd to speak of a first book as a life's work, but the questions animating this book have been among those I've been asking since I was a small child. Indeed, the members of my extended family were my first mentors along the winding path that ultimately led to this publication. My paternal grandmother, Nellie Herrera, became perhaps the first champion of my research method when I was about seven years old, and she defended my predilection, peculiar to some, for reading and watching television at the same time (a skill that would become invaluable to my professional development as a scholar of popular performance). For his part, my grandfather, Max Herrera, seemed never to tire of my telling him all about my favorite stars and the different shows in which they appeared. With my cousins, Judi Garduño-Gallegos and Terri Mares, I first practiced what I now recognize as the techniques of critical fandom, as we together parsed the career choices of the "Spanish" (and "Spanish-ish") actors and actresses who so fascinated us. In ways both large and small, my maternal grandparents, Ed and Ida Ehrman, provided unflagging emotional and material support of my educational aspirations. My sister, Saudi Herrera, became my first pupil in the fine arts of "rewatching" and pop cultural connoisseurship. My parents, Richard and Diana Herrera, taught me early on to recognize and value the hard work of principled, gifted educators. Their stewardship of my schooling in New Mexico and Saudi Arabia provided me with a foundation I treasure to this day. When the time came for me to choose a high school, my father—mistrustful of the boarding-school options open to me as an expat kid in Saudi Arabia—opted to leave his highly remunerative job abroad and bring the family back to New Mexico, where I might attend the award-winning high school in our home district. Of course, at the time, I was outraged, but today I am humbled by my father's foresight. At Manzano High School in Albuquerque, New Mexico, I not only encountered the band of brainy misfits who became my lifelong friends but I also entered the classrooms of formidable public school teachers like Clara Sanchez, who introduced me to the power of both Chicana poetry and close reading, and Joyce Briscoe, who opened my eyes to the fact that history is as much about art, literature, and ideas as it is about maps, generals, and dates. My parents also encouraged me to go far away from New Mexico to Brown University for college, where mentors like Martin

U. Martel, George Houston Bass, Tori Haring-Smith, Paula Vogel, and David Savran prompted and prodded me to become the peculiar kind of historian I clearly wanted to be. It shakes me a bit to realize how many of these treasured mentors have passed on, many during the years since I began this project, and so I offer this book as a small tribute to the legacy of these many educators (some possessing college degrees, some not) who together provided me with the intellectual foundations on which I built not only this work but all the work that I do.

My parents also believed that friends are family, and my friends have only confirmed their faith. My archival passions were first stirred by my beloved friend since childhood, Nilz (Inez Na-gig) Fullerton, whose pre-ternatural gift for making art from scraps of the past never fails to aston-ish me. Tanya Ward Goodman's example—as a seeker, as a companion, as a parent, as a daughter, but especially as a writer—always reminds me that I first must do the hard work so that I might be ready to recognize its reward. At an important crossroads in my life, as I struggled to find my footing, Kari Main offered me her steady hand; I will forever remain in her debt for that simple yet enormous act of friendship. I am also deeply grateful to the many friends, like Tim, Joe, and especially Leanne, who taught me to recognize the perils of my own grandiosity and (along with hundreds of others whose last names I'll never know) tutored me to stay rigorously honest and keep things simple. I feel incredibly fortunate that my most stalwart friend, Brad Griffith, is also an omnivorous culture hound and that he has always been game to be my most vigorous sound-ing board whenever a new idea starts to simmer.

Finally, when I began this project, I had not yet met the man who would become my partner. Michael Quanci started out as my friend, became my sweetheart, and is now my family. The life we have built together over the past ten years has housed this project, for better and for worse. This book arrives to you, in no small part, because of Michael's forthright belief that I could, that I should, and that I would write it. I thank him for his faith in me, and for so much more. And I know we are both ready for me to send this book out into the world. So here goes.

Brian Eugenio Herrera
Princeton, New Jersey

Contents

Latina/o visibility through *Time*. *Clockwise from top left:* in 1978, "Hispanic Americans. Soon: The Biggest Minority"; in 1988, "*¡Magnifico!* Hispanic Culture Breaks Out of the Barrio"; in 1999, "Latin Music Goes Pop!"; and in 2012, "*Yo Decido.* Why Latinos Will Pick the Next President." (Cover images by permission of Time, Inc.)

Prologue

In early 2012, as the nation anticipated the upcoming presidential election and considered the US Census Bureau's recent projections that non-Hispanic whites would likely become a minority within three or four decades, the question of Latino voter participation loomed large. *Time* magazine's cover—"*Yo Decido*. Why Latinos Will Pick the Next President" (March 5, 2012)—both named and framed the uncertainties surrounding the anticipated impact of shifting Latino demographics on US electoral politics. The cover's dual declamations provoked vague curiosity— at once ominous and auspicious, as much a threat as a promise—about what Latinos were about to do in ways both highly contemporary and utterly familiar. While the "*Yo Decido*" cover was clearly about the very contemporary questions of voter participation, it also brought to mind another *Time*.

More than thirty years earlier, on October 16, 1978, *Time* dedicated its first cover to US Latinos: "Hispanic Americans. Soon: The Biggest Minority."[1] Both the 2012 and 1978 covers depict diversities intrinsic to US Latinidad, with 1978's rough collage of faces refracting 2012's precise mosaic of squared pictures (which might be equally suitable for a passport photo or an online profile). Both covers stir the same sense of inevitability, a comparable concern over the apparent fact that this startlingly disparate group, called "Hispanic" in one decade and "Latino" in another, is somehow "next," is "soon," is about to matter to American life. Indeed, while these two covers are as different as 2012 was from

1978, something about these two moments in *Time* seems strikingly similar. Because, as these two magazine covers remind us, Latinos have been
about to become important for a good long while.

In 1978, Latinas/os were "soon" to become the biggest minority.
(The feature accompanying the 1978 cover was titled "It's Your Turn in
the Sun.") In 1988, Latinas/os were "*¡Magnifico!* Hispanic Culture Breaks
Out of the Barrio"—and this *Time* devoted a special issue to the cultural influence of Latinos within US popular performance and culture.[2]
Then, in 1999, Latinas/os went pop! (In the 1999 "Latin Music Goes
Pop!" feature, *Time* appointed Puerto Rican music star Ricky Martin as
the photogenic poster boy for the magazine's investigation of Latinas/
os as an important new cultural force.) The 1999 feature story enthused,
"[W]ith Hispanics poised to become America's largest minority group
within the next few years, [Latin] music might just be the sound of your
future."[3] Indeed, by 2012, *Time*'s sudden "discoveries" of US Latinas/os
had become something of a tradition.

But Ricky Martin's solo status as 1999's breakout Latin act did not
last long. Soon, even as his hit song "Livin' La Vida Loca" continued to
lead the pop charts through the summer of 1999, Martin was only the
first of a number of Latin artists to "pop" that season. Indeed, just six
weeks after Martin headlined for *Time*, the magazine's main competition
upped the ante.

On July 12, 1999, *Newsweek* ran its own "Latin" cover—"Latin U.S.A.:
How Young Hispanics Are Changing America."[4] In contrast to *Time*'s
Ricky Martin feature (a single Latin going pop), the *Newsweek* cover carefully created a composite portrait of "Latin U.S.A." Slightly foreground-
ed in the cover image, with his arms prominently crossed, stood Oscar
De La Hoya, the then undefeated welterweight boxer, Olympic medalist
(having won gold for the United States at the 1992 Barcelona games),
and second-generation Mexican American, born and raised in Los Angeles.[5] At the rear stood acclaimed author Junot Díaz—born in the Dominican Republic and raised since the age of six in central New Jersey—
the breakout literary phenomenon, whose debut short story collection,
Drown, had been released to an avalanche of acclaim in 1996.[6] Between
these two men stood Shakira, the Colombia-born singer-songwriter who
had just released her greatest international hit album and, with the support of producer Emilio Estefan, had recently begun to headquarter her
career in the United States.[7] Thus, *Newsweek*'s visual representation of
"Latin U.S.A." evocatively featured three prominent twenty-something
Latinos—an athlete, a musician, and an author—each ostensibly repre-

sentative of three distinct histories of Latina/o immigration (a recent immigrant, a member of the 1.5 generation, and an American-born child of immigrants), together representing three key regional vectors of recent (as well as historical) Latina/o immigration to the United States: Mexico, the Caribbean, and Latin America. These three—Shakira, Díaz, and De La Hoya—were emblematic of the cover story's main interests: how young Hispanics are changing America (as stated on the cover) and (as the magazine's table of contents proclaimed) how "Hispanics are hip, hot, and about to make history."[8]

But *Newsweek* was not the last of the major weeklies to focus on the cultural impact of Latinas/os as its feature story. On September 6, 1999, an actual "Latin Explosion" happened on the cover of *New York* magazine, which (for the first time in its history) changed its name and published its early fall issue under the banner *Nueva York*, with actress-cum-recording-star Jennifer Lopez posed provocatively in the cover image.[9] At the time of its publication of the *Nueva York* issue, *New York* magazine reported finding only one previous feature story on Latino culture and style in its archive (a short fashion piece in the early 1970s). As cultural critic Juan Flores pointedly observed, "[T]he theme of *Nueva York*, after all is 'The Latin Explosion,' those words emblazoned in bold yellow and white lettering across the half-exposed midsection of Jennifer Lopez. The Nuyorican actress, singer, and pop idol is surely 'Miss *Nueva York*' in our time." Flores added, "Latino fever is gripping U.S. popular culture at a pitch unprecedented in the protracted history of that continental seduction."[10]

As the summer of 1999 ended, the first Latino cast member of *Saturday Night Live*, Horatio Sanz—in the second episode of his second season as a featured player on the late-night television sketch comedy series—offered an "editorial" segment on that episode's "Weekend Update," the program's feature satirizing current events in the style of a nightly news broadcast. In his commentary, the Chile-born, Chicago-raised Sanz asked, "What Latin Explosion? There are . . . like . . . three. When Matchbox 20, Third Eye Blind, and The Offspring were all on the Top 20, no one called it a jackass explosion."[11] Sanz's comedic critique addressed a general sentiment that imbued 1999's "Latin explosion"—one shared by Latina/o and non-Latina/o audiences alike, and one apt for any such "boom" in interest in US Latinas/os. Was this sudden fascination with Latina/o cultural influence in the United States really a new thing? A really big deal? Or was it a marketing thing? A boilerplate publishing trend in a slow news cycle? Or might Hispanics actually be "hip, hot, and about to make history"?[12]

As Sanz's quip suggests, the "Latin explosion" does not necessarily describe an actual proliferation of Latina/o cultural workers. Rather, this peculiar phenomenon of fascinated discovery of Latinas/os is its own form of recurring, spectacular entertainment. In this book, I offer the term *Latin numbers* to describe such moments of spectacular proliferation of Latinos on the varied stages of US popular performance. Defined as much by its quick dissipation as its sudden eruption, a "Latin number" (like 1999's purported "Latin explosion") enacts the notion that Latinos are—in one way or another—newly significant arrivals to US culture. Each Latin number typically begins with an excited discovery of Latinos ("their" distinctiveness, youth, diversity, religiosity, cultural flavor, and sheer numbers), and this discovery spectacularizes a somehow transformative challenge Latinos are about to present to mainstream US culture. I use the term *Latin number* to mark the discrete historical moments in which a briefly intensified media interest queries the ways in which Latinos might soon be important within US culture, life, and politics. I also use *Latin number* to hail these moments of fleeting fascination with Latino individuals, Latino stories, and Latino cultural forms. (Whether everyone is "suddenly" doing the tango in the 1920s, the mambo in the 1950s, or the macarena in the 1990s, you can be sure that—in any Latin number— the rhythm is gonna get you.) A "Latin number" is a mainstream cultural fascination with Latino-ness, which both highlights and obscures the cultural presence, influence, and impact of actual Latinas/os.

As a phenomenon of fascinated discovery and casual disregard, the "Latin number"—like 1999's Latin explosion—typically manifests within a cycle of heightened Latina/o visibility in all media. In such historical moments, Latina/o cultural workers and expressive forms become novelties requiring both introduction and translation, in ways that somehow forget that US audiences already know a little (or a lot) about Carmen Miranda, Speedy Gonzales, Charo, and George Lopez (each of whom became iconic while enacting previous "Latin numbers"). In such moments of amplified Latina/o media presence, the "Latin number" also prompts discursive postures of studied uncertainty as to whether, where, and how Latinas/os might fit within existing cultural systems of power— racial hierarchies, legitimated citizenship, educational achievement, and electoral participation—while also eliding the diverse histories of political struggle for inclusion enacted by prior generations of Latina/o cultural activists. Then the fascination with all things "Latin" dissipates just as abruptly it began, when mainstream cultural attention deflects interest from the "Latin fad" to something—to anything—else. As a performance scenario, then, each historical "Latin number" rehearses audiences and actors in the spectacular notion that Latino cultural influence is new, Latino cultural forms are foreign, and Latinos themselves do not yet fit within US cultural systems. At the same time, the "Latin number" scenario makes Latinos freshly legible (and the category of Latino newly "real") to and for US audiences. In short, each "Latin number" makes Latinos "new" all over again, thereby making historical amnesia an entertaining diversion for Latino and non-Latino audiences alike.

"Latin numbers" typically burst onto the stages of US popular performance like flashy fireworks. First there is an attention-grabbing pop, followed by an often spectacular display, which gathers some measure of excited attention and then fizzles, leaving the perhaps breathless (perhaps weary) audience to other diversions until the next Latin number explodes on the scene. (Which might happen, if the last forty years of *Time* magazine are to be believed, in ten or twelve years.) By reenacting this scenario of discovery, fascination, and disposal, each "Latin number" also prompts audiences to delight in Latino cultural workers and cultural forms as perpetual novelties—as always already unfamiliar, exotic, and best enjoyed as a diversion from more "serious" forms of entertainment—a recurrent contemporaneity that harks back to earlier centuries while reminding audiences to think back only a handful of years.

Each Latin number's rhythm of discovery, fascination, and discard is like a dance, one that might feel momentarily new but has actually been long rehearsed. And much that is enduring does come from each of these "Latin numbers." Careers can be fortified. Miranda and Montalban, Olmos and Estefan, Ricky and Jennifer . . . most of the most enduring Latina/o figures in US popular performance became iconic amid the surging swirl of one or another of these periods of faddish fascination. The fleeting fixation on Latin numbers often accelerates the production and distribution of Latina/o-themed film, television, theatre, and other performance projects. Some such projects even enter the repertoire, the canon, or reruns as a result. Indeed, as recurring scenarios of emphatic contemporaneity, Latin numbers typically do not make or change history, but the performances animated by them—the careers, the compositions, the characters, the conventions—often do.

Playing Latino

Latin Numbers does not endeavor to create a comprehensive catalog of US Latinos/as in twentieth-century popular entertainment and performance. The story follows a loose chronology, but it is not necessarily a sequential story. Rather, *Latin Numbers* narrates a set of overlapping historical moments in which an evident fascination with the people, regions, traditions, and styles we might today recognize as Latina/o absorbed significant interest and attention within popular film, theatre, and television. Some of these epochs were conspicuous and spectacular; others were more subtle and subtextual. Some accumulated around particular performances, others around questions of form in performance, and still others seemed to be only incidentally about Latinas/os at all. But in each "Latin number," we can see a historical proliferation of presence—of either Latina/o actors or Latina/o characters or both simultaneously—and at such moments we can also evince the performance strategies that rehearsed and conventionalized the act of "playing Latino."

The formulation of "playing Latino" that I rehearse in *Latin Numbers* has been guided by the clarifying example provided by other scholars of racialized ethnicity in US popular culture, entertainment, and performance, perhaps most especially the work of Philip J. Deloria in *Playing Indian* (1998) and Henry Bial in *Acting Jewish: Negotiating Ethnicity on the American Stage and Screen* (2005).[13] In these two very different works, Deloria and Bial take bold, multidisciplinary approaches to a diverse assortment of performance strategies and styles, as they chart what Deloria calls "the persistent tradition in American culture" of performing ethnic otherness (respectively, "playing Indian" and "acting Jewish") within and for mainstream American culture. In their different ways, both authors explicate what Bial calls "the specific means and mechanisms by which a performance can communicate one message" to those being performed "while simultaneously communicating another, often contradictory message" to the broader audiences for which the performance is intended.[14]

Yet, even as I am inspired by the affinities between Deloria and Bial, *Latin Numbers* also moves in the conceptual space mapped by their differences. Just as Deloria's *Playing Indian* examines how "savage Indians served Americans as oppositional figures against whom one might imagine a civilized National self," *Latin Numbers* explicates how performing "the Latin" became a particularly expedient mechanism through which to rehearse the racialization of certain "types" of ethnicities, and in so doing helped to consolidate a normative American whiteness.[15] At the same time, riffing on Bial's central intervention in *Acting Jewish*, *Latin Numbers* argues that "a performance-based analysis of significant performances" involving Latina/o characters, narratives, and performers in twentieth-century US theater, film, and television is "essential to understanding the formulation" of US Latina/o identity over the same period.[16] So—not unlike Deloria—I wrote *Latin Numbers* to examine popular performance as a complex racializing mode, even as I—not unlike Bial—also study how popular performance offers a clarifying measure of the shifting articulations of ethnic identity formation over time.

So, although this book might just as easily have easily been called *Playing Latino* or *Acting Latino*, I offer it under the title *Latin Numbers: Playing Latino in Twentieth-Century Popular Performance* precisely because *Latin numbers* captures my interest in the historical specificity of this fascination, while *playing Latino* amplifies my interest in the always dynamic and processual dimensions of racializing performance—always in rehearsal and never finally performed. I therefore offer the overlain ideas of "Latin numbers" and of "playing Latino" to prompt a simultaneous consideration of the historical and processual ubiquity (rather than the novelty) of Latina/o influence in US expressive culture and popular performance in the twentieth century. In this way, this book also responds to the challenge posed by pathbreaking Chicana historian Vicki Ruiz in her 2006 presidential address before the membership of the Organization of American Historians. In her remarks, Ruiz called for historians of the United States to "reimagin[e] an American narrative with Latinos as meaningful actors,"[17] and a "reperiodized" United States using key dates—1848, 1898, and 1948—of relevance and significance to Latina/o history. As a historian of Latinas/os in US popular performance, I find Ruiz's phrasing—"reimagining an American narrative with Latinos as meaningful actors"—dually significant for my work in this book. For not only do I endeavor to consider Latinos as meaningful actors in US history but I also aim to offer Latina/o actors themselves— the performers who have captivated Latino/a and non-Latina/o audiences alike throughout the twentieth century—as historical actors, or as agents of historical change over time. In particular, this study explores how Latina/o performers were historically significant—and occasionally instrumental—in the historical processes of racialization of Latinas/os as an aggregate ethnoracial group in the United States in the twentieth century.

Each chapter of *Latin Numbers* asks variants of a question: how did popular performance rehearse US audiences in recognizing a "new" ethnoracial category of distinction for Mexicans, Puerto Ricans, and Cubans—peoples considered to be ethnically, nationally, and even racially distinct in the United States at the beginning of the twentieth century—and so categorize them as "Hispanics" or "Latinos" by century's end? Or, put another way, how did playing Latino rehearse the idea that Latinos were a distinct (and distinctly "nonwhite") ethnic group in the United States? This study looks to the performance venues of mainstream theatre, film, and television for answers. Through a selection of case studies—or "Latin numbers"—I investigate how particular historical moments in US popular performance enacted and enlivened changing twentieth-century North American notions of race and ethnicity, bringing these shifts in racial formation "to life" for audiences in the United States. In so doing, popular performance proved crucially instrumental in developing "Hispanic" and "Latino" as viable categories of ethnoracial aggregation for these ethnically, culturally, and regionally distinct peoples in the United States.

To "play Latino" is to enact Latina/o racial formation before an audience. Sometimes a playing-Latino performance works, capturing the imagination and attention of an audience for a moment. Sometimes a playing-Latino performance is a smash, reaching a vast array of audiences and establishing new genres, styles, and conventions for subsequent eras. And sometimes a playing-Latino performance bombs. However, each performance in which the choice is made to play Latino stages an encounter: between ideologies of racial purity and histories of miscegenation, at the juncture of a nationalized US border and the contiguities of hemispheric cultural transmission, and in the exchange between "Latin" performances and variously "American" audiences. More generally, playing Latino is a specific model for understanding how popular performance—in theatre, film, television, and live expressive culture—is instrumental in processes of racial formation in US cultural history for all ethnoracial groups in the United States. *Latin Numbers* examines an assortment of such playing-Latino performances in an array of venues (amateur theatricals, Hollywood films, Broadway musicals, broadcast television) to explicate how popular performance has been instrumental in enlivening and enacting shifting notions of race and ethnicity at specific, historical moments. *Latin Numbers* integrates these three typically segregated historical narratives—US social and cultural history, Latina/o history, and performance history—through particular case studies of genres, conventions, and styles of performance practice.

Popular Performance

When I began this project more than a decade ago, much excavation in the terrain of Latina/o presence in US popular culture remained to be done. In the intervening years, I have benefitted greatly as an array of scholars in a host of disciplines have published exemplary works evincing how Latina/o presence in US popular cultures expresses and explains core premises of US Latina/o identity, experience, culture, and history.[18] The accident of my delay provided an additional benefit. As my own thinking, teaching, and research continued to incubate within the redolent intellectual environment configured by these works, my rooting questions confirmed my own stake in this conversation: I am a performance historian intent on excavating the broad intermedial landscape of US popular entertainment through the lens of performance. More simply, I count myself a historian of US popular performance.

I define *popular performance* as those practices and products within expressive culture that are (1) animated by a performer's voice, body, and words; and (2) developed to be "widely accessible and widely accessed; widely disseminated; and widely viewed or heard or read."[19] Although other, more familiar terms (*commercial entertainments, mass culture,* or *popular culture*) might seem apt, my use of *popular performance* aims to emphasize the particular collaborative processes, techniques, and methods of performance that compose the products of commercial, mass, and popular entertainment, whether on the stage of a Broadway theatre or on the soundstage of a Hollywood studio. In this way, my work follows that of David Román, who has invited performance scholars and cultural historians to interrogate the "romance with the indigenous" that tends toward a "valorization" of "what is thought to be natural," "unmediated," or "seemingly authentic." For Román "the romance with the indigenous" reflects a "bias toward the grassroots and the community-based," and it also asserts a concomitant predisposition against "commercialism, commodity culture, or mainstream tastes" as somehow suspect or contaminated.[20] Román's notion of "grassroots-ism" endeavors, in part, to critique the monolithic view of the culture industries that is commonplace in the US academy while simultaneously broadening the definition of what qualifies as a performance worthy of and available for critical historical study.[21] My own approach both heeds Román's challenge and extends its reach.

To explain: as a performance historian, I go where performers go. As a performance historian specializing in the twentieth century, this means I often encounter both the opportunity and the obligation to follow a particular performer's, phenomenon's, or text's movements between and among venues. Yet, within the academy, such migrations—between film, television, and theatre; between "popular" and "fine" arts; between live and mediatized performance—often defy disciplinary convention. Even (or especially) in the emphatically defiant interdiscipline of performance studies, inceptive arguments over whether the ontology of performance inheres in the "live" event haunt even the boldest inquiries by performance scholars.[22] My approach to performances of the past admittedly does draw from a theatrical model in which rehearsals and improvisations configure an anticipated enactment. Perhaps as a result, while I do not dismiss either the ostensive or ontological differences imposed by the mediatized frame or the proscenium, I do scrutinize movies, radio, and television programs, as well as Broadway shows and amateur theatricals, for evidence of the production choices made during the crafting and execution of whatever performance is ultimately made available to the presumptive audience.[23] Perhaps emboldened by the work of my generational cohort in performance studies (and also by the critical intermedial lucidity modeled by my colleagues in dance studies),[24] I offer *Latin Numbers* as a study of how the performer's work (as an artist and a laborer) moves among industries, disciplines, and media in ways that document not only the general importance of performance within twentieth-century life but also the particular work that performers are asked do in times of cultural, demographic, and political upheaval.

As a term, *popular performance* also cues my critical investment in the process by which some constellation of performance-makers made performance, an interest that well exceeds my curiosity about what audiences thought about that work. This, too, defies academic convention. Just as the "live" in performance studies has anchored a critical orientation toward the meanings made between the performer and the audience, long traditions of inquiry into popular and mass culture have been primarily concerned with what mass entertainments said or did to a mass audience—or, by turn, what those audiences said or did back. My approach, however, is disinclined to assess what a given work said to or about its presumptive audience, just as I do not emphasize what that work's actual audience said about or to it. Instead, I look to the embedded logic expressed by the performance work itself: a group of highly skilled, ambitious, and creative artists made this set of performance choices because, in their best estimation, they thought those choices would serve their intended performance. By evaluating the operation of a creative choice (like the decision to cast a Mexican American actor to play a Japanese Kabuki master in a very serious role in a very serious mid-century film), I seek to divine neither the creative collaborators' intentions nor the audience's response but rather to discern some instructive cues as to why certain choices "made sense" in given historical moments.

Popular performance archives the commonsense conventions of the past. In the pages that follow, I discuss big hits and major misses, canonical works and nearly forgotten obscurities, enduring artistic triumphs, and ill-begotten disasters. When I consider a composer's biggest hit in the same discussion as one of his or her perhaps deservedly unperformed lyrics, or when I examined a film's deleted scenes or a show's dropped numbers, I seek insight beyond just the choices that did work; I also examine which choices this particular set of performance-makers also thought *might* work. Indeed, whether a creative choice lands on or misses its mark, the fact of its being a fully executed choice documents the parameters of plausibility at a particular historical moment.

But not everything in popular performance is a big hit or a major miss, and the banal middle of popular performance offers perhaps the deepest repository of the commonsense conventions of the past. To that end, I consciously assess popular performance's ever-widening midsection of works that are neither revered nor reviled but vividly confirm the viability of certain performance conventions. I look to the careers of middle-tier performance-makers, when I can, just as readily as I engage the work of their more uniformly acclaimed peers. My objective in such instances is not simply to recuperate and reclaim the relevance of these lives and works, in the same way that I do not necessarily hope to unveil previously undiscovered archives or narratives of resistance. Rather, I intend to show how the jobs taken by jobbing actors (rather than stars) or the scripts written for nearly forgotten plays, films, or television programs document at least as much—if not more—about what kinds of performance choices made sense at a particular historical moment. Indeed, for all their inconsistencies and incongruities, I submit that some of the most illuminating examples of the past's commonsense conventions derive most readily from popular performance's middling successes and minor failures.

Finally, and perhaps most necessarily, I define performance-makers as those who compose performances in shared space and time on a stage. Within this category, I count dramatic writers (playwrights, librettists, composers, choreographers) who not infrequently perform their own material (in development, rehearsal, and performance) and so craft their compositions within and through the act of performing. At the same time, I count actors, singers, and dancers not as vessels or vehicles for the compositions of others or as star-icon texts to be read and interpreted. Rather, I begin by considering each actor, singer, and dancer as a possible coauthor of the performance he or she is charged with enacting. Just as I consider it a foundational mistake to privilege performers' work on a theatre stage while ignoring or diminishing their often contemporaneous work on a soundstage, I likewise consider it fundamental to affirm that, even in the most hierarchical of productions, performers are always already both historical agents and creative collaborators. I thereby presume that every performer's on-stage choice also documents both the possibilities and limits scripted by the commonsense conventions of a given historical moment.

Playing Latin/a/o

Problems of terminology pose important questions in Latino studies, sustaining the scholarly convention of devoting significant prefatory attention to the particularities of labels and nomenclature, especially when such terminologies address ethnic, national, political, and cultural distinctions. As Nicholas De Genova and Ana Y. Ramos-Zayas have argued, "[T]he intrinsic incoherence of social categories such as 'Latino' or 'Hispanic,' combined with their persistent meaningfulness, are telltale indicators of the ongoing reconfiguration of 'Latinos' as a racial formation in the United States."[25] For the purposes of this project, my nomenclature decisions aim for simplicity and clarity, in terms of both style and content. While I prefer the term *Latino* to *Hispanic*, I utilize both to evoke the distinct political implications of each. As a general rule, I use *Latino* to describe histories, communities, and individuals, while reserving *Hispanic* for descriptions of government policies and mainstream cultural attitudes. When appropriate, important, or instructive, I adopt a more precise regional, national, or cultural descriptor. For example, I might refer to Ricardo Montalban as Mexican, Mexican American, Hispanic, or Latino, each term being factually correct, depending on context. Likewise, I typically reserve *Latina/o* for narrative moments when gender diversity and inclusivity are (or should be) relevant vectors of analysis or description. By specifying these terminological choices, I hope to assure readers that my use of this array of terms signals neither inconsistency nor assertions of "correctness" on my part. Rather, I hope to utilize the diversity of this range of terminological options to achieve descriptive precision in both tone and content.[26]

Some readers may already have been surprised by my use of the term *Latin* to describe the performance tradition analyzed in *Latin Numbers*, as well as the performers and performances "playing Latino" therein. To be sure, *Latin* is hardly an innocent or transparent term. Alberto

Sandoval-Sánchez has succinctly—and to my mind accurately—defined *Latin* as "a denomination imposed by an Anglo-American system of power," an "act of cultural appropriation" that "accommodates Anglo-American ways of seeing and cultural discursive models of the other."[27] Most Latina/o studies scholars have approached the term *Latin* (and its corollary, *Latinization*) along these lines. Frances R. Aparicio and Susana Chávez-Silverman have described Latinization as the "commodification" and "reformulation of cultural icons by the dominant sector."[28] Thus, the terms *Latin, Latinization,* and *Latin-ness* describe cultural mechanisms of appropriation and, just as often, misunderstanding. In no small part, my conscious use of the word *Latin* aims to evoke Chicano activist César Chavez's lucid cynicism when he commented on the US cultural appropriation of Latino cultural materials in 1974 by saying, "[T]hey take what they want and ridicule the rest."[29]

My use of *Latin* aims to prompt a critical lucidity regarding the often ridiculous appropriation of Latina/o characters, narratives, styles, and forms within US popular performance. At the same time, the archive from which this project draws—commercial film, theatre, and television; amateur theatricals; and the ephemera of the popular media—operates almost entirely in a realm where such commodification and appropriation occurs almost as a matter of course. To excavate the archive of popular performance is also to privilege those "Latin numbers" in which the act of playing Latino documents the processes of cultural appropriation, bastardization, and misapprehension. Still, I do not prize these performances as exemplary confirmations of insidious racism, cultural insensitivity, or obdurate inauthenticity. I take it for granted that the archive of popular performance is also an archive of popular racism.

Yet, within the middlebrow conventions of playing Latino, I find another archive hidden in plain sight. By attending to both the "good" and "bad" modes of playing Latino, and by not cordoning "authentic" depictions from "inauthentic" ones, I endeavor to excavate the full incoherence of what it has meant for actors—Latina/o and non-Latina/o alike—to play Latino in mainstream US entertainments. *Latin,* then, operates for me not simply as a term of critical abuse or dismissal but rather as a privileged signifier of the very constructedness—inaccuracies and inauthenticities—of such racializing performances. The terms *Latin* and *Latin-ness* provide a necessary marker of the recurrent—often sizable—distance between a Latin performance and actual Latina/o peoples, communities, and audiences.

Put simply, in my use of these terms, *Hispanic* and *Latino* refer to populations, respectively defined from without and within. *Latin* describes stylized constructions that operate in popular performance through some alchemy of racialization, commodification, and appropriation. Terms like *Latina* (along with regional, national, or cultural descriptors like *Cuban American* or *Chicana*) aim for descriptive precision. (In chapter 5, I also develop a bit of creative nomenclature—*Latin/o*—to animate the tensions that arise when the impulse to "diversify" or "include" Latina/o characters collides with the obdurate, fetishistic pleasures of familiar "Latin" types, styles, and scenarios.) Throughout, my use of this terminological repertoire aims to be aptly descriptive and abstains from making prescriptive claims as to what is or is not authentically Latina/o.

Some readers might be perplexed—or even alarmed—by my somewhat unconventional choice to emphasize works in which non-Latina/o performance-makers opt to play Latino opposite, alongside, or instead of Latina and Latino performance-makers. The styles, conventions, and scenarios that comprise the repertoire of playing Latino in twentieth-century popular performance emerged in the encounter between Latina/o and non-Latina/o performance-makers, and to emphasize one at the expense of the other would contribute only a partial portrait. My choice to disaggregate playing Latino from being Latino derives from my interest in excavating the archive of popular performance as an essential arena for the performative inauguration of racial meaning.

I submit that performance animates raciality as simultaneously real and unreal. Race is an artificial construct that bears the very real experiences of violence, exclusion, and oppression. Performance is also a conspicuously constructed artifice that bears its most palpable impacts when it feels real. This parallel anchors my conviction that historical analysis of the practices of performance can reveal the process of racial formation, especially those rehearsed through enactment to feel undeniably real. To this end, my analysis looks to performance-makers—or those whose creative choices compose performances—and to the ways those choices also compose or prompt performances of raciality. This project aims to offer a historical investigation of the racialization of Latinos as nonwhite by assessing racial formation as an essentially performative process of cultural meaning construction.

The dynamic interplay between racial formation and performativity operates in each of my "Latin number" case studies. When a performance-maker stages an enactment of racial, cultural, or ethnic distinction, as he or she sings, dances, or speaks before an audience's eyes, these distinctions aspire to become experientially real, however fleetingly and antifactually, at least for the duration of the performance. Not all of the choices made by performance-makers make sense, and not all find appreciative audiences. Yet the processes of crafting a playing-Latino performance—almost inevitably collaborative, involving at least a few and often a few hundred people—rehearse ideas about race, ethnicity, and "America" that, when approached as an archive, also document changing ideas about being Latino in the United States in the twentieth century.

Latin Numbers is guided by a fascination with how the categories of "Latino" and "Hispanic" emerged as aggregate ethnoracial distinctions in the twentieth century. At the beginning of the twentieth century, the three main national groups constituting the US federal category of Hispanic—Mexicans, Puerto Ricans, and Cubans—were listed among the catalog of disparate "races" comprising the American landscape.[30] And yet, even as Celts, Poles, and Jews accessed provisional claims on whiteness over the course of the twentieth century, Mexicans, Puerto Ricans, and Cubans were segregated from this same midcentury expansion of whiteness as a racial category.[31] This historical phenomenon—the exemption of the populations that we might now consider Latino from the racial category of whiteness—frames the interests of this study. How did it come to "make sense" to innovate a new racialized category for Latinos? Even more, does "Latino" delineate a racial or ethnic distinction? I approach these questions through the lens of racial formation theory as originally formulated by Michael Omi and Howard Winant. Racial formation theory, in its simplest configuration, is defined as "the sociohistorical process by which racial categories are created, inhabited, transformed, and destroyed" within which "race is a matter of both social structure and cultural representation."[32] Racial formation describes the "creation of racial meanings," which is reciprocally interdependent with the social structures of politics, economics, and culture.

I am most interested in demonstrating how popular performance in the twentieth century charts the racial formation of "Latino" and "Hispanic" as a racial category, neither black nor white, but clearly distinct from both. In *Latin Numbers*, I contend that popular performance operates as an especially relevant site of such "racialization." Omi and Winant define *racialization* as "signify[ing] the extension of racial meaning to a previously racially unclassified relationship, social practice, or group."[33] An ever-growing scholarly canon describes racial performance as a vector of racial meanings, or a place in which racial meanings are archived, reanimated, and reconfigured. I consider myself a part of the impulse, as Sarah Chinn evocatively describes it, "to recogniz[e] that racialization is a totalizing force, a kind of ideological extruder that shapes everything that passes through it into recognizable forms."[34]

In *Latin Numbers*, I do not seek the racial origins of particular performance practices, nor do I allege that certain performance practices cause racialization. Rather, I look to popular performance as a rehearsal space, a cultural platform on which ideas about raciality are practiced and enacted, sometimes to enter the social or cultural repertoire, sometimes not. I approach popular performance as an important social structure that operates at the nexus of politics, economics, and culture. This approach aligns in important ways with performance theorist Jon McKenzie's "speculative forecast" that "performance will be to the twentieth and twenty-first centuries what discipline was to the eighteenth and nineteenth centuries, that is, an onto-historical formation of power and knowledge."[35] Along these same lines, this study explores how popular performance operates as an instantiating venue for the conventionalization and distribution of racial knowledge in the United States. Specifically, I examine how performed entertainments inaugurated popular ways of knowing about Latinos as a distinct—and distinctly nonwhite—aggregate ethnoracial group in the United States during the twentieth century.

Latin Numbers is organized into five overlapping chapters, each of which tells a particular story of how playing Latino animated distinct modes of understanding Latina/o ethnoracial distinction within and through US popular performance. First, chapter 1, "Conga! Latin Numbers and the Good Neighbor Era," details the emergence and refinement of the signature vocal, visual, and staging conventions that configured spectacularly musical Latin numbers during the Good Neighbor era. Chapter 2, "Stealth Latinos: Casting the Limits of Racial Legibility at Midcentury," describes how a performer's ethnic or racial legibility as Latino varied wildly depending on the audience, the role, or both. I give a detailed explication of the casting profiles of three actors (Mexican American Ricardo Montalban, Puerto Rican Juano Hernandez, and Cuban American Mel Ferrer), whose careers document the general casting practices and aesthetics of the era. Chapter 3, "How The Sharks Became Puerto Rican," traces the history of *West Side Story*'s genesis, development, and circulation. It explicates not only how this canonical American musical became an enduringly contentious performance text but also how it offered an inaugural performance of one of the most enduring stock characters in the performance of Latino-ness in twentieth-century US popular performance: the Latino gang member.

Chapter 4, "Executing the Stereotype," explicates how Latina/o performers and playwrights since the 1960s have executed the stereotype—enacted the stereotype so as to eliminate it—within an array of performances and in so doing devised an influential theorization of how to intervene in the conventions of racial representation. Chapter 5, "Carlos Comes Out: Gay Latin/o Lovers in the AIDS Era," examines how the appearance of the Carlos doll (an anatomically "complete" novelty figurine introduced in 1998) confirmed the emergence of the gay Latin/o lover as a stock character within mainstream television, film, and theatrical narratives of gay intimacy in the 1990s. Throughout, *Latin Numbers* affirms that the performance of Latin-ness rehearsed shifting ideas of Latina/o raciality, bringing these ideas to (pretend) life on the myriad stages of US popular performance (for better and for worse) throughout the twentieth century.

In each chapter, *Latin Numbers* adopts a distinct mode of "playing Latino"—or the constellation of styles and strategies configuring how the idea of "Latino" was rehearsed and performed (by Latinos and non-Latinos alike) in popular film, theatre, and television. First, I examine playing Latino as a constitutive part of the popular vogue of "Latin" musical stagings, wherein playing Latino became an option available to all, irrespective of ethnicity, yet especially charged for some precisely because of it. I then explore what playing Latino meant for seriously working actors of Mexican, Puerto Rican, and Cuban descent, as they built and rebuilt careers in the 1950s. Next, I explicate how notions of playing Latino scripted *West Side Story*'s explosive success as perhaps the first canonical work of American theater to place Latina/o characters at center stage. Then I inquire into the efforts by activist Latina/o artists to remake the performance vocabulary of playing Latino and how such interventions revealed the complex persistence of that repertoire. Finally, I engage the unpredictable utility of playing Latino when deployed as a mechanism to articulate queer difference and desire in the context of a miniboom in gay Latin/o lovers in film, television, and theatre of the gay 1990s. Each "Latin number"—spectacularly enacted and then conspicuously forgotten—displays another among the ever-changing ways of playing Latino and thereby unveils important changes in Latina/o racial legibility throughout the twentieth century. Taken together, these "Latin numbers" confirm how popular performance is often where such ideas about race, ethnicity and nation stir to life, die dramatic deaths, and find resurrection in the most startling yet entertaining of ways.

CHAPTER 1

Conga!

Latin Numbers and the
Good Neighbor Era

————— ✥ —————

The conga made Danny Kaye a star. In early 1940, the song-and-dance man was struggling to transform his success on the summertime "borscht belt" circuit into a year-round career when a one-week booking at a new Manhattan nightclub changed everything. As the story goes, Kaye's set of original comedy songs showcased his most reliable bits (including "Anatole of Paris," which relied on Kaye's gift for rapid-fire, foreign-sounding gibberish), but the act languished before the self-consciously swank patrons of La Martinique. Fearing a mediocre review, Kaye had to be convinced to go on for his eleven o'clock set. In spite of his anxieties, the later set was such a smash that Kaye exhausted his prepared material during several encores and was compelled to add a spontaneous "conga" as his finale.

While the band improvised a simple Latin-style tune, Kaye made up some Spanish-sounding nonsense lyrics as he kicked off a conga line that snaked through the club. By the song's end, the dancing line included the entire audience, nearly all of La Martinique's serving staff, and most of the band—all periodically shouting "Conga!" at Kaye's behest. The next day's papers delivered rave reviews, and Kaye's act—with its notorious conga finale—soon became "a favorite among New York's chic nighttime crowd."[1] Subsequently Kaye's one-week booking extended to thirteen weeks, ending only when he left to join the cast of *Lady in the Dark* on Broadway.[2] Thereafter, the conga became a signature feature of Kaye's repertoire, figuring prominently both in his return to La Martinique the following year (at six times his original pay) and in his feature film debut several years later.[3]

Although the conga made him a star, Danny Kaye did not introduce it to US audiences. The conga—with its ever-expanding line of dancers (who only have to give a quick kick on the fourth beat, if that)—has several potential points of arrival in US popular performance. An adaptation of a long-standing Cuban *carnaval* tradition, "conga line" performances had been seen in commercial venues in the United States and United Kingdom since at least 1935.[4] However, it was not until Desi Arnaz began incorporating the conga drum (whose percussive rhythm cues the simple movement obliged by the dance) into his nightclub act that the conga line began to be popularized among US audiences. Arnaz claims a kind of authorship of the dance in his autobiography, asserting that "the conga dance had never been done in the United States" until he began incorporating it into his nightclub performances. The "tipping point" for the conga's legibility within US popular performance seemed to come when Arnaz led the conga dance in the Rodgers and Hart musical *Too Many Girls*. In both the 1939 stage musical and its 1940 film adaptation, the Cuban actor portrayed an Argentine kicker playing for a New Mexico college football team, who, in a fiery first-act finale, led the entire company in a conga-line/pep rally. The George Abbot stage production, which coincided with Arnaz's burgeoning popularity as headliner at the genteel La Conga supper club, proved successful, and his conga number was among the otherwise unremarkable musical's most acclaimed moments. Kaye's conga finale at La Martinique was widely appreciated as a lampoon of Arnaz's breakout success in New York on both the stage and nightclub scenes.

That same year Carmen Miranda made her sensational stage debut in 1939's *Streets of Paris*. Indeed, the Broadway season of 1939–40 emerges as a nodal, historical moment during which US audiences seemed to discover—all of a sudden—what to do when someone shouted "Conga!" and to realize that there was something of interest going on "South American Way." By the end of the theatrical season, both Arnaz and Miranda were adapting their respective theatrical successes for the Hollywood soundstage. Indeed, by October, Arnaz would lead an onscreen conga in the film version of *Too Many Girls* (1940), and Miranda would reprise "South American Way" for moviegoers headed *Down Argentine Way* (1940).

Thus, within the span of less than a year, incremental lessons in the conventions of such conspicuously "Latin" musical numbers were rehearsed on US stages for increasingly broader audiences. This chapter examines the historical formalization of the "Latin number," or the stylized mode of musical-theatrical presentation that deployed a shifting constellation of visual, musical, and linguistic cues to enact a distilled fantasy of Latin American peoples, places, and traditions, presumably for US audiences. Characterized by flashy colors, prominent percussive rhythms, and a frequently nonsensical mix of English, Spanish, and Portuguese phrases, the Latin number was formalized on stage and screen during the height of the Good Neighbor Era, a period that began in the mid-1930s and was amplified throughout World War II. The "Good Neighbor Policy" was a rhetorical shorthand introduced by President Franklin Delano Roosevelt to describe the guiding diplomatic orientation of his administration (1933–45) toward Latin America and to encourage "friendly" commercial, cultural, and military relations among neighboring American republics. Whether the 1930s and 1940s vogue for Latin numbers was a popular trend repurposed as political propaganda or vice versa, the Good Neighbor Era also incubated the genre conventions of the Latin number, which would persist as one of the most ubiquitously repurposed modes of musical comedy presentation for US theatre, cabaret, film, and television for decades, long after the "policy" imperatives of the Good Neighbor Era had passed.

Previous scholars have shown intermittent interest the Good Neighbor Era's commingling of political priorities and musical performance practice. Ethnomusicologist John Storm Roberts has termed the period's "sudden development of a music scene that was stylistically Latin" as "latinoid," while cultural historian Gustavo Pérez Firmat has noted the proliferation in the 1930s and 1940s of what he calls "latunes," pop songs enacting "a fusion of Latin beats and English syllables." For my purposes, the theatrical and cinematic staging of such songs was marked by legible shifts in how the conventions of the Latin number were deployed. This period began with the diverting interludes in "the so-called maraca musicals that gave Latin-curious Americans the opportunity to sightsee and tune in without ever leaving their theater seats" in the 1930s,[5] moving through the spectacular phantasms of Busby Berkeley and Walt Disney in the 1940s, and concluding with the baroque abstractions of Broadway songs like *Candide*'s "I Am Easily Assimilated" and *Peter Pan*'s "Captain Hook's Tango" in the 1950s.

The shifting deployments of Latin musical numbers on stage and screen during the Good Neighbor Era provide perhaps the clearest introduction of the cycle of discovery, disidentification, and dissolution that, as I argue throughout this book, attend the recurrent phenomenon of fleeting fascination with Latin-ness within US popular performance. These Latin musical numbers, like the mostly nonmusical "Latin numbers" I examine in subsequent chapters,[6] perform their fixation on Latin-ness in three legible, overlapping modes. The first Latin musical numbers usually enact the excitement of discovery, typically through a naively enthusiastic encounter with the Good Neighbor idea generally or the thrill of a particular site, song, or style of musical performance. Next the Latin numbers demonstrate a sophisticated familiarity with such sites and styles, as well as the Good Neighbor impetus that compels such engagement with Latin rhythms and modes. This sophisticated familiarity also enacts a kind of disidentification, in which a particular Latin number might selectively embrace (or identify with) some aspects of the Good Neighbor ethos while simultaneously disavowing (or disidentifying with) others.[7] The resulting musical staging thereby recycles and repurposes the cultural logics embedded within the Good Neighbor idea toward a sometimes celebratory but more frequently cynical reframing of it within the spectacular frame of a musical number. Finally, in the later years (especially after the ostensible dismantling of the Good Neighbor Policy), Latin numbers effect a dissolution of the Good Neighbor idea, devolving it within an abstractly deconstructive pastiche of the ostensibly Latin stock styles, characters, and techniques now rearranged without clear reference to the Good Neighbor premise that instigated their circulation within US popular performance.

My description of the typical "Latin number" cycle—discovery to disidentification to dissolution—borrows heavily from the work of academic theorist Bert O. States and its further elaboration by playwright and teacher Paula Vogel. In *Irony and Drama*, States argues, in terms simultaneously schematic and theoretical, that innovations in dramatic form develop along a pattern of intelligibility for both artist and audience. States identifies three primary stages in the innovation cycle. First comes the "naive" phase of "true discovery," in which the artist and audience alike delight in their introduction to or initiation within a previously unfamiliar dramatic convention. Next these conventions are developed in what States terms the "sophisticated" or "mature" phase, which follows (or overlaps with) the naive encounter and is characterized by a "worldly, complex, subtilized" deployment of these conventions. Finally, States names as "decadent" the third overlapping phase, in which "a great deal of original use" is made of the "old" conventions, often toward intentionally absurd ends—and occasionally within what becomes a new naive phase of innovation.[8]

While States's formulation has largely lapsed into obscurity within the critical lexicon, Vogel has rehearsed this schema (which States called an essential "part of the dramatist's toolbox") with succeeding generations of students for the past thirty years.[9] In Vogel's elaboration of the naive-sophisticated-decadent paradigm, the triad not only describes the historical evolution of particular forms (from simplicity to complexity to self-referentiality) but also evinces the ways in which artist and audience alike apprehend the operation of form within a theatrical work, within a artist's oeuvre, within an artistic movement, or within a historical moment.

I invoke my teacher Paula Vogel's elaboration of her mentor Bert O. States's paradigm not simply for purposes of intellectual genealogy. Rather, Vogel amplifies the practical dimensions of States's critical paradigm, reminding her students that a performance-maker's independently creative choices always operate strategically within and through evolving aesthetic contexts. I follow the lead of States—and especially Vogel—in my contention that the strategic and creative deployment of theatrical conventions (like those of the "Latin number") might also be understood, historically, as documentation of broader shifts in critical, creative consciousness guiding these performances.

In the pages that follow, I demonstrate how the changing deployment of Latin-themed musical numbers during the Good Neighbor Era also rehearsed US audiences in the idea of cultural encounters between citizens of the United States and those of "other" American republics. My account will first offer a brief historical overview of the Good Neighbor Policy and its various promoters— in both government and entertainment—during the 1930s and 1940s. For illustration, I will offer two examples of composer-lyricist Harold Rome's work at the height of the Good Neighbor Era—specifically two songs, "Be a Good Neighbor" and "South America (Take It Away)"—as exemplary of the transition from fascinated discovery to sophisticated disidentification of the Good Neighbor ethos. I argue that Rome's work demonstrates how cultural workers in the Good Neighbor Era used performance to distinguish "Americans" from citizens of the "other American republics" of the southern hemisphere. In so doing, these songs moved from fascination to familiarization and finally to formalization of specific performance conventions in presenting such "differences."

To chart this arc even more precisely, I examine the shifts in strategy and tone guiding the "conga" scene in the various adaptations of Ruth McKenney's *My Sister Eileen* stories, as the work moved from print to stage and film in the later 1930s and 1940s, before being taken up again in the 1950s as two different musicals on stage and screen. My discussion concludes with a summary overview of the legibility, functionality, and generic formation of the Latin number as a mode of musical staging on stages and screens throughout the 1950s. This decade saw the Latin number transformed from a mediated ritual of putative cultural encounter to a conventionalized staging style, one that both rehearsed the idea of "Latin" cultural aggregation and elided pricklier questions of raciality.

The Good Neighbor Era

While the Good Neighbor Policy only remained a government priority until the end of World War II, the Good Neighbor Era stands as the period when the US government most openly enlisted the culture industries—of Broadway and especially Hollywood—to rehearse inter-American audiences in the idea of cultural encounters between citizens of the United States and citizens of the "other American republics." Even so, the Good Neighbor Policy was never actually a policy but rather a rhetorical flourish that, over time, accrued the ideological force and impact of a presidential proclamation.[10] Indeed, when Franklin Delano Roosevelt dedicated his administration to "the policy of the good neighbor" in January 1933, the new president likely neither intended nor expected his single inaugural statement on world affairs to become the rhetorical umbrella that would describe a dizzying array of heavily promoted activities (governmental, nongovernmental, commercial, and volunteer) performing "Pan-American" cooperation for the next two decades.

Even so, Roosevelt's 1933 declaration that the United States would be "the neighbor who respects his obligations and respects the sanctity of his agreements in and with a world of neighbors" heralded what seemed to be the United States' new stance toward the "other American republics" occupying the Western Hemisphere.[11] Within the year, while attending the Seventh International Conference of American States, held in Uruguay, FDR's secretary of state, Cordell Hull, assured the audience of the US position "that no state has the right to intervene in the internal or external affairs of another." In so doing, Hull also affirmed that FDR's dedication to "the policy of the good neighbor" would eschew military intervention in favor of economic, political, and cultural cooperation with its "neighbors" to the south.

This ethos—that the United States would behave as a good neighbor "who resolutely respects himself and, because he does so, respects the rights of others"—endeavored to enhance "inter-American" cooperation and goodwill within the Western Hemisphere, so the United States might maintain its relative remove from the political, military, and economic crises roiling European stability throughout the Good Neighbor Era. For my purposes, the Good Neighbor Era comprises roughly the two decades characterized by the prominent deployment of the Good Neighbor idea. From its initial goal of championing US economic interests within the hemisphere (1933–39) to its amplification as a propaganda tool during wartime (1940–45) to its deliquescence in the post–World War II era (1946–55), Good Neighbor rhetoric always served a dual purpose: to sustain growth and expansion opportunities for US industry and to promote an ideal of "neighborly" cultural encounter, exchange, and understanding.

Throughout the Good Neighbor Era, performances and entertainments served as prominent mechanisms for inter-American "exchange." Throughout the United States—especially on or near Pan-American Day on April 14—women's clubs hosted lecture luncheons and visits to traveling art exhibits. Military bands played music by Latin American composers. Elementary and high school students staged Pan-American pageants and reported on their activities through Pan-American pen pal clubs.[12] Hollywood stars headlined international goodwill tours. In commercial entertainments on stage and screen, highly stylized musical interludes used song and dance to enact "Good Neighbor" narratives of cultural encounter and exchange. These interludes began to punctuate Broadway and Hollywood productions, often irrespective of whether the narratives had anything to do with Latin America. This targeted use of Latin American song and dance styles within enactments of inter-American exchange marks a departure from earlier "Latin" fads, like the "Carmen craze" of the 1890s or the "Tango Rage" of the 1910s. As Adrián Pérez Melgosa has noted in his account of the "Carioca" scene in *Flying Down to Rio* (1933), the "depiction of Latin American identity as an act of transformation within a musical number" emerges in "the inaugural moment of cinematic U.S.-centered Pan-Americanism."[13]

Notably, the producer of *Flying Down to Rio* was Nelson Rockefeller, Roosevelt's 1940 appointee to lead the Office for the Coordination of Inter-American Affairs (OCIAA). Rockefeller's office was housed within the State Department, and he reported directly to the president. Rock-efeller believed the "relatively modest expenditure of funds" required by "cultural investments" to be the most effective way to fortify inter-American goodwill and, by extension, hemispheric security. Addition-ally, Rockefeller believed that "culture could serve as valuable public relations" for US business interests as they expanded their activities in Latin America.[14] Thus, from the time of the OCIAA's founding in early 1940 through its dissolution in 1945, Rockefeller actively encouraged US culture industries to cultivate an interest in these "other American republics."[15] The OCIAA—especially through its work with Hollywood studios and the US military's "Special Services" division—became one of the most significant forces shaping the cultural fascination with the performers, styles, and scenarios that conventionalized the Latin musi-cal number as a mode of staging within the entertainments of the Good Neighbor Era. To elaborate on this idea, I turn now to an account of composer-lyricist Harold Rome's work at the height of the Good Neigh-bor Era. His work marks the Latin number's shift from a device with which to stage an encounter of fascinated discovery to a mechanism used to enact sophisticated disidentification.

Be a Good Neighbor

Few embraced the ethos of the Good Neighbor Era with the verve of Harold Rome. Known best for his work on the 1937 International Ladies Garment Workers smash hit musical *Pins and Needles*, songsmith Harold Rome was celebrated for his "idea songs"—tunes in popular styles that addressed topical themes, often with cleverly satirical wordplay. Rome's "socially pointed" songs, as one historian observes, "brought together traditions of the vaudeville stage and the radical theater, of workers choruses and Tin Pan Alley."[16] A Yale-trained architect, Rome paid for his studies by playing and arranging music for local clubs and dance halls. Upon graduation, he discovered that he could make better money writing, playing, and arranging songs, and he soon abandoned archi-tecture for a career as a theatrical composer-lyricist. Over the next four decades, Harold Rome wrote the music and lyrics for such diverse shows as the musical fantasy *The Little Dog Laughed* (1940), the summer resort farce *Wish You Were Here* (1952), the Wild West romper *Destry Rides Again* (1959), the garment factory romance *I Can Get It for You Wholesale* (1962), the folksy intercultural drama *The Zulu and the Zayda* (1965), and the single authorized musical adaptation of *Gone with the Wind* (which pre-miered in Tokyo, London, and Los Angeles in the early 1970s but never made it to Broadway).

Throughout his career, though, Rome was perhaps best known for his "idea" songs—comedy songs on serious subjects—which led to his famously (if perhaps somewhat apocryphally) being called "Nöel Cow-ard with a social conscience" by a 1930s critic.[17] With songs like "Sing Me a Song of Social Significance" and "History Eight to the Bar," Rome was widely admired for what one contemporary called his "running fire of sardonic commentary on our foreign affairs and American social scheme," which invited audiences to "come to laugh and [to] go out thinking."[18] When pressed in a 1973 interview about whether he wrote with hopes of "converting others" to his own "way of thinking," Rome demurred, "You don't write to convince. . . . You write to amuse and move."[19] Elsewhere, in a column about songwriting, Rome elaborated, "[I]t's the idea that counts. . . . You state your idea as simply and clearly as possible—never getting away from it—approaching it from different sides—getting all the fun out of it you can. . . . But in every case—music, rhyme, meter, jokes . . . they all come *after* the idea."[20]

The Good Neighbor Policy was ripe for his mix of sardonic style and progressive sensibility, and so it is not surprising that Rome—without even a nudge from the OCIAA—was perhaps the first composer-lyricist to embrace the Good Neighbor Policy as a narrative premise for a stage musical. Nor is it surprising that a Rome song would express "good-humored irritation at the fad of Latin music and musicals."[21] Indeed, a comparison of two Harold Rome songs—one an obscurity from 1941, one his greatest popular hit from 1946—provides a productive glimpse into how the Good Neighbor ethos circulated and changed within US popular performance in the 1940s. Rome's 1941 song "Be a Good Neighbor" depicts a fascinated, naive encounter with (and sometimes an all-consuming embrace of) the Good Neighbor ethos. The 1946 song "South America (Take It Away)" displays how a sophisticated familiarity with the Good Neighbor idea compels both a simultaneous affiliation with and dissociation from that same ethos. The paragraphs below detail this shift from discovery to disidentification.

In May 1941, actor-producer Sam Byrd announced that he would present a new musical, "Give a Viva," on Broadway later that year. Harold Rome would serve as composer and lyricist, in collaboration with novelist Erskine Caldwell as book writer. Stage comedian Jimmy Savo and "Mexi-can Spitfire" Lupe Vélez were already in talks to take on principal roles.[22] In the previous decade, Rome and Caldwell had both accomplished notable commercial success (Rome with *Pins and Needles* and Caldwell with *Tobacco Road*) by elaborating their left-leaning social concerns within crowd-pleasing genres.[23] Their "Give a Viva" (which had been initially titled "Man from Mexicana") promised to tell a story premised within the imperatives of the Good Neighbor Era. In it, Cordoba (the newly and reluctantly inaugurated president of a fictional Latin American country) becomes the unwitting object of attention from Carmen, a Hollywood starlet joining a team from the US State Department sent to assess the new president's neighborliness. With its mix of love ballads, comedic character songs, and rousing group numbers—all presented within a romantic narrative that nonetheless interrogated the limits and liabilities of the US government's new strategies of cultural diplomacy—"Give a Viva" aimed for the crowd-pleasing mix of socially conscious comedy and critique typical of both Rome and Caldwell.

For Harold Rome, the Good Neighbor Era provided many of the punny incongruities the lyricist typically mined when crafting his comedic, topical "idea" songs. Lines like "All I get for my work is aggravations / Ladies bat me in the eye/ When I cuddle close and try / To promote some Pan-American relations" punctuate songs throughout "Give a Viva." One song in particular demonstrates Rome's acuity as a lyricist, even as it also documents some of the ways that the Good Neighbor Policy was understood in 1941. In the opening verse and chorus of "Be a Good Neighbor," the leader of the US delegation to "Maxcatan" details how US policy makers and performers collaborated to communicate Good Neighbor imperatives. The song begins as the delegate identifies how the US government's interest in his trip ("When it got around in the U.S.A / That I was traveling down this way/") was informed by its own uncertain strategies ("The State Department was in a state of flux/") for dealing with the region. The singer then sets up the central conceit of the song ("All the big guys and the high mucky-mucks / They asked me to cocktails and to tea / And very confidentially . . .") before launching into a name-checking litany ("Rockafella—told me / Fiorella—told me / Franklin Della—told me") importuning the singer to "Be a Good Neighbor!" The next verse repeats the formula ("Eleanor, she told me / I repeat she told me / Don Ameche told me/") as a refrain ("Be a Good Neighbor!"). A brief sloganeering bridge ("The Department of State is waiting / So get together and start cooperating!") launches another name-checking chorus ("Sumner Welles, he told me / Orson also told me/"), which concludes the song with "Dolores said to do what I could / To be a good, good neighbor!"[24]

Rome's intricate patter name-checks key cultural ambassadors of the

FDR administration's policy initiatives. These include Nelson Rockefeller, head of the OCIAA; Fiorello LaGuardia, the charismatic New York City mayor and reliable FDR ally; Sumner Welles, FDR's lead policy strategist for Latin American affairs; and the president and Mrs. Roosevelt themselves. Rome's list also layers the names of significant workers in the US culture industries who were affiliated with Latin American projects or roles: Don Ameche, who by early 1941 had already appeared as a tropical swain in several Hollywood musicals set in Latin American locales; Orson (presumably) Welles, who was the target of the OCIAA's active and public recruitment to helm a prestige film project to be filmed in Latin America;[25] and Dolores (arguably) Del Rio, whose status as Hollywood's leading Latin lady had been established for more than a decade.

By hailing these performers and politicos in a single lyric, Rome underscored the centrality of performance within the US government's "policy," in a musical that, for all its frivolous frippery, exploited an imagined inter-American encounter as its dramatic scenario under the rhetorical exhortation (to character and audience alike) to "Be a Good Neighbor." Thus, when considered within the genre of Latin numbers that emerged in the Good Neighbor Era, Rome's "Be a Good Neighbor" stands out for the way it hails the collusion among US politicians and performers in the promotion of the Good Neighbor Policy.[26]

If "Be a Good Neighbor" is notable for the overtness of its commentary, Rome's song is also negligible, because it was never performed, at least not publicly. Rome and Caldwell's "Give a Viva" did not open on Broadway in October 1941 as promised. Producer Sam Byrd did present *Good Neighbor*, a play that—despite its title—has nothing to do with the Good Neighbor Policy, instead exploring anti-Semitism and the limits of interracial tolerance in the Deep South.[27] Also arriving on Broadway in place of "Give a Viva" that fall was the notorious *Viva O'Brien*, the legendary "aquamusical" (so termed because of its massive on-stage swimming pool), which followed the hijinks of a troupe of partygoers traveling from Miami to Yucatan on a putative quest for a sacred singing stone. Brooks Atkinson described *Viva O'Brien* as "one of the strangest experiences offered on Broadway."[28] In addition to the massive on-stage pool (into which several Olympic divers leapt during the first act finale), *Viva O'Brien* also featured Victoria Cordova, a petite nightclub singer billed as "The Mexican Monsoon," and an appearance by a character called "Secretary of the Mexican Consulate" (played by Mexican American radio singer Terry La Franconi), who presented a "noble speech at the end about our star-spangled friendship with Mexico" immediately before the grand, splashing finale.[29] Featuring such songs as "Wrap Me in Your Serape" and "Mexican Bad Men," one critic noted that *Viva O'Brien* "will win us no Good Neighbors," while another discerned the aquamusical's intercultural inconsistencies: "You could tell the Latins from the Americans very easily. The Latins called Mexico 'Mehico' while the Americans called it 'Mexico.'"[30]

Neither *Viva O'Brien* nor *Good Neighbor* lasted through October. (In fact, *Good Neighbor* closed after a single performance.) Still, even in their failure, we can see the ubiquity of the "Good Neighbor" idea and its increasing alignment with the spectacular musical. Although Harold Rome's "Give a Viva" might have failed just as spectacularly as *Viva O'Brien* and *Good Neighbor* had it opened as planned in October 1941, Rome's never-performed lyrics to "Be a Good Neighbor'" further document how those musical entertainments deployed in service of the Good Neighbor idea were necessarily devoid of comedic commentary on that ethos.

Although the Good Neighbor Era collaborations among political appointees at the US State Department and practitioners within the US culture industries were never secret, they mostly transpired behind the scenes in the OCIAA, under the leadership of Nelson Rockefeller. A longtime collector of Mexican and pre-Columbian art, Rockefeller (presumably the "Rockefella" of Harold Rome's "Be a Good Neighbor" lyric) supervised a wide program of activities initiated by the OCIAA, carefully selecting, sponsoring, and censoring literary translations, magazine and pamphlet productions, musical tours, and more—all for circulation among Latin American audiences. But perhaps the OCIAA's most prominent contributions came through its Motion Picture Section, under the watchful eye of its director, John Hay "Jock" Whitney. Shortly after his appointment in 1941, Whitney declared, "Wherever the motion picture can do a basic job of spreading the gospel of the Americas' common stake in [the struggle against the menace of Nazism and its allied doctrines], there that job must and shall be done."[31]

Hollywood studios responded swiftly to OCIAA's call, immediately producing a spate of films (shorts, cartoons, and features) using Latin and South American themes, characters, or locales. All such productions were subject to either direct or indirect supervisory advisement by the OCIAA. Sometimes, this supervision caught things just in the nick of time, as in the case of Twentieth Century Fox's 1941 release *That Night in Rio*, an Alice Faye vehicle featuring Carmen Miranda and Don Ameche (as noted in Rome's lyric). *That Night in Rio*'s songwriters, Mack Gordon and Harry Warren, wrote a number of tuneful ditties with Spanish lyrics, not remembering or not knowing that most people in Brazil speak Portuguese. Intervention by the OCIAA supplied the production with a Brazilian technical advisor to translate the lyrics before seeking approval of the songs and script from the Brazilian embassy.

Such supervision provided no guarantees, however, and OCIAA's supervisory structure proved ill-equipped to catch the many cultural elisions that quickly became typical within Good Neighbor Era productions. For example, another 1941 Faye-Miranda-Ameche vehicle from Fox, *Weekend in Havana,* boasted Technicolor background shots filmed in Havana as a signal feature of its authentic depiction of Cuban nightlife. Back on the Hollywood soundstage, though, studio production personnel routinely incorporated Mexican costume elements and architectural details into film's visual vocabulary, perhaps most comically when the dashing Cesar Romero whisks Alice Faye into a thrilling Havana nightspot, passing a snoozing sombrero- and serapé-wearing señor taking his siesta.

The OCIAA not only supervised productions, but in several notable instances it actually sponsored them. Perhaps most memorably, Jock Whitney's Motion Picture Section partnered with the struggling Walt Disney Studios to "show the truth of the American way" and be "the first Hollywood producer of motion pictures specifically intended to carry a message of democracy and friendship below the Rio Grande."[32] Whitney was struck by the popularity—especially in South America—of the animation produced by the Disney studio, and he thought animation a potentially efficient means of resisting the growth of pro-Axis sentiment in the hemisphere. (Whitney even had an animated character he wanted Walt to develop—"Miss PanAmerica.")

So, in the summer of 1941, Whitney paid for Walt Disney—and an entourage of artists, animators, and film technicians—to tour Brazil, Argentina, Bolivia, and Chile, where they accumulated the research necessary for the lively blend of music, animation, and live action footage that would comprise much of *Saludos Amigos!* and *The Three Caballeros.* Although they never realized Jock Whitney's hope for a new animated character named Miss PanAmerica, the Disney projects quite literally animated the OCIAA's philosophic aggregation of Latin American nations and cultures as uniformly distinct from a normalized model of English-only, US-only "American"-ness, thus bringing the Good Neighbor Policy to life right before the audience's eyes.[33]

By early 1942, with mobilization for the war effort at full pace, the OCIAA also indirectly oversaw stage productions developed by "Special

Services" military personnel. Within the Special Services units, enlisted men with specialized skills in the performing arts were charged with developing entertainments to boost morale, both in the field and on the home front. Two notable early Special Services productions—both of which toured commercially in 1942—were Irving Berlin's all-soldier revue *This Is the Army* and the youth revue *Let Freedom Sing* (in which Betty Garrett got enthusiastic notices for her rendition of the Harold Rome tune "Give a Viva!," the only song from Rome's abandoned Good Neighbor musical to be publically performed).[34] *This Is the Army* and *Let Freedom Sing* both rehearsed the aesthetic of volunteer authenticity that would inform the emergence of the "all soldier" musical revue for which the Special Services unit became most known. Berlin's opening chorus announced, "But beneath the powder and beneath the paint / There's a soldier brave and true / If some guy in Congress tells you that we ain't / Let him do what we had to do."[35]

Corporal Harold Rome was among the many artists who were assigned to the Special Services unit at Fort Hamilton. There Rome and other writers churned out new songs and skits that would be distributed in semimonthly dispatches for use in the amateur theatricals staged by the entertainment directors of military training camps around the world or—quite literally—in the trenches as "jeep shows." A jeep show was a form of instant theatre in which three or so men (occasionally accompanied by a United Service Organization [USO] celebrity or two) traveled to the front lines—in a jeep—to put on a show. Made somewhat famous by the 1944 Twentieth Century Fox release *Four Jills in a Jeep* (featuring Betty Grable, Alice Faye, and Carmen Miranda, among other World War II era performers), jeep show performers played instruments that could be transported easily (guitar, banjo, accordion) and upon arrival at their destination, would present songs, skits, jokes, and occasionally dances and pantomimes, depending on who was on the jeep.[36]

Conspicuously "Latin" musical numbers, typically featuring at least one soldier dressed in quick Carmen Miranda–style drag for a comedic dance duet, were a stock feature—along with blackface minstrelsy sketches and square dance routines—of World War II jeep shows and field camp theatricals alike.[37] Corporal Harold Rome developed songs in every genre for such revues, and his songs were featured in the two main soldier shows that toured commercially during the war—*Skirts* (1944) and *Stars and Gripes* (1944). Rome was also the primary composer-lyricist for the single postwar soldier show that proved to be a major hit, *Call Me Mister* (1946).[38]

Call Me Mister opened on Broadway in the spring of 1946 and soon emerged as one of the surprise hits of the season. The musical comedy revue's sketches and songs depicted the experiences of demobilization for the many Americans whose lives had been transformed by the war effort. *Call Me Mister* boasted a cast composed entirely of former service members. The program listed the branch of the military in which each of the nearly thirty male performers had served during wartime, while also noting whether the fifteen or so women cast members were from the Women's Army Corps (WAC), the Navy's Women Accepted for Volunteer Emergency Service (WAVES), or (most frequently) the War Department's USO. The premise of the show was signaled with its "infectiously jaunty" title song about the paradoxes of giving up one's wartime identity on returning to civilian life.[39] The show ranged in tone from romantic (as in the four songs recounting how the war shaped a young couple's love) to anthemic (as in "The Face on the Dime," a tribute to Franklin Delano Roosevelt) to the folk-tinged "Going Home Train," which followed an ensemble of veterans as each was delivered by rail to his home, concluding poignantly with an African American soldier's arrival in a still segregated America. Befitting Harold Rome's strengths, though, most of *Call Me Mister*'s songs and sketches were comedic commentaries, like those sung by the ensemble's breakout star, Betty Garrett.

Betty Garrett's featured contributions to *Call Me Mister* signaled the show's overarching comedic tone. In the sketch "Welcome Home" (which came early in the first act), Garrett played a returning GI's mother who remained a bit too enthusiastic about protecting the home front. Just two numbers later she appeared as a waitress at a luncheonette and sang "Little Surplus Me," a comedic lament, which detailed her loss of both economic and romantic opportunities with the closure of a nearby military base. Over the course of show, Garrett also appeared as a WAVE, a society matron, and a member of the ensemble, but the song that garnered her the most attention (and provided *Call Me Mister*'s breakout pop hit) was Harold Rome's arch riff on the Latin dance styles so popular in USO halls during the war, "South America (Take It Away)."

Toward the end of *Call Me Mister*'s second act—and immediately after the concluding episode of its recurring love story (in which the young couple sang to their newborn baby)—Betty Garrett's final entrance signaled an abrupt change in tone. Dressed in "a tight fitting evening dress [and] wearing a banner across her chest labeled 'Hostess,'"[40] Garrett began to sing: "Up here in the land of the hot dog stand / The atom bomb and the Good Humor man / We think our South American neigh-

Call Me Mister's weary USO hostess, Betty Garrett, sings "South America (Take It Away)" in 1946. (Image by permission of *Photofest*)

bors are grand." Complete with a yodeled "babalu" or two, the song's opening cued that "South America (Take It Away)" would be a conspicuously "Latin" number performed by a USO hostess. The lyric before the first chorus set up the song's running joke: "You beautiful lands below don't know what you began / To put it plainly / I'm tired of shaking my Pan-American can."

Four uniformed soldiers approached Garrett, each hoping for a dance. As the increasingly weary USO hostess continued to sing, she did dance with each of the soldiers—sometimes in turn, sometimes two at a time, sometimes all at once. As she did, she listed the dance styles she was expected to perform on command ("Take back your samba! Ay! Your rhumba! Ay! Your conga! Ay, yay, yay!") interspersed with a repeated rhyme scheme, noting the particular strains of these rhythmic exertions—be they physical ("All this makin' of the quakin' / And the shakin' of the bacon / Leaves me achin'"), emotional ("Though I like these neighborly relations / All these up and down gyrations / Try my patience"), or even possibly sexual ("All this goin' and this comin' / To this fancy Latin drummin' / Numbs my plumbin'"). Thus, through music, dance, and rhyme, "South America (Take It Away)" distilled the cultural imperatives of the Good Neighbor ethos for comedic effect.

Indeed, although "South America (Take It Away)" was a repurposed trunk song added by Rome late in the process to inject some humor into *Call Me Mister*'s self-serious second act,[41] Garrett's harried USO hostess became *Call Me Mister*'s breakout hit. Though not featured in any of the show's original publicity materials, pictures of Garrett's USO hostess— always wearing her beaded dress, often before a group of smiling GIs— soon appeared in popular reports of the show's success, including *Life* and *Dance* magazines.[42] Even beyond Garrett's celebrated performance,[43] the song moved on to become perhaps Harold Rome's biggest commercial hit. In the summer of 1946, two different recordings of "South America (Take It Away)" (both with male performers singing the lead lyric) were released for radio and jukebox play. Xavier Cugat's Orchestra, featuring crooner Buddy Clark, released the first version in July 1946, as the B-side to Clark's popular cover of the "Chiquita Banana Song."[44] Bing Crosby and the Andrews Sisters released a second version in August, and it went on to become one of the year's most popular songs, with Billboard listing the Crosby cover as one the year's "Top Tunes" in both radio and jukebox play.[45]

Such popularity led the limited entry of "South America (Take It Away)" into the repertoire for the next decade or so. One of the few songs retained for the much transformed 1951 film version of *Call Me Mister* (reset amid the Korean conflict and in which World War II icon Betty Grable performed the song), "South America (Take It Away)" also became a standard on the big band circuit and entered the television variety show acts of comediennes like Eve Arden and Dody Goodman. Due perhaps to the 1940s contemporaneity of Rome's lyrics, however, the song fell into a kind of obscurity by the end of the 1950s. Thereafter, it occasionally garnered critical attention from Latina/o cultural studies scholars mapping the peculiar popularity of Latin American musical performers, styles, and rhythms during the 1940s. Alberto Sandoval-Sánchez describes Betty Garrett's performance as an "unforgettable parody [of] Miranda's hypnotizing hip movements and stylized mannerisms [and] in the refrain . . . none other than Desi Arnaz is parodied," while Gustavo Pérez Firmat describes it as the "definitive anti-Latin music hymn of all time."[46]

It is not incorrect to read "South America (Take It Away)" as an "anti–Latin music" parody. Indeed, the song's title seems an acerbic tweak on 1939's "South American Way," the song that introduced Carmen Miranda to US stardom and became one of the most ubiquitous songs heralding the Good Neighbor ethos in the early 1940s. The song's (and the star's) popularity instigated almost immediate parody. Imogene Coca's spoof in 1939's *The Straw Hat Review* stands as perhaps the first parody of Miranda's acclaimed debut, appearing only a few months after *The Streets of Paris* opened. Yet Coca's "Soused American Way" is perhaps most noteworthy for the fact that Carmen Miranda herself taught Coca both the song and her own signature moves, effectively cocrafting Coca's comic parody of Miranda's ostensibly "authentic" on-stage persona.[47] Over the next few years, overt parodies of Miranda's persona (likely authored without her input) were delivered by Bugs Bunny, Mickey Rooney, Milton Berle, and other celebrities, as well as in innumerable soldier shows. Indeed, by 1946 parodic riffs on Miranda's career-making song were neither new nor noteworthy. Additionally, Harold Rome was among the writers who had contributed to *The Streets of Paris* in 1939, the show in which Miranda introduced "South American Way" and for which Rome composed a special interlude featuring her in the show's finale. In this context, and when considered against Rome's draft lyric "Be a Good Neighbor" (which was likely penned in 1939 or 1940), it would seem that the comedy of Rome's "South America (Take It Away)" might operate in a slightly different contemporary register. Indeed, the breakout commercial and popular success of Rome's "South America (Take It Away)" cues the subtle but significant pop cultural shift in attitude toward Latin musical performers, styles, and rhythms, which had become quite evident by 1946.[48]

Call Me Mister's USO hostess in "South America (Take It Away)" disidentifies with Latin music fads by demonstrating her familiarity with and competence within the conventions of these performance modes, while also disavowing their relevance within her contemporary US life. The USO hostess's change in disposition toward Latin musical styles signals the cultural shift happening within pop cultural elaborations of the

Good Neighbor ethos at the end of World War II. This shift coincided with the decommissioning of the OCIAA in 1945 and the subsequent deprioritization of Good Neighbor imperatives within US cultural diplomacy, as the techniques developed under OCIAA's supervision were redeployed in the postwar era away from Pan-American collaborations and toward proto–Cold War engagements. Even as long-standing inter-American cultural exchanges did persist, they continued with greatly diminished federal support. Thus, Betty Garrett's weary USO hostess emerges as a provocative stage surrogate for the decommissioning of the Good Neighbor Policy—an all-American supporter of the war effort, clearly competent with the Latin musical styles, declaring her lack of sustained investment in the Good Neighbor ethos. Indeed, if the sincerity of Rome's "Be a Good Neighbor" announces the popular inauguration of the Good Neighbor Era in 1940, the acerbic "South America (Take It Away)" proclaims its nearly immediate demobilization in 1946.

Even as the success of "South America (Take It Away)" documented the demobilization of the Good Neighbor ethos, it also inspired at least two retorts—by Desi Arnaz and Harold Rome—each of which, in very different ways, used comedy to cue the distinct styles through which the Latin musical number continued to thrive in US popular performance. In his direct retort to "South America (Take It Away)" (first performed in early 1947), Arnaz referenced Rome's lyrics ("Folks are saying that when they do the rumba / they crack / their sacroiliac") before launching his own comedic critique of the aural and physical assaults of swing dance styles, noting, "If I try keeping up with this jive / I'll need doctors to keep me alive" and "You can't even hear yourself dance / with the rhumba you may find romance." Whereas Arnaz's "I'll Take the Rhumba" (which became a minor success for the bandleader, both in his nightclub act and as a recording) recuperated the romantic pleasures of Latin music styles, Rome's retort—in an unpublished (and possibly never performed) song titled alternately "South America Strikes Back" or "Up North America Way"—rendered a particularly mocking critique of US popular cultural excess.

Adopting the same rhythmic and rhyme scheme of his previous hit, Rome's self-satirizing lyric addresses a hypothetically Latin American listener: "Come with me to the land of the good neighbor plan / Where they've got Frank Sinatra, the schmoo and Superman" and where "in every Yankee movie and show / They always have a big finale / Where all the actors get gay / And wiggle below the belly / What they call the South American Way." Together, Arnaz's and Rome's ironic rebuttals to "South America (Take It Away)" signal how the conspicuously "Latin" musical number, in the decades after World War II, ceased operating primarily to exploit dramatically (or comedically) the novelty of cultural encounter, emerging instead as a device to evoke either nostalgic romance or comedic chaos or both.[49]

To better explain this cycle, and to show how naive cultural discovery evolves into sophisticated disidentification before dissolving into decadent convention, I now turn to *My Sister Eileen* and her potent solicitation to "conga!"

My Sister Eileen

Beginning in early 1937, Ruth McKenney published a recurring series of "light sketches" in the *New Yorker* magazine. Episodic and loosely autobiographical, McKenney's humorous stories featured the author (a cub reporter) and her younger, prettier, and blonder sister Eileen, an aspiring actress. McKenney recounted the girls' adventures growing up in Ohio, as well as their tribulations as young, single women living in New York's Greenwich Village in the 1930s.[50] The response to McKenney's first two stories (published in January 1937) was so positive that editor Katherine S. White commissioned more, and by the summer McKenney was publishing roughly two stories a month. By the beginning of 1938, plans were in place to collect McKenney's *New Yorker* stories in a single volume later that year, to be published under the title *My Sister Eileen*. The final story presented in *My Sister Eileen*—"Beware the Brazilian Navy"—was nearly a word-for-word reprint of one originally published in the summer of 1937. In ways McKenney could never have anticipated, this story provided the basis for *My Sister Eileen*'s famed "conga" episode, which would emerge as perhaps the most memorable sequence in subsequent adaptations of McKenney's work, and to which my discussion will now turn.[51]

The collection of stories in *My Sister Eileen* was an immediate hit, ranking second on the *New York Times* best-seller list the week of its July 1937 release. Also a featured Book-of-the-Month Club selection, *My Sister Eileen* was in its eighth hardcover printing by the end of 1938. The book's success drew the attention of several playwriting teams interested in capturing *My Sister Eileen* for the stage. After several rounds of interviews and pitches, Joseph Fields and Jerome Chodorov were selected for the task, and their Broadway stage version—directed by powerhouse George S. Kaufman, with rising star Shirley Booth in the role of Ruth—opened on

Broadway in the final days of December 1940. The play ran for nearly nine hundred performances.[52]

The immediate and formidable success of the stage play drew the attention of Hollywood, and in September 1942 Columbia Pictures released a film version, with Fields and Chodorov serving as screenwriters. The film *My Sister Eileen* went on to become Columbia's biggest hit of the year and earned its star, Rosalind Russell, her first of four Oscar nominations for her turn as Ruth. Legal wrangling foreclosed several attempts at a radio serial adaptation (including one featuring Lucille Ball) in the latter half of the 1940s.[53] Nonetheless, the popularity of *My Sister Eileen* continued unabated throughout the decade. McKenney's book never went out of print; Fields and Chodorov's stage play entered the repertoire of school, community, and summer stock theatres.[54] By 1952 a Broadway musical version was in the works, once again featuring Rosalind Russell in a script adapted by Fields and Chodorov, but this time featuring new music by Leonard Bernstein and lyrics by Betty Comden and Adolph Green.

The stage musical version of *My Sister Eileen*—titled *Wonderful Town*—opened on Broadway in early 1953 and proved an immediate popular and critical hit, earning Tony awards in six categories (including one for Russell and the prize for Best Musical). Once again, the show's Broadway success garnered Hollywood's interest, but Columbia Pictures (which retained ownership of Fields and Chodorov's 1942 screenplay) balked at the cost of the Broadway property. Instead, it opted to adapt the 1942 film version, inserting specially commissioned songs. In 1955 Columbia released a movie musical version of *My Sister Eileen* (with Betty Garrett as Ruth) to—for the first time in the property's history—only middling success. A television presentation of *Wonderful Town* followed in 1958 (with Russell again reprising her performance as Ruth), and a short-lived TV sitcom version of *My Sister Eileen* premiered on CBS in 1960–61 (with Elaine Stritch starring as Ruth). All told, with multiple variants appearing in print, on stage, and on screen, *My Sister Eileen* was rarely far from the mainstream of US popular performance from 1937 to 1961.

My attention to *My Sister Eileen* derives not simply from the fact that its life cycle of adaptations happens to span the same quarter century marking the Good Neighbor Era. Rather, changes within a particular, prominent episode in *My Sister Eileen*—the encounter with the "Brazilian" Navy—also provide an instructive measure of the shifts in what the "Latin number" accomplished at distinct historical junctures in the Good Neighbor Era. As *My Sister Eileen*'s conga episode changes from the page to the stage to the screen (and then as it is reinvented for the musical stage and screen), I detail how each of these media melded music, dance, and narrative to stage the fraught encounter between the "All-American" Ruth and her "Pan-American" admirals. At the same time, these variants chart legible shifts in the dramaturgical utility of the musical "Latin number" in US popular performance—from discovery to disidentification to dissolution. The variations on the "conga" scene within different iterations of *My Sister Eileen* demonstrate not only how this particular Latin number works, but also how the phenomenon of any "Latin number" cycle operates. *My Sister Eileen*'s "conga" episode rehearses the particular cultural styles, techniques, and forms that enter the repertoire of US popular performance through the overlapping phases of naive discovery, sophisticated disidentification, and decadent dissolution. *My Sister Eileen*'s "conga" episode thus emerges as both an exemplary Latin number and an exemplar of the "Latin number" process more broadly.

In the first iteration of what becomes *My Sister Eileen*'s "conga" episode, the conga does not figure at all. Even so, in the story "Beware the Brazilian Navy"—which first appears in the *New Yorker* in July 1937 and is later republished as the final story in *My Sister Eileen* (1938)—Ruth McKenney crafts the encounter between two all-American girls from Ohio and the "future admirals from Brazil" into a dramatic scenario of naive discovery that would function as a pivotal—even climactic—incident in subsequent adaptations of her stories. In the story (subtitled for the book as "Almost the Worst Thing That Ever Happened to Us"), McKenney recounts how, one hot summer day, she arrived at the Brooklyn shipyards to report on the landing of a Brazilian military vessel. She found that not only was she the only reporter there but she was also the only "American peacherino" present to "welcom[e] the flower of Brazilian manhood."

In McKenney's telling, Ruth is seized upon by the ship's captain and suddenly becomes the uncomprehending center of attention for the "gorgeous future admirals," who mistake her for someone of significance. After thrusting her business card into the captain's hand, Ruth escapes to her newspaper office. The "future admirals" follow, first to her office and then to the home she shares with her sister Eileen. ("The five Brazilians now sat down in a happy row . . . staring with five pairs of gleaming black eyes at my pretty sister.") Thwarted ludicrously by a language barrier, the sisters guide the future admirals to a nearby restaurant, where the men tip the orchestra to play familiar songs. After wrangling herself a break "to repair the ravages of several rumbas with Number Three,"

Ruth recalls returning to "the horrid sight" of "my sister and the Number One boy from Brazil . . . prowling around each other while the orchestra played a sneaky, sinister rumba" and as other patrons "were lined up around the dance floor, three deep, jaws agape."[55] Confounded by the "delicate situation" of how they might return to their apartment without the admirals, the sisters just march "smartly home, the fine brave sea dogs singing some little Portuguese sea chanty in tango time and trotting along." The evening and the story resolve as the sisters sneak—with some farcical bait-and-switch trickery—into their own apartment, leaving the frustrated future admirals to serenade and fight until morning. In the story's final moment, Ruth opens the door only a crack and is relieved to discover that the "Brazilian Navy were gone. . . . I guess they were pretty disappointed in American girls."[56]

"Beware the Brazilian Navy" was one of only two stories from McKenney's collection that playwrights Joseph Fields and Jerome Chodorov adapted for their 1940 script for the play *My Sister Eileen*. To McKenney's combination of cultural incomprehension, Latin music, and libidinal threat, the playwrights added just a little bit of conga. In so doing, they created a rollicking scene of comedic conflict and chaos that would comprise their play's second act finale and eventually become one of its most iconic episodes. Where McKenney's "Beware the Brazilian Navy" distilled the naïveté of cultural encounter and discovery, Fields and Chodorov refined it toward comedic ends. Additionally, by integrating the contemporary conga fad of 1940, the playwrights also transformed "almost the worst thing that ever happened to us" into one of *My Sister Eileen*'s most incongruously comedic on-stage sequences.[57]

In the stage play, the scenario of Ruth's encounter with the Brazilian Navy remains the same—she goes to the naval yard and is followed home by the Brazilian sailors, and the "Future Admirals" (their character designation in the playscript) dance with the two sisters, instigating a comedic spectacle. Several differences are noteworthy in the Fields and Chodorov adaptation. First, because the play *My Sister Eileen* takes place entirely within the sisters' basement apartment, the episode begins as Ruth returns home with six "very handsome" Future Admirals in tow, "[t]heir dark skins contrast[ing] brilliantly with their immaculate tropical white uniforms." Ruth explains, "They've been on my tail ever since I left the Brooklyn Navy Yard. There were another dozen when we started out, but they got lost on the subway." Some obligatory language-barrier jokes follow, and the dancing begins when one of the sailors "discovers the phonograph." Then, "a conga blares forth loudly, . . . and the dance is on with great gusto, despite the girls' protests." The spectacle of the "men laughing and dancing excitedly" in Ruth and Eileen's apartment soon musters the attention of their neighbors, and before long, neighbors, passersby, and onlookers have joined the line, which begins snaking in, out, and through the apartment. Thus, in the 1940 stage version, while maintaining the sexual threat implied within the musical culture clash, Fields and Chodorov replace the sailors' repeatedly requested rumbas with a single recorded conga, transforming the episode into both a farcical set piece and a dance interlude in an otherwise nonmusical play.[58]

When Fields and Chodorov adapted their stage play for Hollywood the following year, they made comparatively few changes to the dramatic structure and dialogue, aside from adding a brief Ohio prologue and resetting selected scenes in locations other than the sisters' basement apartment. One of the script's more conspicuous stage-to-screen changes came at the behest of Jock Whitney's film office. The OCIAA's auditors balked at the script's depiction of the Brazilian Navy's "Future Admirals" and insisted that all references to Brazil's military be excised from the film. Thus, with just a few emendations to the shooting script, the conga-ing Brazilian Navy cadets became "Future Admirals" of the Portuguese Merchant Marine.

The archive remains unclear as to whether the OCIAA, Columbia Pictures, or Fields and Chodorov suggested the substitution of Portugal's commercial shipping fleet for Brazil's maritime military force, but the filmed screenplay confirms that the production simply switched out the words. Even the script's single throwaway reference to the Good Neighbor idea was retained. This line comes in the final moments of the play and the film when the maritime commander arrives to deliver a formal apology to Eileen for her inconvenience in having been jailed for inciting the conga riot, which was actually caused by the sailors. Ruth then returns their hats with a mordant salute. On stage, Shirley Booth's Ruth says "[T]o Brazil, from your good neighbors in Greenwich Village." On screen, Rosalind Russell's Ruth offers a tribute "To the Merchant Marine," thereby rhetorically incorporating the Iberian Peninsula under the inter-American umbrella.

In this way, the 1942 film version of *My Sister Eileen*'s conga episode bears the era's hallmarks of a quick and easy substitution of one "Latin" for another, as compelled by directives from the OCIAA, resulting in glib cultural inaccuracies. Even so, the film version's conga episode (even with the Merchant Marine substitution) distills the dramaturgic utility of the "Future Admirals" to their essence: a "romance" language barrier

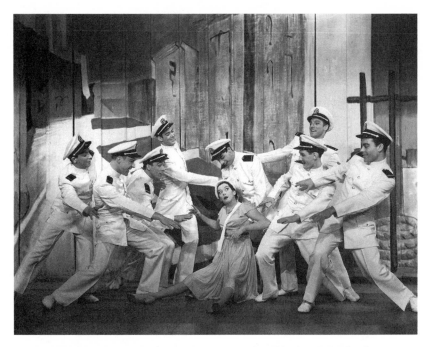

Rosalind Russell congas with the "Future Admirals" in *Wonderful Town* (1953). (Image by permission of *Photofest*)

that leads to libidinal threat, which finds incongruous release through a ludicrous conga line. Thus, in the five years separating McKenney's first account of the Brazilian Navy's rapacious rumbas from Hollywood's good neighborly depiction of the conga-ing Portuguese Merchant Marine, we can see how the scenario was transformed from an episode of naive discovery and cultural encounter to an example of sophisticated disidentification.[59]

The dramatic utility of *My Sister Eileen*'s conga episode becomes even more apparent in the piece's next adaptation ten years later, when the Ruth, Eileen, and the Future Admirals do their one-two-three kicks in the Broadway musical *Wonderful Town* (1953). Guided again by the authorship of Joseph Fields and Jerome Chodorov, *Wonderful Town* is also shaped by the contributions of its star Rosalind Russell, composer Leonard Bernstein, and lyricist team Betty Comden and Adolph Green. Three central points of reconceptualization distinguish *Wonderful Town* from previous adaptations. First, in 1953 the story of two Ohioan sisters arriving in "Greenwich Village in the '30s" is reframed as a nostalgia piece, and the mortifying details that animated Ruth McKenney's magazine stories are recast as quaint reminiscences of a simpler time. This nostalgia is on prominent display in the musical's opening "Christopher Street" number, in which tourists follow a guide through a mix of modern dancers, radical painters, and various others who comprise the "interesting people living on Christopher Street." Next, *Wonderful Town* reimagines *My Sister Eileen* as a star vehicle for Rosalind Russell in the role of Ruth.[60] As such, several musical episodes (including "One Hundred Easy Ways," "Swing!," and "Conga!") showcase Russell's verbal dexterity with intricately witty lyrics. Finally, a two-act dramatic structure uses the first act to introduce Ruth, Eileen, and a host of complicating characters, all of whom snarl into a chaotic apex in the first act finale and are subsequently untangled in the long denouement of the musical's second act.

Wonderful Town's version of the conga episode—which comprises the first act finale, "Conga!"—contributes pivotally to each of the musical's reformulations of its source material. First, during Ruth's encounter with the (once again) Brazilian Navy cadets, she sings the song's chorus: "Good neighbors—Good neighbors, / Remember our policy / Good neighbors—I'll help you / If you'll just help me." As a feeble attempt to repel the future admirals' one-two-three kicks across the language barrier, Ruth's admonition to "remember our policy" also reanimates inter-American rhetoric in a nostalgic register, evoking the Good Neighbor ethos as a quaint policy of the past. At the same time, in each verse of the song Comden and Green's lyrics name-check the contemporary trends of the 1930s (in a manner reminiscent of Harold Rome's comedic commentaries). With each verse, Ruth struggles to maintain her reporterly decorum by asking the Future Admirals for their thoughts about the idiosyncrasies of "American" life ("What do you think of the USA—NRA—TVA, / What do you think of our Mother's Day"), but at the end of each verse, the cadets' calls for "Conga!" whisk Ruth back into the dance line, as if to confirm the fundamental limits of Pan-American communication. Finally, as the "Conga!" number kicks its way from the shipyard back to Greenwich Village, *Wonderful Town* uses the snaking dance line to weave every plot thread into a rousing chaotic musical finale in which hearts are broken, betrayals are revealed, and Eileen is carted off to jail. The musical's second act is dedicated to untangling the myriad plot complications snarled during the first act's "Conga!" finale, anchoring the conga episode not only as one of the musical's most memorable sequences but also as one of its most structurally significant.[61]

The conga episode in the 1955 Columbia Pictures musical film version of *My Sister Eileen* operates somewhat differently. By most measures, the musical film augments the narrative rudiments of the 1942 movie by inserting songs and dance interludes at specific dramatic junctures. Because of legal challenges from both the team of Fields and Chodorov and Ruth McKenney herself, writer-director Richard Quine (along with his coscreenwriter Blake Edwards) were obliged to avoid any appearance of copying the narrative placement of musical numbers in *Wonderful Town*—with one exception. Because the 1942 film had its own conga episode, so does the 1955 movie. In contrast to *Wonderful Town*'s "Conga!" (which serves as the stage musical's climactic pivot point), "What Happened to the Conga?" serves as both the movie musical's last number and its closing credit finale. The episode begins as Ruth arrives at the shipyard, is immediately thronged by dozens of naval cadets, and escapes down the pier with a mob of sailors running in pursuit. Seven of these sailors chase Ruth to the apartment she shares with Eileen, in which, after an abbreviated version of the familiar language-barrier comic bits, one sailor sits at the piano and the others indicate their desire to dance. Betty Garrett's Ruth rebuffs them: "My sister doesn't rumba / She doesn't samba either / We don't even do the conga!"

Ruth's mere mention of the conga instigates an extended dance number in which Ruth, Eileen, and their landlord engage in a farcical hide-and-seek dance with the exuberant sailors, all to a conga beat. When an unseen someone calls out, "[L]et's join the party!," throngs of neighbors, passersby, and onlookers join the conga line until the police arrive (thus instigating the jailings that compel the romantic reconciliations necessary for the story's conclusion). Notably, in the film's final moments, when Ruth and Eileen receive the apology of the Brazilian official on the exterior steps of their apartment, Ruth makes no mention of the Good Neighbor idea as she avers, "[A]ctually we didn't do anything—all I did was say something about the conga!" Of course, Ruth's "conga" utterance incites an eruption of exuberant merriment among all assembled, and the screen fills with hundreds of conga-ing bodies as the film's end title appears.[62]

Notably, in *Wonderful Town*, when Ruth first asks the Brazilian sailors for their thoughts on America, they answer, "American dance—Conga!" Ruth's correction ("No, no! Conga's a Brazilian dance!") is itself corrected by the Future Admirals ("No—Cubano! Conga *American* dance! You show conga!"). Yet, even though *Wonderful Town*'s "Conga!" actually corrects some of the cultural elisions that were features of the 1940s versions of the conga episode, the joke of the number depends on the collision between Ruth's most intricate lyric commentary on 1930s US culture and the libidinal frenzy unleashed among the sailors by the mere mention of the word *conga*. In this way, *Wonderful Town*'s variation on the conga episode offers a sophisticated commentary on the naïveté of the Good Neighbor idea, even as it also delights in manipulating the excesses of the conspicuously "Latin" musical number's established conventions.

Wonderful Town thus distills within its "Conga!" number all the different ways in which the charged encounter between Ruth, Eileen, and the crew of libidinal, dance-inclined, Portuguese-speaking "Future Admirals" operated in each version of the story. From its most naive first encounter in McKenney's original stories through its more sophisticated elaborations by Fields and Chodorov in the 1940s and its highly self-conscious distillation and abstraction in the musicals of the 1950s, we can see the ways in which *My Sister Eileen*'s conga episode emerged as a readily reconfigurable dramaturgic device, handy both to exploit the musical-comedic entertainment value of such an intercultural encounter and to confirm the intransigent cultural differences between the all-American sisters and their Pan-American others.

Wonderful Town's conga episode demonstrates how, by the early 1950s, the conventions of the Latin number had become so absorbed within the repertoire of musical theatrical presentation that the simplest invocation—conga!—could simultaneously animate a cultural encounter (discovery) that confirms distinctions of difference (disidentification) and prompt a largely nonsensical display of choreographic, musical, and comedic excess (dissolution). Indeed, by the 1950s, the Good Neighbor idea may have been a "policy of the past," but its productions—especially those deploying the conspicuously "Latin" musical number—remained current, ongoing, and increasingly ubiquitous on the musical stages of both Broadway and Hollywood. The many postwar (and post–"Good Neighbor") conspicuously "Latin" musical numbers distilled an enduring mode of theatrical staging that recast the cultural novelty of inter-American encounter as a stylized novelty routine characterized by color, chaos, and carnality. This mode—however inadvertently—would establish the "Latin number" as among the most enduring legacies of the Good Neighbor Era.

Color, Chaos, and Carnality

The decommissioning of the OCIAA in 1946 signaled an official dissolution of the imperatives guiding the Good Neighbor ethos. As the techniques of cultural diplomacy pioneered under the Good Neighbor umbrella were reoriented toward the uncertain nuclear futures of Asia, Europe, and the United States, efforts to foster neighborly relations among the other American republics did persist, mostly within educational contexts such as schools, libraries, and museums. At the same time, the conspicuously "Latin" musical number—that stylishly stylized mode of musical theatrical presentation so central to Good Neighbor productions—became even more ubiquitous (and ever more ridiculous) in productions featured in nightclubs, theatres, and movie houses across the country. Bandleaders included "Latin" sets, songs, and soloists in their acts with such regularity that reporters for the entertainment trade magazine *Variety* started snidely categorizing any such number as a "latune" as early as 1946.[63] Broadway and Hollywood productions began using the signature flourishes of the Latin number—the colorful costumes, the carnal rhythms, the chaotic energy—to stage narratives and songs with no diegetic connection to the peoples, cultures, or geographies of Latin America. Indeed, as it became increasingly untethered from even the vaguest diplomatic obligation, the Latin number refined a performance style increasingly divorced from intercultural substance, and this cultural divorce would haunt the enactment of Latin-ness in US popular performance for the next half century.

In his comparative analysis of "latunes" of the 1930s and 1940s, Gustavo Pérez Firmat repurposes the *Variety* reporter's epithetic neologism as a scholarly term with which to describe the genre of US popular song that featured both "a Latin beat and an English language lyric" and typically expressed a fascination with "Latin" geography, musicality, or sensuality.[64] During the late 1940s and 1950s, the staging of such numbers for Broadway and Hollywood musicals not only evoked these distinct fascinations—geography, musicality, and sensuality—but also distilled them into an aggregated fantasy of incoherently coherent Latin-ness. Generations of scholars have rightly faulted these conspicuously "Latin" musical numbers for their many inaccuracies and cultural elisions. Yet their percussive, brightly hued, ruffled twirls and haphazard Spanish-ish verbal tics cued not only a genre but also an idea. Indeed, in its dissolution of the good neighborly specificities of Latin American cultural forms, the conspicuously "Latin" musical number in the later 1940s and 1950s also rehearsed US audiences in the practice, pleasure, and privilege of perceiving all "Latins" as being alike in their difference.

On the Broadway stage of the 1950s, there emerged a peculiar ubiquity of musical scenarios rehearsing and delighting in this generalizing fantasy of conspicuous Latin-ness. *Wonderful Town's* conga episode (in which all-American Ruth encounters the sailors of Brazilian fleet, whose craving for the conga is strongly suggestive of other desires) typifies the ways in which ostensibly "Latin" musical numbers on Broadway simultaneously evoked Latin American geography, musicality, and sensuality, even as they also instigated some measure of often comedic chaos. Indeed, examples from this period exploit this particular admixture of color, carnality, and comedic chaos, often in nonsensical ways. Sometimes these musical scenarios cued escape from societal expectations, as in "Hernando's Hideaway," in which a percussive tango guides intrepid venturers beyond their inhibitions and to the discovery of an after-hours nightclub in *The Pajama Game* (1954). In more metaphorical forays like "Mu-Cha-Cha" from *Bells Are Ringing* (1956), learning a "foreign" dance (and singing nonsense lyrics) opens a world of new romantic confidence for the musical's uncertain heroine.

Occasionally, a Latin musical number might cue a character's demonstration of intercultural dexterity, as in the mock-multilingual mashup "I Am Easily Assimilated" from *Candide* (1956), or it might demonstrate a character's enumeration of his or her unique abilities, as when the self-proclaimed "Senorita Lolita Rodriguez Hernando" endeavors to seduce a reluctant baseball player in "Whatever Lola Wants" from *Damn Yankees* (1955). And from time to time, in the tradition of songs like "South America (Take It Away)," a Broadway Latin number might prompt a bit of parody, as when athletic men enact the physicality of certain dance styles in "Who's Got the Pain," also from *Damn Yankees*, or the crafty queen tricks her unsuspecting nemesis into doing "The Spanish Panic" (described by one character as "only the most complicated, exhausting dance in the entire world") in *Once upon a Mattress* (1959).[65]

These few examples—in tandem with others in musicals as stylistically disparate as *Guys and Dolls*, *Peter Pan*, *Call Me Madam*, and *Wish You Were Here*—confirm that such emphatically "Latin" musical numbers were not primarily used in the handful of shows featuring characters, settings, or story lines from Latin America or the Caribbean. Rather, in the decade or so after the official decommissioning of the Good Neighbor Policy, the Latin number continued to function as a ready stylistic and dramatic device to inject a jolt of colorful unpredictability and energetic physicality into any (and nearly every) musical of the period.

Berlin's "Heat Wave"—a mildly suggestive song about a woman's capacity to raise temperatures with a simple move of her body—was introduced on Broadway by a sultry and elegant Ethel Waters and was subsequently popularized in a jaunty swing version by Ethel Merman in the 1938 film *Alexander's Ragtime Band*. For 1954's *There's No Business Like Show Business,* "Heat Wave" was reimagined as a Latin rumba, which both Ethel Merman's matriarch vaudevillian and Marilyn Monroe's ambitious show singer plan to perform at nightclub in Miami. Ultimately, Monroe's "Heat Wave" takes the stage, leaving Merman's team to strategize an alternate use for their newly purchased Latin costumes. Musically, Monroe "exaggerates the calypso rhythms the song always had, highlighting them through conga drums,"[66] while also augmenting the original lyrics with spoken interjections that confirm the locale as both definitively—but also abstractly—somewhere in the Caribbean. The set is bare but for outlines of foliage against a darkly red scrim. An ensemble of male dancers—referred to by Monroe as Pablo, Chico, and Miguelito—wear tight, striped outfits that expose their makeup-darkened arms and abdomens. As Monroe sings the simple lyric, the men circle around, variously drawn to and repelled by the elaborate swirl of her fuchsia-clad hips. A spectacular musical set piece, with choreography by Jack Cole and art direction by John DeCuir and Lyle R. Wheeler, the staging of "Heat Wave" bears all the lush yet ludicrous hallmarks of the Latin number—color, carnality, and congas—with just enough controlled chaos to keep it enthralling.

So scooped by Monroe, Ethel Merman's team opts to perform a "Latin" version of "Anything You Can Do"—Berlin's comedic challenge duet introduced by Merman in 1946's *Annie Get Your Gun*. Merman retains the twangy inflections of her original Annie Oakley characterization, even as she reperforms the song "maraca style." Merman and her costar Dan Dailey sing the first verse of the song's call-and-response lyric, interpolating the occasional twirl and an exclaimed *olé* or two, while churning their arms rumba style. As Merman (who wears a black sequined gown accented with tangerine and fuchsia ruffles) steps to a circular side platform, Dailey (who wears a bolero hat, flamenco pants, and a lavishly ruffled pink and yellow shirt) welcomes Mitzi Gaynor and Donald O'Connor (whose outfits complement Dailey's) for an extended dance break.

As Dailey leads a three-person rumba-ish cha-cha, Merman shakes her maracas on the side and leads the group in routinely Spanish musical exclamations (*Olé! Sí sí! Ajua! Arriba! Viva los Donahues!*) until the song ends. Producer Daryl Zanuck cut the song from the film (reportedly in the interests of reducing its long running time), and the only remnant of this Latinized version of "Anything You Can Do" in the final film comes when Merman and family, still in costume, rush to catch the tale end of Monroe's "Heat Wave."[67] Considered together, however, the two sequences confirm the coordinating conventions of Hollywood's use of the conspicuously "Latin" musical number as a stock staging style.

It might seem that the many such musical episodes filling the stages and screens of the 1950s with congas, ruffled shirts, and arbitrary *olés* signal the Good Neighbor Era's final moments of devolution, the moment when the Pan-American imperative devolved into camp incoherence. And, on some levels, that is true. At the same time, however, there is a kind of sense to the insensibilities of the Latin number of the 1950s. The decadent dissolution of the Latin number in musicals like *Damn Yankees* or *There's No Business Like Show Business*—in which Latin-ness floats freely as a vague abstraction and operates primarily as a dramatic device or staging strategy—remains tethered to the polyglot Pan-Americanisms and mambo-dancing sophisticates of the previous decade. Indeed, in each phase of its cycle, the pleasures of the conspicuously "Latin" musical number for US audiences were predicated on the premise that galvanized all those "other" American republics into a singular and presumptively shared Latin-ness. Like the Good Neighbor idea, such musical episodes rehearsed the notion that the "other" American republics were similar in their cultural differences from the United States. Such spectacularly musical rehearsals of difference usually stopped just short of drawing racial distinctions between "Latins" and "Americans," rarely emphasizing particularities of racial difference and instead affirming an aggregated cultural otherness. Still, raciality haunts every "Latin number," even though questions of race only rarely take center stage within any particular "Latin number" itself.

Of course, there are conspicuously "Latin" musical numbers that do experiment with raciality, and though they prove no rules within the incoherent landscape of popular performance, the incongruity of such exceptions does confirm that the Latin number was not generally used as a device to rehearse Latina/o racial distinction. One film from 1944—the historical moment when the Latin musical number stopped discovering the novelty of cultural difference and began to develop sophisticated strategies of disidentification with regard to Latin American cultural practices and forms—offers two such exceptions.

Broadway Rhythm

The undistinguished finale in the storied *Broadway Melody* franchise, 1944's *Broadway Rhythm,* was a routine backstage romance that followed

Ginny Simms in "Amor" from *Broadway Rhythm* (1944). (Publicity still, collection of the author)

a successful Broadway producer Johnny Demming (played by future US senator George Murphy) as he scouted talent for his new hit show, all while ignoring the pleas of his reluctantly retired musician father and star-struck sister. At the same time, Demming is interested in dating—but not hiring—movie star Helen Hoyt (Ginny Simms), who has come to New York in search of a suitable stage role. When the Brazilian singer "La Polita" arrives to audition, Demming fails to recognize Simms's Hoyt in a

Lena Horne in "Brazilian Boogie Woogie" from *Broadway Rhythm* (1944).
(Publicity still, collection of the author)

disguise, which consists of an elaborately brocaded gown, mantilla, fan, and—of all things—a blonde wig. Undeterred by the Brazilian La Polita's high Castilian getup, Murphy's Demming swoons, as Simms's Hoyt lyrically sings "Amor" (a bolero by Gabriel Ruiz, who also composed the Carmen Miranda hit "Cuanto le Gusta"), while an ensemble of matador dancers flap their capes on an elaborate set filled with the Moorish arches and planes of Andalusia.

Of course, Demming hires La Polita on the spot, and once the disguises fall away, the Broadway producer and Hollywood actress begin scouting talent at a series of elaborately themed Manhattan nightclubs, such as the Jungle Room, where Fernway de la Fer (Lena Horne) is the headliner. Horne's first of two featured numbers is "Brazilian Boogie Woogie," a swinging Latin-inflected number, which Horne performs along with an ensemble of tropically attired dancers (that included notable African American dance figures Marie Bryant and Lennie Bluett, among others). Clad in a loose, full-length skirt that is slit to the hip and a midriff-exposing short-sleeved halter, Horne's attire is demure compared to that of the microskirted chorines, in their ruffled halters and feathered headwraps, and her male partners, each wearing tight clamdiggers and half shirts. The song, as arranged by Horne's *Broadway Rhythm* costar Hazel Scott (who, like Horne, appeared in two easily censored scenes), told a story typical of Latin musical numbers, albeit with a conspicuous racial twist: "Down in Brazil they do a dance that's gonna give you a thrill / It's just a half-breed / Because its mammy was a samba and its pappy was swing / They got together and made a nice kind of thing." Horne's performance of "Brazilian Boogie Woogie" captivates both the Broadway producer and the Hollywood actress, but neither interacts onscreen with Horne's Fernway de la Fer.

The paradox implicit in each of *Broadway Rhythm*'s two conspicuously "Latin" musical numbers is underscored by their close narrative juxtaposition. Both Simms's disguise as La Polita and Lena Horne's as Fernway de la Fer are apprehended diegetically as Brazilian, with no acknowledgment of either Simms's conspicuous whiteness or Horne's apparent blackness. Likewise, both numbers rehearse an idea of Brazil that is visually and aurally inclusive of both Iberian bolero and African American boogie-woogie. For generations, scholars have noted how Latin music fads of the 1930s, 1940s, and 1950s deracinated and denationalized authentic Latin American traditions for popular consumption in the United States. While this is certainly the case, the peculiarly juxtaposed yet conspicuously "Latin" musical numbers in 1944's *Broadway Rhythm*— neither of which is performed by a Latina—also underscore how the Latin numbers of this period also rehearsed a racial silence within their celebration of the "other" American republics. The Latin musical number's free-floating cultural signifiers were thus capable of evoking colorful, concupiscent inter-American pleasures while, at the outset of the civil rights era, also avoiding the more precarious paradoxes of integration, miscegenation, and race consciousness. Indeed, the incongruously juxtaposed "Latin" musical numbers in 1944's *Broadway Rhythm* provide a compelling reminder that the fundamental work of the Good Neighbor Era Latin number, in all its modalities, was to rehearse for US audiences how an aggregated Latin-ness might look, sound, and feel. Central to that enactment was an assiduous inattention to the realities of raciality and racial distinction off stage.

The handful of conspicuously "Latin" musical numbers that amplify questions of racial legibility also introduce the complicated questions of recognizing race within the bodies and performances of Latina/o actors.

Aptly, the unspoken question of Latin raciality manifests in *Broadway Rhythm* in the context of a casting scenario within which a performer's distinctive qualities and abilities are assessed when determining their suitability for a particular role. And it is to such questions of casting—specifically the ways in which Latino actors were assigned roles during the postwar era—that my next chapter turns.

CHAPTER 2

Stealth Latinos

Casting the Limits of Racial
Legibility at Midcentury

—— ❧ ——

In 1950 the Academy of Motion Picture Arts and Sciences named Puerto Rican actor José Ferrer the year's "Best Actor" for his performance as the title character in *Cyrano de Bergerac*. Ferrer's recognition at the twenty-third annual awards ceremony was neither the actor's first Oscar nod, having been nominated two years before for his supporting performance in *Joan of Arc*, nor his first award for this particular role, having received the Tony for his Broadway performance as Cyrano in 1947. Still, Ferrer's recognition as Best Actor marked the first time an actor of Latin American heritage had ever won an Oscar. It was also the only occasion in the twentieth century when a Latino was recognized as Best Actor or Best Actress (a distinction Ferrer held into the second decade of the twenty-first century). But Ferrer's status as "first Latino to win an Oscar"—however conspicuous in historical retrospect—occasioned little comment in 1950. Ferrer's Puerto Rican heritage received scant mention in press accounts, with attention to the actor's stage-to-screen success (and impending testimony before the House Un-American Activities Committee) overwhelming any potential interest in the relevance of his win for other "Latin" or "Spanish" actors.[1]

Even before Ferrer's 1948 *Joan of Arc* nomination, Thomas Gomez's gregarious portrayal of a humble New Mexican carousel owner in

1947's *Ride the Pink Horse* earned the veteran actor a Best Supporting Actor nomination in the Oscars' twentieth year. More significant, perhaps, in the decade or so that followed Ferrer's *Cyrano* win, one or more Latina/o actors were nominated for Oscar recognition every other year or so, marking the years between 1947 and 1965 as a Latin boom of sorts, a time when more Latinos were nominated for and won Oscars than any other period in Academy Award history. Between 1947 and 1964, six Latina/o performers—Thomas Gomez, José Ferrer, Anthony Quinn, Katy Jurado, Susan Kohner, and Rita Moreno—earned a total of eleven nominations. (Both Ferrer and Quinn were nominated multiple times, with three nominations for Ferrer and four for Quinn.) Three of the six nominated performers took home the trophy a total of four times. (Quinn won twice, and Ferrer and Moreno were each awarded once.) The trend toward awarding Latina/o actors came to an abrupt end in the mid-1960s, however. After Anthony Quinn was honored with his fourth and final career Oscar nomination for *Zorba the Greek* in 1965, no Latina/o actors were recognized with nominations until Argentinian actress Norma Aleandro's 1987 Best Supporting Actress nod for *Gaby: A True Story* broke a two-decade streak of nonrecognition.[2]

So bracketed by two separate twenty-year periods of nonrecognition, the midcentury proliferation of Oscar recognition for Latina/o actors between 1947 and 1964 might seem a simple anomaly, a symptom of the peculiar vicissitudes of the entertainment industry. At the same time, the incongruity of a Latina/o actorly presence within the Academy Awards mainstream at midcentury becomes conspicuous, compared not only to the Latina/o absence in adjacent decades but also to the patterns of recognition for other minority actors. During the same periods, the recognition of African American actors increased in begrudging increments. In the first forty years of the Academy Awards (1927–66), African Americans were nominated six times, winning only twice (Hattie McDaniel for Best Supporting Actress in 1939 and Sidney Poitier for Best Actor in 1963). The next twenty years (1967–86) brought only fifteen nominations and a single win (Louis Gossett Jr. in 1982). In the thirty-five years between 1987 and 2012, however, African American actors (and actors of African descent) earned forty nominations, winning eleven times. For Asian and Asian American actors, as well as Native American actors, recognition arrived more sporadically, if at all. The ratio of accomplishment for Latina/o performers in this period is all the more remarkable considering that more Latina/o actors won awards between 1947 and 1964 than in the nearly fifty years since.[3]

Additional scrutiny of this minor midcentury explosion of Latino/a actors at the Oscars reveals additional anomalies. In particular, Latina/o actors were nominated for both "Latin" and "non-Latin" roles. Perhaps most conspicuously—especially from a contemporary vantage point— only three Latina/o actors were nominated for playing Latina/o roles. While Thomas Gomez (whose ancestry could be traced to Spanish colonial New Orleans) portrayed a contemporary Hispano in New Mexico, Puerto Rican José Ferrer's nominations all came for his portrayals of elite French men. Anthony Quinn's came for his depictions of, in turn, a Mexican, a Frenchman, an Italian, and a Greek. Among the three Latinas nominated, only Rita Moreno was recognized for her portrayal of a Latina (Anita in *West Side Story*), while both Mexican actress Katy Jurado and Mexican American Susan Kohner were nominated for cross-racial performances as indigenous and black characters, respectively. (Though best remembered for her portrayal of the Hispana saloon owner in 1952's *High Noon*, Jurado's sole career Oscar nomination came for her turn as Spencer Tracy's Comanche wife in 1953's *Broken Lance*; Susan Kohner—daughter of Mexican actress Lupita Tovar and film producer Paul Kohner—was nominated for her portrayal of the rebellious Sarah Jane in 1957's *Imitation of Life*.)

The midcentury Latina/o presence at the Academy Awards has been viewed as a peculiar aberration. Some observers have considered the eleven nominations and six wins to be a constellation of coincidences or (because of cross-racial performance practices within, by, and opposite the Latina/o nominations) a confirmation of Hollywood's incoherent traditions of racial representation.[4] Such interpretations are not necessarily incorrect. At the same time, this Latina/o boomlet of Academy Awards also provides a provocative thumbnail portrait of a broader range of practices and assumptions guiding the ways in which Latina/o actors were assigned roles at midcentury.

In the pages that follow, I examine the particular ways Latina/o actors were cast in the 1950s and document how Latina/o actors—through the roles they were hired to play in film, television, and theatre—rehearsed the racial limits of the color line in US popular performance. As an illustration, I offer a detailed discussion of the lives, careers, and roles performed by three Latino actors who worked prolifically during this period: Mexican American Ricardo Montalban, Puerto Rican Juano Hernandez, and Cuban American Mel Ferrer. A brief biography of each man details how his particular life and career intersects with the broader patterns of im/migration from Mexico, Puerto Rico, and Cuba in the postwar period. My close examination of each man's body of work will help to explain three central aspects of how casting practices of the period deployed the presumptive racial fluidity of known Latina/o actors through narrative depictions of the limits of legibility (Montalban), the permeability of the color line (Hernandez), and the perils of passing (Ferrer).

My discussion concludes with a summary overview of how the "stealth Latino" casting practices rehearsed at midcentury endured into the 1960s and 1970s, when emerging Latina/o actors like Raquel Welch and Henry Darrow opted to "closet" their Latina/o identities to avoid the ossifications of racial typecasting, even as performers like Montalban and Moreno maintained some limited access to the diversity of roles they enjoyed at midcentury. Even though the question of "why" a given actor may have been assigned a particular role may never be fully explained, careful attention to the results of such casting decisions—to the roles Latina/o actors were actually hired to play—provides historical documentation of the ways in which US popular performance rehearsed and enacted emerging notions of Latina/o raciality in the 1950s, revealing some of the presumptions about Latina/o racial legibility, fluidity, and interchangeability that continue to inform casting practices to this day.

Casting

The casting of Latina/o actors in commercial film, television, and theatre productions at midcentury documents the logics and limits of racial intelligibility during the first decades of the Cold War era. The diversity of film, television, and theatre roles assigned to Latina/o actors, especially during the later 1940s through the early 1960s, deployed the Latina/o actor's known Latin-ness both to amplify and to elide the raciality of a broad array of performance narratives. The roles assigned to Latina/o actors in this period both mark and measure the limits of racial intelligibility generally, while also rehearsing particular modes of Latina/o enactment and legibility that endured through subsequent decades. By assessing casting as a form of cultural documentation, we can see how the familiar fluidity of interchangeably "Latin" actors is deployed in the postwar years, within increasingly racializing performances that themselves rehearse and confirm the nonwhite raciality of the Latina/o performer.

Casting—or the process by which actors are assigned roles to perform—is a topic that has largely eluded historical inquiry. For the most part, critical examinations of casting by scholars and practitioners alike have drawn lightly on the history of casting as a practice, even as they have developed productive analyses of casting processes. Typically, these studies are oriented toward some combination of three aspects of the casting process: the logistical, the metaphysical, or the political. Logistical approaches elaborate "how to" cast (or how to be cast in) a production, while metaphysical discussions appreciate casting's affective impact (as when the author of one introductory theatre textbook enthuses, "There is good casting and bad casting, of course, and there is also inspired casting").[5] Logistical and metaphysical approaches to casting both seek to make sense of what another textbook calls the "complicated and finally, irrational" mechanisms of choice that guide the casting of a particular role or production. By contrast, political approaches to casting advocate specific interventions into such casting mechanisms as a means of achieving social, economic, or cultural goals beyond a particular production.

With specific regard to questions of racial casting, the logistical approach is perhaps most evident in the late-twentieth-century movement toward "Non-Traditional" casting, which affirms particular strategies for expanding the ways in which actors of color might be assigned roles in particular productions. The metaphysical aspect is most evident in myriad commentaries on the "miscasting" of particular roles or productions, evincing the particular insensibility of casting John Wayne as Genghis Khan or Puerto Rican Jennifer Lopez as Mexican American Selena. Meanwhile, efforts by actors' labor unions, minority advocacy groups, and other activist voices have articulated the political registers of casting in a variety of campaigns, aimed both toward expanding casting opportunities for minority actors and toward challenging racialist assumptions and traditions embedded within conventional casting practices. Yet, even as particular casting decisions are routinely identified as "proof" in many of these critical discussions, the ways in which casting practices and assumptions from the past might document the historical operation of raciality in twentieth-century performance have yet to be methodically explored.

Although a full history of the material practices of casting in the United States is beyond my task here, a cursory sketch of that history will help to underscore how the racial aesthetics of casting changed dramatically in the 1950s, moving from an inherited regime dominated by racial mimicry toward an emerging aesthetic more compelled by racial congruity. For my purposes, "racial mimicry" describes the imitative practices of racial impersonation, wherein performers of any cultural or racial background might—through a variety of physical, vocal, and visual performance techniques—present themselves as characters of an apparent, distinct, and different ethnoracial background. Likewise, "racial congruity" references the principle that performers should, in some meaningful way, be of a kind with the character being portrayed, and that such congruence (of gender, race, physicality, ability, etc.) necessarily amplifies the aptness of the subsequent performance. The casting practices of the 1950s cue the pivot point from the established tradition of mimicry toward an emerging regime that purported to prioritize congruity.

For more than one hundred years, the guiding tradition for assigning parts within US commercial entertainments borrowed from the European "*emploi*" model, in which a particular performer was expected to specialize in one or more "lines of business," or stock character impersonations, cued by specific physical, vocal, and presentational techniques (including makeup, wigs, and costumes). Although some "stars" could set their own repertoire, most working actors in the mid-nineteenth century were hired based on their skilled capacity to play more than one particular line of business, which might include a selection of the many "ethnic" impersonations popular on the nineteenth-century stage. As the US entertainment industry became increasingly industrialized in the late nineteenth and early twentieth centuries, producers and casting offices increasingly relied on an actor's known specialties—or the types of stock characters he or she could readily play—to streamline the hiring process. Within such a structure, racially and ethnically specific characters were usually considered stock characters—or "types" that actors might portray—provided their impersonations displayed the expected physical, vocal, and visual techniques of racial mimicry.

Beginning in the 1920s and 1930s, with increased interest in cinematic verisimilitude and theatrical innovation, some performance-makers in both New York and Los Angeles began to resist racial imitation as a practice of the past. These innovators sought modern performance modes and forms, which sometimes included hiring African American and Asian actors to play roles that might otherwise be portrayed by white impersonators. By the later 1940s, mobilization by actor unions on both coasts, in tandem with protests organized by prominent social advocacy groups, such as the National Organization for the Advancement of Colored People (NAACP), placed increasing economic, social, and media pressure on producers to hire minority actors to play minority characters, especially in the portrayal of African and African American characters on US stages and screens. Yet, even as expectations of racial congruity increasingly guided the casting of black roles in 1950s, such interest in congruence did not immediately displace racial mimicry within all casting practices. Rather, the shift away from a casting regime in which white actors played most nonwhite roles in blackface (or yellowface, brownface, or redface) was gradual, and these ostensibly counterpointed aesthetics of racial casting were both at work—at times simultaneously—throughout the 1950s.

The casting of Latina/o actors at midcentury is one compelling indicator that the 1950s marks a crucial shift toward a casting aesthetic rooted in racial congruity. Comparable to the kind of cultural fluidity rehearsed by the "Latin" narratives of the Good Neighbor Era, similar logics of interchangeability informed the development of an array of distinctly racialized and racializing casting strategies for Latina/o actors in the 1950s. In addition, the casting decisions evident in past productions document meaningful shifts in the racial legibility of Latinos in the same period. I submit that Latina/o actors were especially useful to producers and directors during this time, as they provided a racially intermediary caste of actors who could mobilize both aesthetics simultaneously. As Latina/o actors portrayed a diverse array of nonwhite characters, their racial mimicries were stealthily fortified by the question of whether—as actors of Latin American heritage—they existed beyond the US white-black color line. Yet such impersonations did not function as cultural rituals confirming Latina/o entrance into whiteness. Rather, these "stealth Latino" performances rehearsed the distinctive legibility of Latina/o nonwhiteness in US popular performance.

As a critical conceit, "stealth Latino" hails those particular instances in which an actor's known or perceived Latina/o identity haunts his or her portrayal of a particular role in ways that, not infrequently, contribute to the performance's effectiveness in its contemporary moment. Some "stealth Latino" performances might highlight the presumed authenticity of a given portrayal, as perhaps in Rita Moreno's Oscar-winning performance in *West Side Story* (1961). More often, however, "stealth Latino" performances exploit the uncertain or mixed raciality of Latina/o performers to amplify themes of racial distinction, legibility, and violation that are central to the dramatic narrative being performed. For example, in two widely seen performances offered in the years prior to *West Side Story*, Rita Moreno also portrayed a charismatic supporting character whose presence and actions compelled dramatic encounters that directly opened questions of racial difference within the broader narrative. In each, and in contrast to her portrayal of *West Side Story*'s

Anita, Puerto Rican Moreno played a character of Asian descent. In the film version of *The King and I* (1956), Moreno portrayed Tuptim, the enslaved Burmese woman whose resistance to her imperially authorized concubinage results in tragedy. In the "Fair Exchange" episode (1958) of the television comedy series *Father Knows Best* (1954–60), Moreno played Chanthini, a college exchange student from India, whose initial distaste for American football reminds the all-American Anderson family that intercultural communication is a two-way street. For each of these very different (but surprisingly similar) roles, Moreno's performance choices efficiently inject a measure of distinctive and racially tinged ethnic difference into the particular homogeneities of each scenario.[6] By deploying Moreno's known ethnicity—while also effacing it within a cross-racial impersonation—Moreno's casting as both Tuptim and as Chanthini enables both *The King and I* and *Father Knows Best* to present the interethnic encounters required by their racially charged plots with some measure of verisimilitude, while not violating the racial proprieties of the late 1950s.

I offer Moreno's Tuptim and Chanthini as examples of my "stealth Latino" premise, not because Moreno's casting in these roles was exceptional but rather because such practices were typical of how Latina/o actors like Moreno were cast throughout the 1950s.

Typecasting the Stealth Latino

Ricardo Montalban, Juano Hernandez, and Mel Ferrer are actors who, by most measures, appear to have little in common. Mexican American Ricardo Montalban spent the first two decades of his career almost being a major star. As a Metro Goldwyn Mayer (MGM) contract player (hired specifically to play "Latin lover" type roles), Montalban appeared in a number of big-budget romances, often opposite a leading lady like Esther Williams or Lana Turner, as well as within the ensemble of large-cast prestige dramas like *Battleground* (1949) and *Across the Wide Missouri* (1951). In his work both for MGM and in the raft of independent dramas for which he was contracted out, Montalban played Latin American or Latino characters as frequently as he played characters of indigenous, Asian, Middle Eastern, and African descent. In contrast, Puerto Rican Juano Hernandez mostly portrayed African American characters, with only a handful of notable exceptions. A veteran trouper who had supported himself since childhood by performing as an acrobat, an athlete, and as an actor throughout the Americas, Hernandez emerged in the 1950s as one of the most significant supporting presences in socially conscious dramas of the period, all while precisely affirming the fact of his Puerto Rican heritage. In contrast to the diligent strivings of both Montalban and Hernandez, Cuban American Mel Ferrer was a reluctant star. After dropping out of Princeton (where he earned national notice as a playwright), Ferrer worked variously as a dancer, writer, and director before moving to Hollywood where be began taking acting roles in small-ish films, mostly to maintain access to the industry (where what he really wanted to do was direct). When his 1954 marriage to actress Audrey Hepburn made him a celebrity of sorts, Ferrer's career felt the boost, and the actor began appearing in the elaborate Technicolor romances for which he became best known.

Montalban, Hernandez, and Ferrer each began his respective US film career in the later 1940s. Although he was more than twenty years older than either Ferrer or Montalban, and had worked seriously as a stage and radio actor for nearly two decades, Hernandez's first Hollywood film was 1949's drama of southern justice *Intruder in the Dust*, which came out the same year as Ferrer's leading turn in the "racial passing" saga *Lost Boundaries* and two years after Montalban's US film debut in the musical bullfighting extravaganza *Fiesta* (1947). Over the next decade or so, Montalban, Hernandez, and Ferrer remained actively jobbing actors playing a diversity of roles in an array of theatre, television, and film productions. Each appeared in more films in the 1950s than in any other period in his long career. From the outset, each actor's particular Latin American heritage became a familiar aspect within his personal and professional persona. Even so, Montalban, Hernandez, and Ferrer almost never worked together and would rarely have been considered for similar roles. Though not among the small cohort of Latino actors (which included Anthony Quinn and José Ferrer) to receive significant critical or award recognition, Montalban, Hernandez, and Ferrer each reliably received early credit billing for his work and stood prominently among the battery of Los Angeles–based actors we might now recognize as Latina/o who worked regularly in Hollywood at midcentury.

Though their film careers all began in the late 1940s, the routes that Montalban, Hernandez, and Ferrer took to Hollywood differed in ways that reflected the longer histories of Mexican, Puerto Rican, and Cuban migration to, from, and within the United States before World War II. Mel Ferrer's father emigrated from Cuba to New York City in the 1870s to study medicine. Like many of his Cuban emigrant contemporaries in cities like New York and New Orleans, Ferrer's father opted to remain in the United States as a Cuban expatriate upon the completion of his studies, both to benefit from professional opportunities available to him in the United States and to avoid the tumult of the Cuban political scene in the late nineteenth century. He became an affluent physician and late in life married an Irish American socialite, with whom he had four children, the youngest (Melchor) born not quite two years before the elder Ferrer's death in 1920.

In stark contrast, Juano Hernandez was born in San Juan, a year or two before—or after, depending on your source—the United States annexed Puerto Rico. After a childhood spent between San Juan and São Paolo, Hernandez in his early teens supported himself busking as an acrobat and athlete before joining a small circus with which he toured the Caribbean and the US Gulf Coast, eventually leaving to hit the US vaudeville circuit in the late 1910s. By the early 1930s, Hernandez had become a reliable presence within the burgeoning African American theatre scene in New York, and by the 1940s he was supporting himself performing roles of every race, nationality, and educational background as a member of the stock company of the *Cavalcade of America* radio show.

Ricardo Montalban's early life was neither so affluent nor so hardscrabble. Born to a proudly Spanish family in Mexico City, Montalban spent his early youth in northern Mexico before migrating with his older brother Carlos to Los Angeles, where he attended high school. After a brief jaunt to New York (where he was cast in his first stage and film roles), Montalban returned to Mexico to tend his ailing mother, even as he continued to pursue an acting career. After performing in a few movies in the booming Mexican cinema, he caught the attention of MGM talent scouts.

For these actors, the decade of the 1950s marked a period of both great professional success and significant struggle, within which the roles they played, in tandem with their known Latino heritage, charted what I will argue are particular modes of Latin/o legibility. These actors were often cast in roles that inhabited the edges of raciality, occupying the borderlands of racial distinction marking whiteness apart from blackness, Nativeness, and Asian-ness. Ricardo Montalban, who entered the US film industry as a "Latin lover" type, was assigned a broad range of both Latin/o and non-Latin/o roles. Yet, whether in realist "social problem" dramas, neo-noir thrillers, elaborately costumed adventures, or tropical musical diversions, Montalban's work throughout the 1950s often enacted the thrills (both pleasurable and perilous) of traversing the various color lines. Juano Hernandez, cast almost exclusively in African American roles, became especially well known for characters who, whether through their actions or their beings, highlighted the conspicuous construction of racial distinction, placing special pressure on the propriety, permanence, and permeability of the color line. In contrast, Mel Ferrer was routinely put in roles that underscored the problem of "passing" outside one's culture, race, or religion of origin; that were often the troubling, tainting third in a love triangle; and that were always a threat to the fine calibrations required for social equilibrium.

The kind of "stealth Latino" typecasting I am evincing here must be distinguished from conventional critical discussions of typecasting. Typically, in academic discussions, to typecast is to stereotype—or to apply evaluative generalizations about a particular group to all perceived members of that group, either in social life or in creative practice. (Although I take up this discourse of stereotyping in performance in greater detail in chapter 4, I should note here that my work in this chapter remains indebted to foundational taxonomies of ethnic stereotypes in film developed by scholars such as Donald Bogle, Allen L. Woll, Robert G. Lee, and Charles Ramírez Berg, among others, even as my work applies different theoretical pressure to their taxonomic model of typecasting.)[7] Among performance practitioners, however, *to typecast* can operate in a dual register. On the one hand, *to typecast* might describe the practice wherein a typically brisk visual assessment of an actor's physical attributes determines that actor's suitability for a given role, thereby "typing" him or her in or out of consideration accordingly. On the other, *to typecast* might describe the way an actor's performance in a prior role (or series of roles) informs whether or not he or she is deemed suitable for another, either by confirming the relevance of the actor's demonstrated skills or by evoking perceived affective qualities that threaten (or promise) to "ghost" the taking on of this different role. Each particular iteration of typecasting—whether it deploys stereotype as performance, exploits an actor's physical appearance as visual characterization, or reanimates an actor's past performances within or against his or her current work— underscores the efficiency of typecasting as a storytelling technique.[8]

The typecasting of Ricardo Montalban, Juano Hernandez, and Mel Ferrer in this period is not singly about stereotype, type, or star persona. Rather, by evincing the particular patterns of casting within the careers of these very different actors, we can see the operation of a stealthier mode of typecasting—what I call "stealth Latino" casting—which relies less on an actor's accent, appearance, or affect than on these Latino actors themselves (and Latina/o actors more generally) to enact roles that animate the limits of racial legibility in the 1950s. By thus attending to the ways in which Latino actors like Richardo Montalban, Juano Hernandez, and Mel Ferrer "worked" (through, literally, the roles they were hired to portray), we might discern how Latina/o actors were "used" in midcentury popular performances to rehearse what race might mean for Mexican Americans, Puerto Ricans, Cuban Americans, and other Latinas/os in the United States.

The peculiar perversities of casting also suggest a haphazard, intuitive experiment in how best to "use" Latino performing bodies, both to configure and to confirm the outer limits of racial convention, rehearsing how the color line was shifting in the racial sand. Moreover, the working histories of actors like Montalban, Hernandez, and Ferrer—and any other seriously jobbing Latina/o actors in this period, including the Oscar winners— not only document the erratic shifts in racial logics during the civil rights era but also reveal the instructive gestures toward the racial rationales used by the US government and other institutions to define "Hispanic" as an aggregate ethnoracial grouping in the early 1970s.

Performance-makers of the 1950s seemed almost inevitably inclined to cast Latina/o actors in roles that enacted racial crises, hybridities, and futurities, as well the complex social, political, and erotic complications of complexion. Montalban, Hernandez, and Ferrer played Latin, Latino, or Latin American characters, even as they also played African American characters, with each also taking on various roles of other racialized ethnicities (indigenous, Middle Eastern, Asian, and Jewish). This racial fluidity, especially as rehearsed by the peculiar perversities of stealth Latino typecasting, had the reciprocal effect of racializing the Latina/o actor's body of work and, perhaps by extension, the Latina/o actor's body itself. At the same time, the "stealth Latino" typecasting of Montalban, Hernandez, and Ferrer also reveals the reciprocal ways in which their performances rehearsed the apprehension of the Latino actors themselves as neither precisely white nor black.

Indeed, for Latina/o actors at midcentury, performing such racial surrogations did not confirm their passage to or within the privileges of whiteness, as scholars have argued to be the collateral benefit of blackface performances by Irish, Jewish, and other immigrants in previous epochs.[9] Instead, these stealth Latino typecastings confirmed that Latinos were something other than simply white or black. As the preferred enactors within narratives of racial crossings and interracial intimacies, of collapsing color lines and the perils of passing, the "stealth Latino" performances of actors like Montalban, Hernandez, and Ferrer unexpectedly rehearsed the verisimilitude of the racial borderlands of Latinoness at midcentury.

Ricardo Montalban

Ricardo Montalban was born in Mexico City in 1920. The youngest of four children, he spent his childhood in Torreon, in north-central Mexico, and returned to Mexico City for boarding school. Upon graduation, Montalban joined his eldest brother Carlos, an entrepreneur and sometime actor, in a move to Los Angeles. At his brother's insistence, Ricardo continued his schooling in the United States, enrolling first in Los Angeles's Belmont High—a school dedicated to students for whom English was a second language—until he passed the test necessary to permit his attendance at Fairfax High, where he began appearing in school plays and soon attracted the interest of a talent scout at MGM. Carlos Montalban's business interests intervened, however, and the brothers moved to New York.

In New York, Ricardo Montalban quickly landed a gig as a background player for a company producing "soundies," the short musical films played on the Panoram movie jukeboxes, which, in early 1940, had become the rage in New York's bars, bowling alleys, hotels, and transit stations. A shooting mistake required a hasty reshoot of Gus Van's novelty song "Latin from Staten Island," and Ricardo Montalban stepped in to mouth the lyrics. The appearance helped Montalban to secure an agent, and shortly afterward he landed his first stage job opposite Tallulah Bankhead in a summer "straw hat" circuit production of *Her Cardboard Lover.* The role led to a subsequent string of comparable gigs, including a 1941 production of *Our Betters,* in which he portrayed a gigolo named Pepi D'Costa, who wooed Elsa Maxwell's Duchess de Surennes with an incongruous conga. Montalban's stage work garnered him another invitation to test for MGM, but when his mother suddenly took ill, the youngest Montalban returned to Torreon to assist with her care.[10]

With World War II under way, Montalban opted to stay in Mexico after his mother's convalescence, but he relocated to Mexico City to pursue acting work. With the assistance of some family friends, he soon landed a small part opposite Cantinflas. This led to more work—both in Mexican films and in films by US exiles—and ultimately a major part as the gypsy bullfighter Jarameno in the 1943 film *Santa,* which established the young actor's star status within Mexico's burgeoning film industry. Montalban would make more than a dozen films in Mexico before MGM approached him again, this time to play opposite Esther Williams in the bullfighting-themed *Fiesta* (1947). Filmed in Puebla, Mexico, *Fiesta* tells the story of a legendary torero's twin children, Maria (Williams) and Mario (Montalban). Anointed from birth as his father's successor, Montalban's Mario shows no special talent or passion for bullfighting and instead aspires to be a classical composer. (This being an MGM musical feature, Williams's Maria of course demonstrates natural talents in the ring, a predisposition to mischief, and a startling resemblance to her brother—they're twins!—all of which leads to ostensibly comedic deceptions, spectacular bullfights, intermittent musical interludes, and a requisitely contented resolution.) *Fiesta*'s display of Montalban's on-screen charisma and athletic musicality (both in the ring and in dance numbers with Cyd Charisse) earned polite notices ("a nice departure [from] the Valentino type but [not] socko in any other direction").[11] Montalban's turn in *Fiesta* also earned the Mexican actor a multiyear contract with MGM, and he spent the next seven years as one of its most heavily featured stars.

The studio hired Ricardo Montalban to play "Latin lover" roles, which he did from 1947 to 1953, mostly opposite Esther Williams and a handful of MGM's other leading ladies, including Jane Powell and Lana Turner. Fifteen years later the actor reflected on the implications of his hiring. "My countrymen wanted to disown me," Montalban recalled. "I was a promising actor in Mexico and then I come up here and play that stereotype—the smiling romantic idiot."[12] Indeed, MGM valued Ricardo Montalban's Latin-ness in particular ways. Even his training at the studio amplified his generic Latin-ness—MGM voice coach Gertrude Fogler sought to refine his speech while also maintaining his accent—and the studio assigned him variously "Latin" roles ("South American" tycoon, dream Cuban tango dancer, and Brazilian landowner) in the musical romances *Neptune's Daughter* (1949), *Two Weeks with Love* (1950), and *Latin Lovers* (1953), respectively.[13]

At the same time, the studio kept Montalban busy in an array of more "serious" nonmusical films, in nearly all of which he portrayed Mexican or Mexican American characters. In 1949 he appeared in both the neo-noir crime procedural *Border Incident* and the genre-busting war epic *Battleground*. As *Battleground*'s sympathetic Roderigues, the sweet-spirited GI from East Los Angeles who has never seen snow, Montalban provided a sentimental anchor for the sprawling ensemble narrative. In *Border Inci-*

dent, as Mexican federal agent Pablo Rodriguez, Montalban goes under-
cover and risks his life to reveal the gruesome abuse and criminal exploitation of Mexican bracero workers within the US agricultural industry.

Montalban followed *Battleground* and *Border Incident* with other sen-
sitively grounded performances of Mexican American characters (not
always named Rodriguez) in a host of minor MGM genre pictures. In
1950 he appeared in both the crime thriller *Mystery Street*, in which his
Detective Pete Morales races to catch a vicious killer, and the boxing
melodrama *Right Cross*, in which his Johnny Monterez spars outside the
ring with sportswriter Dick Powell in a contest for the affections of June
Allyson. In the next few years, Montalban would continue to portray
characters in whimsical fantasies of Latin American life, as in 1953's
fascinating adaptation of Josephine Niggli's folktales, *Sombrero*, and the
darker side of the Mexican American experience, as in 1952's *My Man
and I*, in which Montalban plays the newly naturalized ChuChu Ramirez,
who is intent on rescuing a boozy blonde waitress played by Shelley Win-
ters. With only one exception—as the bare-chested and bronzed Black-
foot leader Ironshirt in the 1951 Clark Gable frontier melodrama *Across
the Wide Missouri*—Montalban played Latino and Latin American roles
throughout his MGM years.

When MGM dropped his contract in the fall of 1953, however, Montalban was obliged to seek work beyond the studio gates. Not infrequently, he found this work in roles that obliged him to be as interchangeably
ethnic as he had been generically Latin at MGM.[14] In the mid-1950s,
Montalban took on diverse roles in a wide array of film, television, and
theatrical productions. In his first post-MGM gig, he played Don Juan in
a thirty-five-week touring production of George Bernard Shaw's *Don Juan
in Hell* (directed by Agnes Moorehead),[15] before taking to the Broadway
stage opposite Gloria De Haven (as a French variant of his MGM stock
character) in the "calamitous" musical *Seventh Heaven* (1955).

By 1956 Montalban was a reliable presence on all of the major
anthology drama series, mostly appearing in Latino, Latin American,
or (increasingly) Native American roles. A few independent film productions (mostly produced in Italy or Mexico) hired him. In the spring
of 1956, a brief buzz surrounded the Apache melodrama *Broken Arrow*
(which aired on CBS-TV's *20th Century Fox Hour*), in which Montalban
starred as the "great and honorable" Cochise, opposite Rita Moreno as
the winsome Sonseeahray (a Native woman in love with a white man).
Reviews were good ("Moreno develops real individuality for her character [and] Montalban does a good job in a sort of great stone face way"),

Four faces of Ricardo Montalban (1960). (Publicity still, collection of the author)

but ratings for the pilot were not, and the half-hour series version of *Broken Arrow* never materialized.[16] Although Montalban continued to work throughout the mid-1950s—in anthology shows, celebrity appearances, and a half dozen guest spots on his sister-in-law's hit television sitcom, *The Loretta Young Show*—most of the parts relied on his MGM skills: humble Latinos and cosmopolitan Latins, with an Indian chief or two thrown in for variety.

In 1957, Ricardo Montalban took a role that promised to confirm his versatility and ability in a whole new way. He portrayed the Japanese Kabuki master Nakamura in Joshua Logan's screen version of *Sayonara*, James Michener's romantic drama set amid the US occupation of Japan.

Montalban's casting in the role of the Japanese character proved controversial from the outset. ("Millions of Nipponese eyebrows raised in disbelief when Japanese newspapers printed that Latin actor Ricardo Montalban had been cast," wagged one US journalist.)[17] The film's star, Marlon Brando, also expressed doubts about Montalban's casting. In an early press conference, Brando declared, even though he had himself just portrayed a Japanese character in the 1956 comedy *The Teahouse of the August Moon*, that he would never attempt such an impersonation in a "realistic" situation. Japanese American dancer Michiko Iseri (who had appeared in a featured role in 1956's film version of *The King and I*) also questioned Montalban's casting: "All the other Japanese in the picture are being played by Orientals, so why not the Kabuki actor . . . especially the Kabuki actor."[18] Producers even failed to identify a local Kabuki troupe willing to stand in for Montalban's character during the rigorous on-stage dance sequences. ("To ask one of them to double for me," Montalban later observed, "would have been like suggesting to Laurence Olivier that he double for Tony Curtis in *Hamlet*."[19] In a notorious profile of Marlon Brando in the *New Yorker*, Truman Capote noted a different point of comparison: "[O]ne Japanese writer remarked [that it] was much the same as 'asking Ethel Barrymore to be a stand-in.'")[20]

Thus obliged to execute the dance himself, Montalban embarked, with the help of a teacher and translator, on a grueling seven-week training regimen in preparation for the role. "I thought at first this would be easy," he told columnist Mel Heimer. "[A]fter all, I'd swum with Esther Williams, danced [with] Cyd Charisse, and fought bulls in Mexico." But he admitted that the challenge of learning Kabuki had reduced him, regularly, to tears.[21] The question of Montalban's success in the role proved to be a point of fascination prior to the film's release. Stories circulated—in the *Chicago Defender*, the *Kittanning Leader-Times*, and the *Pacific Stars and Stripes*—about Montalban's being mistaken for an authentic Kabuki actor by Japanese locals and US elites alike.[22] Reviewers of Montalban's performance were divided. *The Los Angeles Times* observed that "Montalban astonishes" in "a rather amazing simulation of a Japanese Kabuki performer,"[23] while *the New York Tribune* thought him "placid" and "odd" and the *New York Times* asserted that he was "not up to the illusion."[24]

While Montalban's attempt at racial illusion occasioned commentary from the film's production through its release in late 1957, few contemporary observers asked straight out why he had been hired in the first place. Even director Joshua Logan dodged the question in his own memoir of the production, asserting only that Montalban "was perfect

Ricardo Montalban in *Sayonara* (1957). (Publicity still, collection of the author)

for the part, because he is a fabulous dancer."[25] Subsequent generations of critics, however, have largely assessed Montalban's racial incongruity as a feature of the film's strategic staging of midcentury anxieties surrounding the spectacle of interracial desire. As Gina Marchetti notes, "[T]he fact that Nakamura's part is played by a Latin (Ricardo Montalban), rather than an Asian, actor further removes the threatening racial aspect of the fantasy, while keeping a certain exoticism in place."[26]

I would press this a bit further. In *Sayonara*, Montalban's Nakamura—

in addition to being a Kabuki master whose on-stage performance enflames the interest of an American spectator—also emerges as the putative love interest for that spectator, Patricia Owens's Eileen, the abandoned fiancée of Brando's Sergeant Gruver (who has fallen in love with a Japanese actress). Montalban's Nakamura and Owens's Eileen engage in a measured (and unconsummated) flirtation for much of the film. Even beneath the stylized yellowface apparatus, the physical spectacle of Montalban's performance yet stirs the myriad titillations of cross-cultural (and interracial) fantasy that had long been central to Montalban's presence within US popular performance. Indeed, as he takes on the role of Nakamura, Montalban's presence—including the luxurious display of his exposed, uncostumed body and his slightly Spanish accent—works as it always has: to contain the threat of interracial intimacy within the sensual uncertainties of Latino raciality.

Montalban's particular capacity to both animate and contain the thrill and the threat of interracial intimacy also permeated the role he took on shortly after playing Nakamura—Lena Horne's romantic swain in the Broadway musical *Jamaica*.[27] In what was routinely referred to in the press commentary as a "Negro musical show," *Jamaica* featured a cycle of sixteen faux-calypso songs tethered together by a wisp of a plot (what the *New York Post* called "an epically feeble book")[28] that was somehow lifted to the rafters by the charisma, nerve, and talent of its star, Lena Horne (in her Broadway debut) as Savannah. Ricardo Montalban starred opposite Horne as Koli, Savannah's beloved, whom she will happily abandon on the island should the right opportunity to move to New York come along. Originally conceived as a vehicle for Harry Belafonte (in the role of Koli), composer Harold Arlen and lyricist E. Y. Harburg (with producer David Merrick) retooled the project for Horne's Savannah, with Koli repurposed as second lead.

While it remains unclear how Montalban came to the producing team's attention for the role of Koli, his performance earned generous praise for his on-stage charisma, as well as his appearance. The *Daily Mirror* noted, "Montalban matches the magnificence of Miss Horne," while the *Journal-American* praised him as "a vigorous performer with an engaging voice," and the *New York Post* confirmed him to be "a leading man of force, charm and romantic attractiveness." Meanwhile, the *Daily News* was unenthused: "Miss Horne is a girl on the island, and Montalban is a bare-chested boy." (Walter Kerr also noted Montalban's physique, describing both him and his performance as simply the "bronzed and bare-chested Ricardo Montalban."[29] Only *Variety*'s reviewer commented on "the racial aspect of the show," observing that "there may be raised eyebrows and perhaps increased blood-pressure among Dixiecrats because of the love scenes between Miss Horne and Montalban, even though the latter appears to have been sunlamped considerably." Throughout *Jamaica*'s year-and-a-half run, *Variety* wondered intermittently about the media silence surrounding Montalban's presence in "the otherwise all-Negro legitter," especially given the "fairly torrid love scenes" between Savannah and Koli.[30] Years later Montalban reflected on how "*Jamaica* was considered daring in its time because I, a white man, played a romance with Lena Horne. During the run, I received many letters [but] there is nothing you can do about such hate mail, nothing you can reply."[31] Yet, for most observers, Montalban's presence did not disrupt *Jamaica*'s success (and subsequent remembrance) as one of the most successful black-cast musicals of the 1950s.

Jamaica opened at Broadway's Imperial Theatre about a month before *Sayonara* began its exclusive engagement at New York's Radio City Music Hall, a brisk ten-minute walk away. A couple months earlier he had guest starred as the sophisticated New Orleans gambler Jean LeBec on the premiere episode of the television western *Wagon Train*, and just a month or two later his turn as "the Arab prince who scimitars throat for throat" in *Desert Lovers* (an Italian feature Montalban had filmed in 1956) was released in Europe.[32] Indeed, Montalban's versatility seemed everywhere in evidence. As one newspaper jokingly reminded its readers, "This Frenchman-Japanese-West Indian is actually a very fine Mexican actor."[33] In a 1958 interview, Montalban affirmed that essaying such a diversity of roles would—he hoped—help him to "avoid being typed." He explained, "I first resisted the idea [but now] I consider my part in *Sayonara* one of the most vital in my career. . . . I was very proud when the real Kabuki actors gave me the title of 'Man Who Can Do a Thousand Things.' A few seasons ago I played a Frenchman in another musical comedy, *Seventh Heaven*. Now, of course I am a Jamaican. In *Border Incident*, though, I played a Mexican."[34]

Indeed, although *Sayonara* would go on to become one of the year's most discussed films, and he would continue with *Jamaica* for the full length of its hugely profitable eighteen-month run, the versatility exhibited by Montalban—who, the *Chicago Defender* noted, "has played almost every nationality on the screen"—did little to guarantee him work after his departure from the production forced *Jamaica* to close in the spring of 1959.[35] Two major television projects—Desilu's *Tonight in Havana*, which sought to capitalize on Montalban's persona by casting the actor as "a gay adventurer [who] comes to the aid of damsel in distress," and a variety series starring Ginger Rogers—both failed to find a sponsor, and, for much of the subsequent decade or so, Montalban relied on guest television appearances to get by.[36]

Juano Hernandez

In a roundabout way, being Puerto Rican made Juano Hernandez a star. Early in 1949, movie director Clarence Brown began preproduction on a pet project—a serious film adaptation of William Faulkner's newest novel about southern life, *Intruder in the Dust*. A tale of vigilante justice, in which an independent African American farmer becomes an unlikely hero after being wrongly accused of murder, *Intruder in the Dust* made MGM executives nervous. Despite Brown's clout as one of the studio's top earners, MGM head Louis B. Mayer balked at the prospect of hiring an African American actor to play the pivotal role of the accused, Lucas Beauchamp. As screenwriter Ben Maddow recalls, "a black actor would have been going too far for Metro, at the time." Director Clarence Brown refused to do the film with a white actor in "realistic" black makeup, so a compromise had to be reached. Casting Juano Hernandez (who was, in Brown's words, "a Puerto Rican Negro") proved to be that compromise. In 1949 the veteran stage and radio actor got the role that introduced him to Hollywood, where he would work in films and television programs for the next two decades.[37]

In *Intruder in the Dust*, Hernandez's formidable and charismatic performance earned widespread praise. The *New York Times*' Bosley Crowther praised the "creative art" displayed by Clarence Brown's casting, "especially with Juano Hernandez, who plays the condemned Negro [with] stanch and magnificent integrity." Crowther's review emphasized Hernandez's work ("his carriage, his manner and expression, with never a flinch in his great self-command") as "the bulwark" of the film's success.[38] Crowther was not alone in his praise. In February 1950, the Hollywood Foreign Press Association singled Juano Hernandez out at its annual Golden Globe ceremony as one of the "New Stars of the Year."

Although he may have been a "new star," Hernandez was, by the beginning of the 1950s, well into his fifth decade of work as a professional performer. Born in Puerto Rico in the late 1890s, Hernandez had spent his childhood busking for change on the streets of Rio de Janeiro (where he had been sent to live with an aunt after his mother's death).

By his early teens, Hernandez had joined a series of touring carnivals that traveled to Caribbean seaports, throughout the coasts of South and Central America, and along the US Gulf Coast, until he arrived in New Orleans in 1915. "I did everything from stake-driving and acrobatics, to playing in bands and shilling," Hernandez recalled in 1950. Once in the United States, he sought work on vaudeville and minstrel stages and spent a year on the prizefighting circuit (as "Kid Curley"). Fluent in both Spanish and Portuguese, Hernandez received no formal schooling but had taught himself to read and write in both languages.

Once in the United States, Hernandez "learned quickly [that] if you speak English with an accent people are inclined to laugh at you."[39] Through a mix of correspondence courses and self-tutorials, Hernandez cultivated his diction using the works of Shakespeare and other dramatic texts, even as he continued working on the vaudeville circuit, which ultimately routed him to gigs at the Cotton Club and other New York nightspots. In 1927 Hernandez joined the original cast of *Showboat,* and by the early 1930s, he had become an established presence on the New York theatre circuit. He appeared both in "Negro Revues," such as 1931's *Fast and Furious* (in which he shared the stage with Tim Moore, Jackie Mabley [who was not credited as "Moms" in her early stage performances], and Zora [Neale] Hurston, among others),[40] and in more serious dramas with companies like the Provincetown Players. Commenting on the 1932 Provincetown production of Julian McDonald's *The Marriage of Cana,* Brooks Atkinson praised Hernandez as possessing "the sleek subtlety of an able actor."[41] Around the same time, Hernandez also participated in Chicago's burgeoning African American independent film scene, perhaps most notably as the Cuban racketeer Gomez (under the name "Uano Hernandez") in Oscar Micheaux's *The Girl from Chicago* (1932). In 1933 Hernandez stepped out of the title role in Orson Welles's notorious Mercury Theatre black cast production of *Macbeth* (sometimes referred to as Welles's "Voodoo Macbeth") to take the lead role in the CBS radio serial *John Henry, Black River Boat Giant,*[42] now widely understood to be the first African American hero to anchor a national radio program.[43]

Hernandez's success with *John Henry* led to regular and reliable work (as both an actor and a writer) in commercial radio dramas for much of the next two decades. (The actor also developed a brief dramatic adaptation of *John Henry,* which he made available for bookings on the vaudeville circuit.)[44] In radio, Hernandez's powerful and versatile vocality proved a distinct asset, and throughout the 1930s and 1940s his voice could be heard throughout the United States in soap operas like *We Love and Learn*, juvenile adventures like *Jack Armstrong, the All-American Boy*, religious programs like *The Eternal Light*, and anthology programs like Du Pont's *Cavalcade of America*,[45] and in roles that included Mussolini, Tojo of Japan, Emperor Hirohito, Eduard Benes, and Haile Selassie, among others.[46] During the 1940s, Hernandez also returned to the stage, with widely praised performances in such "race consciousness" dramas as Lillian Smith's lynching melodrama *Strange Fruit* (1945) and Dorothy Heyward's slavery saga *Set My People Free* (1948).[47]

In early 1949, just as Clarence Brown started scouting Mississippi locations for *Intruder in the Dust*, Juano Hernandez and his wife Haydie moved from New York back to Puerto Rico. "We had been planning and saving to go back to Puerto Rico as soon as our daughter finished high school," Hernandez told an Associated Press reporter in 1950, "and just as we got there I was called to Hollywood for *Intruder in the Dust*."[48] In 1950, the University of Puerto Rico awarded Hernandez an honorary doctorate of fine arts and appointed him to a professorship in the English Department, where he was made the head of the new drama program at the university while also maintaining his film career.[49] "Any time there's a good part," Hernandez assured a reporter from the *New York Times* upon the announcement of his faculty appointment, "I can get [to Hollywood] in a day."[50]

Over most of the next decade (which happened to coincide with the busiest phase of his film career), Hernandez split his time between San Juan and Los Angeles, teaching at the university, living on an elaborately appointed estate outside San Juan, and commuting periodically to the mainland for film work or theatrical appearances. (In the early 1950s, Hernandez also performed his twenty-five-minute solo adaptation of Othello—which featured passages in English, Spanish, and "Harlemese"—in venues from New York to San Juan to Oakland.)[51] "It makes a fine arrangement for me—acting in Hollywood and teaching in San Juan," he told Harry Levette of Baltimore's *Afro-American* newspaper in 1955. "I'm afraid, however, the day is coming when I shall have to choose between the two. . . . The present situation does make it difficult for the university officials."[52]

After nearly a decade of balancing his film work, the demands of supervising a university theatre program, and running a small repertory company on his home estate, Hernandez abruptly separated from the University of Puerto Rico in 1958. "Juano Hernandez is furious with the government officials in Puerto Rico," reported gossip columnist Dorothy

Juano Hernandez circa 1957. (Publicity still, collection of the author)

Kilgallen in June 1958. "He was so irked by the strings attached to a grant [to] his acting school that he not only folded the drama academy but took immediate steps to leave the island and settle in Hollywood."[53] The circumstances surrounding Hernandez's departure from the University of Puerto Rico remain unclear, although administrative differences over finances and scheduling—in tandem with uncertainties about Hernandez's unorthodox pedagogy—may have all played a part.[54]

Mere months after leaving the University of Puerto Rico, however, Hernandez opened the Lyceum of Dramatic Art on Los Angeles's Sunset

Boulevard. Originally conceived as a bilingual actor training program,[55] the Lyceum of Dramatic Art would remain open for about three years, during which time it offered a "full course" of "individual instruction" ("no groups") in which "would-be actors and actresses never . . . read a line of dialogue until after the eighteenth lesson."[56] Among Hernandez's faculty were some of his former students from the University of Puerto Rico, including Frank A. Marrero (later an award-winning television producer), who taught courses in directing and stagecraft, and Henry Delgado (later known as *High Chaparral* star Henry Darrow), who offered courses in Spanish pronunciation, accents, and dialects. Throughout the Lyceum's three years of operation, Hernandez took care to promote it as a legitimate school, emphasizing his own career ("directed by film star Juano Hernandez") and credentials ("only actor with a Doctorate in Fine Arts"), as well as the qualifications of the teaching staff ("all my faculty members have degrees"). Juano Hernandez's Lyceum of Dramatic Art closed its doors sometime in 1960.[57]

In 1958 the *Oakland Tribune* published a profile of Juano Hernandez under the headline "Juano Hernandez Plays a Double Role All the Time."[58] Although the story details the delicate balance Hernandez maintained between his two professions (as an actor and as a teacher), the headline also evinces his deft affirmation of his simultaneous identity as both a black man and a Latino. As Miriam Jiménez-Román has suggested, Juano Hernandez "was invariably cast as an African American" actor throughout this period, while Hernandez's public persona continued forcefully to affirm his Puerto Rican heritage.[59] Not unlike Anthony Quinn in this same period (whose Mexican heritage was neither a secret nor a point of media emphasis), Juano Hernandez's Puerto Rican heritage—as well as his island-mainland commute—appeared as a matter of fact in nearly every media profile of the actor. Additionally, not unlike Quinn's choice to headquarter his production company in Mexico and to develop independent film projects centered on figures and events from Mexican history, Hernandez's decision to split his professional time between the island and the mainland earned bemused fascination in media reports.

As an independent actor (with no studio contract and little apparent reliance on an agent, manager, or other staff to guide his career), Hernandez used the Hollywood publicity apparatus to rehearse language that might describe him aptly. For example, an unattributed wire announcement in the fall of 1959 announced simply, "Well-known Puerto Rican actor Juano Hernandez will play the part of Kalanumu, an African priest in the film *Rachel Cade*."[60] At the same time, Hernandez did not shy away from taking a stand on questions affecting African Americans, especially African American actors, lending his name to the NAACP's protest of the television production of *Amos 'n' Andy* in 1952, as one example. Throughout the 1950s, in ways both large and small, Hernandez deftly affirmed the simultaneous fact of his being both black and Puerto Rican.

Perhaps even more forcefully, the roles that Juano Hernandez was hired to play drew on the duality that got him the part in *Intruder in the Dust*—his status as a "Puerto Rican Negro." Thus, he was cast in narratives rehearsing the incongruities of the color line. In some of his first roles after *Intruder*, Hernandez embodies the promise of racial equanimity among white and black men. The gritty noir *The Breaking Point* (1951) frames this promise by staging an unremarkable relationship, born of shared economic circumstances, between the film's lead (John Garfield) and a pivotal supporting player (Juano Hernandez), an on-screen relationship celebrated by one reviewer as "fine evidence of racial feeling."[61] Perhaps comparably, as the aging jazz trumpeter Art Hazzard in 1950's *Young Man with the Horn*, Hernandez provides needed mentorship for a much younger man (played as a boy by Orley Lindgren and as an adult by Lloyd Bridges). Hernandez took on many television and film roles in which he stood at the threshold of the color line. In a few such roles, he stood as an equal (as in a 1957 episode of CBS television's anthology series *Studio One*, "Escape Route," in which his Detective Ricardo Calader unflinchingly interrogates a white suspect) or as an intimate (as in 1956's *Ransom!*, in which he portrays a butler who steadies his employer physically, emotionally, and spiritually through the crisis of a child's abduction). Occasionally, he served as a guide or emissary between worlds, as in another *Studio One* episode ("The Goodwill Ambassador"), in which he played a local doctor attempting to help an American wife adjust to life in a rural South American village.

Most often Hernandez's presence in a role at the threshold of interracial encounter proved to be a catalyzing obstacle, as in 1950's *Stars in My Crown*, in which his performance as a freed slave who refuses to surrender his farm instigates a near riot; as Nat King Cole's disapproving father in 1957's *St. Louis Blues*; or as Amugu, the defiant tribal spiritual leader who defies Sidney Poitier's Christian proselytizing in *Mark of the Hawk*, also in 1957. Yet, almost always, casting Juano Hernandez at the potential threshold of racial equanimity between white and black men enabled television show creators and moviemakers to amplify the conspicuous construction (and implicit permeability) of the color line.

Juano Hernandez as Montezuma with John Baragrey as Cortés in the "Conquest of Mexico—1519" episode of the CBS television series *You Are There* (1953). (Screenshot)

In a compelling handful of instances, Hernandez's "typecasting" in roles marking such racial thresholds enact the compelling incongruities of the color line in narratives about indigenous peoples, Mexican Americans, and Puerto Ricans. The remarkable "Conquest of Mexico—1519" episode of the CBS anthology series *You Are There* (which originally aired in April 1953) restages the encounter between Spanish explorer Hernán Cortés and the legendary Aztec emperor Montezuma. Juano Hernandez plays Montezuma with all the nobility, bluster, and internal conflict of a Shakespearean role. In the episode, directed by Sidney Lumet and featuring Eartha Kitt as Dona Marina, Hernandez's forceful alacrity as Montezuma amplifies the raciality of the Cortés-Montezuma confrontation, with all the Aztecs portrayed by African American actors costumed in "Native" attire. Yet, even within the episode's narrative of colonial submission, Hernandez's meticulous vocal choices deftly avoid twentieth-century idiomatic inflections, while simultaneously confirming Montezuma's nobility in ways that complicate the script's forthright neodocumentary conceits.

Hernandez's turn in 1955's *Trial* two years later offers a comparably complex portrait of conflicted authority. In the courtroom melodrama, Hernandez plays Judge Theodore Motley as he presides over a case (cribbed loosely from the Sleepy Lagoon murders) in which a Mexican American youth (played by Dominican American actor Rafael Campos) is accused of a murder that he probably did not commit. (Oscar-nominated Mexican actress Katy Jurado played the defendant's mother.) Throughout, the competence of Hernandez's Motley to act as the presiding judge becomes a recurrent point of contention, as defense and prosecuting attorneys alike question his ability to be objective on questions of racial discrimination, especially when applied to Mexican Americans. *Trial* exploits Hernandez's presence on the bench both to heighten and to question the racial implications of the trial, amplifying the incongruities of the color line, while also affirming their intransigence.

In the racy noir-ish melodrama *Machete* (1958), Hernandez appears as Bernardo, the "majordomo" of a sugar plantation in rural Puerto Rico. Bernardo is the all-wise supervisor of the vast estate, presciently capable of recognizing suspect motives ("the only thing sharper than his eye is his tongue"). In perhaps his only on-screen performance as a Puerto Rican character, Hernandez's Bernardo monitors the actions of the household, including the landowner, Don Luis Montoya (Albert Dekker), and his new, platinum-blonde "American" wife (Marie Blanchard), as well as Don Luis's foster son (Mexican American Carlos Rivas), housemaid Rita (Puerto Rican Ruth Cains), and Don Luis's violent cousin Miguel (Lee Van Cleef, in slathered brownface makeup). Throughout *Machete*'s torrid betrayals (in which Dekker's Don Luis is cuckolded by Rivas's Carlos, much to the malevolent delight of Van Cleef's Miguel), Hernandez's Bernardo remains the narrative's soulful voice of integrity, guiding the divided and diverse "family" toward the requisite revelations and reconciliations (resulting in the new Anglo wife's expulsion from Don Luis's diversely complexioned and provisionally reconstituted household).

In each of these oddly and arguably "Latino" roles, Juano Hernandez's presence amplifies the incongruities of the color line. His performances guide narratives that explore whether and how established conventions of raciality might (or might not) work within stories about Mexicans, Mexican Americans, and Puerto Ricans.

Juano Hernandez's status as one of the most prominent minority actors working at midcentury is today remembered—when it is remembered—primarily as a pioneering presence within the depiction of African American characters on screen during this period. Donald Bogle identifies Hernandez as "the single black actor in the movies who appeared not to fight the dominant culture, not to be buried under by it, not to have been scarred by it."[62] Yet, as Miriam Jiménez Román reminds us, Hernandez's presence as a seriously working actor in film, television, and theatre also established him as one of the "earliest instructors on Black latinidad."[63] Moreover, Juano Hernandez's work throughout the 1950s—as actor and teacher, on the island and the mainland, in movies and beyond—also documented just how unsettled questions of Latino raciality were at midcentury. His consistent and recurring surrogation of roles that articulated and amplified the conspicuous constructedness of the color line also documents how Hernandez's "stealth Latino" presence rehearsed some of the most enduring—if incoherent—conventions guiding how Latino raciality has been staged and enacted in US popular performance ever since.

Mel Ferrer

What Mel Ferrer really wanted to do was direct. He even professed to hate acting. Still, at crucial junctures in his early career, the Cuban American's work as an actor, both on stage and on camera, provided him access to the industry in which he hoped to write, direct, and produce.

Melchor Gaston Ferrer was born into privilege in New York City in 1917. The fourth and youngest child of Cuban-born José Maria Ferrer (a prominent physician at New York's St. Vincent's Hospital and noted expert on the treatment of pneumonia) and his much younger wife, the Irish American socialite Maria Irene O'Donohue Ferrer, Melchor Ferrer was raised in a cosmopolitan Catholic home on Fifth Avenue. Although his father died when he was still a toddler, the youngest Ferrer was raised speaking Spanish and English, as well as French, and was educated at the elite Bovee School (which bucked New York society convention by admitting not only the sons of actors and musicians but also Jews and Catholics) before matriculating at the Canterbury School in New Milford, Connecticut, the only elite preparatory school with an emphatically Catholic orientation.

Though decidedly disinterested in pursuing his academic studies beyond high school, Melchor Ferrer acceded to his mother's demands that he follow his brother (and their father before them) to Princeton University, where the youngest Ferrer quickly immersed himself in the activities of Princeton's many extracurricular theatre clubs. During his sophomore year, he wrote *Awhile to Work*, a "philosophic comedy" set in New York City's debutante scene. Selected as the winner of an undergraduate student playwriting prize, Ferrer directed a production of *Awhile to Work* (with himself in the lead role) at Princeton's Theatre Intime that spring, earning praise from the university's "resident poet," Archibald MacLeish ("That boy has an ear. . . . I was much impressed"), a small cash prize, and mention in two brief articles in the *New York Times*.[64] The attention paid to *Awhile to Work* also garnered Ferrer a query from the William Morris Agency, which ultimately declined to publish the play but provided Ferrer with a small advance for a possible novel or assortment of short stories.[65]

Awhile to Work's brief brush with independent success inspired Ferrer to drop out of Princeton; to elope with his leading lady, Frances Pilchard; and to move to Mexico, where they both might live as bohemian artists (he as a writer, she as a sculptor). Although they aimed for Taxco, the newlywed Ferrers made it only as far as Juarez, where they struggled (having each been cut off from their "respectable" wealthy families) to make ends meet. After a few months, the offer of an editing job at a small press in Vermont brought the couple back to the states, and by the end of the year, the couple had returned to New York, where Melchor (who had developed the beginnings of a fruitful network of theatre contacts both at Princeton and while working summers at a "straw hat" theatre on Cape Cod) began dancing in the chorus of musical revues, like Cole Porter's *You Never Know* (1938), and acting bit parts in negligible mystery plays, like Edward Chodorov's *Cue for Passion* (1940).

Ferrer's appearances on the New York stage earned further opprobrium from his mortified mother, especially after one critic referred to him as "the only Social Registerite chorus boy." As 1941 began, Ferrer was out of work, his marriage was in collapse, and he experienced the beginnings of a paralysis in his right arm and shoulder that would not be correctly diagnosed as polio until two years later. Unable to work on stage, Ferrer turned to radio ("which required only one hand," he later explained), where he worked as a disc jockey in Arkansas and Texas before landing a job at NBC in New York. At NBC Ferrer wrote, directed, and announced an array of variety and quiz shows, while also acting in several soap operas and developing the Peabody Award–winning spiritual anthology program, *The Eternal Light*. At the same time, after finally receiving a correct diagnosis of his polio-related paralysis, Ferrer began to rebuild his strength and flexibility with punishing daily exercises. By 1944, when his radio success drew the attention of Hollywood's Columbia Pictures, Ferrer was ready to begin his directing career.

Only a few months later, however, Ferrer was out of work again, having been dropped unceremoniously from his seven-year contract with Columbia after he delivered his directorial debut film (the piously earnest girlhood gothic *Girl of the Limberlost*) three days late. Ironically, Melchor Ferrer had just rebuffed his friend José Ferrer's offer of a part in a play ("I informed Joe—loftily—that I was directing my first film and that I intended to keep on that course").[66] The Ferrers shared no filial relation but had become acquainted at Princeton, where Mel's elder brother—also named José—was one of two José Ferrers graduating in the class of 1938. Fortunately for both, the role José offered Melchor remained uncast.

Melchor Ferrer thus returned to New York in the fall of 1945 to take the part of Tracy Deen, the fragile young white man engaged in an interracial love affair with None Anderson, a light-skinned African American woman. The doomed lovers were the central characters in the hotly anticipated stage adaptation of Lillian Smith's best-selling novel, *Strange Fruit*. Directed by Puerto Rican actor José Ferrer, and costarring Juano Hernandez in a pivotal role, Mel Ferrer was cast opposite Jane White, the daughter of the NAACP leader Walter White Jr.[67] José Ferrer had been working closely with first-time dramatist Smith throughout the year, as she struggled to distill the narrative breadth and topical scope of her novel for the stage. Still, as the *New York Times* observed on the play's opening in November 1945, "[I]t is a disagreeable truth but Lillian Smith has not made a satisfying play." Yet, due to the book's notoriety (and Smith's own iconoclastic views), the production drew both protests and publicity in each of its out-of-town tryouts, beginning in Montreal and Toronto (where it ran nearly four hours long), through Boston (where the production was obliged to excise the script's many curse words and racial epithets), to Philadelphia (where the reviewer for Baltimore's *Afro-American* considered it raw but unremarkable documentation of "a blasé social order").[68]

When *Strange Fruit* opened at New York's Royale Theatre in November 1945, the play ran less than three hours, but the production would run only sixty performances, closing in January 1946. Melchor Ferrer's performance as the doomed and crippled Tracy garnered no special praise. (Indeed, only Juano Hernandez's "excellent performance [as] the Negro doctor who has come back to the South to help his people" consistently earned accolades from critics, who appreciated his as one of the few performances to be "acted with sting.")[69] Even so, the notices for *Strange Fruit* did garner the attention of Hollywood, where David O. Selznick, intrigued with his versatility, signed Melchor Ferrer to a "three-way acting, directing, and producing contract" later that year.

Mel Ferrer (he shortened his first name around this time) returned to Hollywood with plans to direct. Selznick, however, had few projects in the pipeline and mostly made money by "loaning" his contracted players to other studios. Ferrer quickly became a lucrative "loan out" for directorial assistant jobs with John Ford and Howard Hughes, as well as for assignments coaching dialogue, staging screen tests, and performing a handful of uncredited roles. Although the contract provided Ferrer with a modest salary, it did not guarantee him much work. Even though the preternaturally industrious Ferrer stayed busy (cofounding a long-standing theatre company,[70] cultivating mentoring relationships, and writing scripts), he soon became restless.

Even so, Ferrer initially rebuffed producer Louis de Rochemont when he was invited to test for an independently produced film, *Lost Boundaries*, in early 1949. The film—an ostensibly true story about a light-complexioned African American doctor in New England who, along with his wife and children, passed as white for decades—was struggling to cast its principal roles. By early 1949, the central role of the doctor remained unassigned, delaying production. Ferrer (ever reluctant to act and at the time "anxious for a Broadway directing job") had declined de Rochemont's overtures without even reading the script. However, Sherlee Weingarten, the "vitally important casting director" for New York's Theater Guild, remembered Ferrer's work in 1945's *Strange Fruit* and "kept bringing [him] up for the part." Seeing only Ferrer's headshot, director Alfred Werker agreed ("that man looks the part"). After some negotiation (in which a reluctant Ferrer required some convincing from his "Broadway pals"), Mel Ferrer agreed to be "loaned out" for the role of Dr. Scott Mason Carter, and he traveled to Portsmouth, New Hampshire, to begin production on the film.[71]

Lost Boundaries, as historians Judith Weisenfeld and Gayle Wald remind us, tells the sort of "passing" story in vogue in the later 1940s, wherein "miscegenation" narratives not infrequently deployed the sentimentality of intergenerational conflict to animate the historical pressures toward integration.[72] As the passing patriarch, Dr. Scott Mason Carter—whose fateful choice not to correct an employer's misapprehension of his race begins as a strategy of short-term survival but expands over two decades—Mel Ferrer offers a distinctive, measured performance. His work deftly dodges the traps of the "tragic mulatto" convention evident in other "passing" performances—both of the period and in this film. Indeed,

Mel Ferrer in *Lost Boundaries* (1949). (Publicity still, collection of the author)

in Ferrer's performance, Carter's choice to pass does lead to conflicts that his character must confront, but even so, the choice to pass, in and of itself, does not define the character's core emotional conflict. Additionally, Ferrer's performance strategies, especially his consistent vocality and affect, confirm that his Carter remains the same African American man whether he is viewed as black or white by those around him.

In a 1951 interview about the role, Ferrer (who seemed ever happy to discuss his career with journalists but rarely his process as an actor) commented on the care with which he approached constructing his performance as Dr. Scott Carter. He nodded to the tacit threat of racial innuendo in Hollywood, as he teased, "[Y]es, I have about a 16th Negro blood in me, but it's not very noticeable." Ferrer evoked his own ancestry only in passing ("being of Spanish descent, I knew something of discrimination"), as he took care to address the controversy, especially in the black press, surrounding the production's casting of nonblack actors to play the Carters. Ferrer emphasized not only the depth of his identification with the character, and his insistence that Hollywood develop better roles for African American writers and actors, but also his subsequent encounters with those convinced, based on his performance in the film, that he "really [was] a Negro."[73]

As a small independent film boasting no real stars, *Lost Boundaries* was surprisingly successful. Within the next couple of years, Mel Ferrer appeared as an actor in a diversity of screen roles in a range of genres, but always in parts that evoked the peculiar perils of passing. Indeed, Ferrer's roles in the first years of the 1950s—a Mexican bullfighter, a waggish painter, a submissive outlaw, and a crippled puppeteer—shared little in common, except for a curious thematic consistency: each character's actions are compelled by his clearly open secret. In 1950's remarkable *The Brave Bulls*, for example, Ferrer leads a cast comprised exclusively of Latina/o and Latin American actors to tell the story of Don Luis Bello, a matador struggling to conceal a debilitating crisis of confidence and conscience. With intense intimacy, especially in scenes opposite Mexican American actors Anthony Quinn (as the matador's best friend and manager) and Eugene Iglesias (as his younger brother), Ferrer's performance reveals how the matador's ostensibly hidden fears (which all can discern in his actions) threaten the survival of those around him. In stark contrast, in 1950's *Born to Be Bad* (Radio-Keith-Orpheum's [RKO's] noirishly effervescent bid to scoop the more prestigious pleasures of Twentieth Century Fox's *All About Eve*), Ferrer appears as Gabriel "Gobby" Broome, a dashing San Francisco artist who delights in the confidences of his wealthy female patrons. Ferrer's Gobby stands among the most overtly and happily gay characterizations to make it to the screen (and stand unpunished) in the Hays Code era, a character whose mercenary (though emphatically nonsexual) interest in his female subjects is a simple fact of the story.

In 1952's Western noir *Rancho Notorious*, Ferrer's ethnically ambiguous Frenchy remains criminally beholden to his lover, Marlene Dietrich, until her death sends him off into the sunset with Arthur Kennedy. In the 1953 musical *Lili*, four puppets (along with Leslie Caron's adoring gaze) reveal the depths of sensitivity within Ferrer's gruff carnival worker. In both *Rancho Notorious* and *Lili*, the thing that is most "off" about Ferrer's character (his blind devotion, his stunted creativity) proves to be his most redeeming feature. Following the surprise success of *Lili*— and especially after his high-profile 1954 marriage to superstar Audrey Hepburn—Ferrer was no longer able to choose under which directors he would work, even as he continued to play "the other man" in big costume epics like *Scaramouche* (1953), *Knights of the Round Table* (1953), and *War and Peace* (1956).

Even in films with more contemporary settings—like 1953's neocolonialist Moroccan soap *Saadia* and 1957's *The Sun Also Rises*—Ferrer continued to play characters whose subtly but emphatically distinct ethnicity (as *Saadia*'s French doctor and *Sun*'s Jewish Robert Cohn) amplified their status as the "other man," both in the film's central romance and within the narrative as a whole. So, in ways established in each of his early 1950s roles, and in ways that would haunt his subsequent bigger budgeted features, Ferrer's casting animates a narrative space (not infrequently at the bum tip of a romantic triangle) that is defined by the subtle intransigence of his ineluctable difference as the "other man."

The capacity of Ferrer's casting to animate the uncertainties of difference is perhaps nowhere so evident as in his performance as the "other man," Benson Thacker, in 1959's postapocalyptic fantasy film *The World, The Flesh and The Devil.* In the film, Harry Belafonte plays Ralph Burton, a black man who happened to be working underground when an unexplained radioactive incident poisoned the entire globe. Belafonte's Ralph puzzles through his isolation in an abandoned New York until he is relieved to encounter another survivor, Sarah (the blonde Inger Stevens). The two become friends, stirring an obliquely but intensely erotic connection that promises both the survival of the species and the elision of preexisting racial distinctions. Then, a third survivor arrives on the horizon. When Belafonte's Ralph introduces himself and Stevens's Sarah as the "total population of New York" to this "other man," he (Mel Ferrer) introduces himself as Ben Thacker, "the total population of the Southern Hemisphere."

After Thacker's arrival, the two male characters (Ferrer and Belafonte) engage in a series of confrontations over Sarah, culminating in a climactic chase in which Ferrer's Thacker hunts Belafonte's Ralph in the urban jungle. The film resolves, somewhat existentially, as Ferrer's Thacker abruptly ceases his pursuit and determines to leave Ralph and Sarah to their future, but he is stopped by Sarah's insistence that the three of them stay together. The film concludes with an extended shot of the three clasping hands, as the concluding title ("The Beginning") rises to fill the screen and the three actors walk hand-in-hand into the urban horizon.

According to one film historian, *The World, The Flesh and The Devil*'s use of a "Rod Serlingesque premise to hammer home a liberal parablel about race relations . . . failed to ignite audience interest."[74] Film his-

Mel Ferrer (*center*), flanked by Harry Belafonte and Inger Stevens, in *The World, The Flesh and The Devil* (1959). (Publicity still, collection of the author)

torian Adilifu Nama has argued that *The World, The Flesh and The Devil* melds "two of America's most visceral social fears"—radioactive contamination and racial contamination—to stage a dystopic fantasy that ultimately confirms the ways in which "the sexual politics of race [are] clearly overdetermined by the societal racial prejudice." Thus, the film "rearticulat[es] racial taboos [even] in a postapocalyptic setting where race supposedly no longer matters."[75] Yet, although his arrival clearly signals the threat posed by white masculine privilege to the integrity of any expression of interracial intimacy, Thacker's whiteness—especially as embodied by Ferrer—is distinctly different from that embodied by Stevens's Sarah. Thacker's migration across the water—as "the entire population of South America"—evokes migratory racial mixtures beyond the black-white racial paradigm initially embodied by the first two survivors. Even when Thacker's backstory is complicated by subsequent revelations, the details confirm that whiteness is not always what it says it is.

Reflecting on his role, Ferrer observed that Belafonte's and Stevens's characters "have a warm and sympathetic relationship. I am definitely the invader."[76] (And, as *Jet* magazine noted following the film's release, "[T]he resulting triangle will almost certainly be bedevilled by the racial problem.")[77] Yet, as an allegory of race relations at the end of the 1950s, I wonder whether "the beginning" of the film's conclusion is singly about the promise of integration. I have to consider that it might also be about a US racial landscape defined by the presence of a not-exactly-white embodiment of the "entire population of South America," migrating across the water and recontextualizing the uneasy but familiar intimacies of whiteness and blackness within the American future.

Stealth Latinos in the 1960s

As the 1960s began, Ricardo Montalban, Juano Hernandez, and Mel Ferrer continued to work as actors, careers they would maintain—to varying degrees—for the rest of their lives.

Juano Hernandez worked fairly steadily throughout the final decade of his life, continuing to inhabit roles that stood at the threshold of interracial encounter, often marking the differences between generations. Throughout the decade—whether in John Ford's western-style drama of the buffalo soldiers, *Sergeant Rutledge* (1960); in Sidney Lumet's mordant portrait of urban despair, *The Pawnbroker* (1965): or in Mark Rydell's film version of William Faulkner's arch homage to southern nostalgia, *The Reivers* (1969)—Hernandez portrayed an African American man struggling to maintain his dignity as the rules of race and society change around him. (Hernandez died in 1970, a few weeks before the release of his final film, the urban crime drama and Sidney Poitier vehicle *They Call Me MISTER Tibbs!*)

While Juano Hernandez worked mostly in US films in the 1960s, both Mel Ferrer and Ricardo Montalban balanced work in international and US features, with both men appearing more and more frequently on television by the end of the decade. (Neither engaged in much stage work after the 1950s.) Ferrer moved casually between negligible adult comedies like 1964's *Sex and the Single Girl* and serious "art" films like 1965's *El Greco*. By the 1970s, Ferrer might be seen as frequently in schlocky horror fare (like 1974's *Antichrist* or Tobe Hooper's *Eaten Alive* in 1977) as he would be in routine television guest appearances on shows like *Marcus Welby, M.D.* or *Hawaii Five-o*. The roles varied (priest, doctor, tycoon), but in most, Ferrer still played the sort of "other man" who carried a barely hidden agenda, as in perhaps his most prominent late career role—the scheming attorney Philip Erikson on the prime-time television soap *Falcon Crest*—which he played from 1981 to 1984. Ferrer retired from acting in the late 1990s and died in 2008.

Not unlike Ferrer, by the late 1960s, Ricardo Montalban had also settled into a career on television, making routine guest appearances as Latino, Latin American, or abstractly European figures in a mix of crime, western, and medical programs. He was also gigging in the 1970s as a television pitchman for, among other products, Chrysler Corporation's "soft Corinthian leather" automobile interiors. By the early 1980s, two roles—his ethnically ambiguous Mr. Roarke on ABC's *Fantasy Island* (1977–84) and the title character in 1982's *Star Trek 2: The Wrath of Khan* (itself a film reprise of one of his best-remembered 1960s television guest spots)—reestablished Montalban as an iconic presence for subsequent generations. The actor continued working, mostly in television and voice actor roles, until the year before his death in 2009.

Although Montalban never stopped working, his frustration with the quality of the opportunities open to him throughout the 1960s led him to cofound Nosotros, an advocacy group for Latina/o film and television actors organized, as announced at a March 1970 press conference, "to enhance the opportunities for Mexican Americans, Latins and all of Spanish-speaking origin to compete for jobs."[78] Montalban's founding of Nosotros stood among several organized responses to questions of typecasting and stereotype that had been circulating—within both industry and activist circles—throughout the decade (some of these organizations I will discuss in detail in chapter 4). Most of these groups—like Nosotros—looked to a broader and more authentic depiction of Latina/o characters and cultures in US popular performance.

At the same time, and even though Montalban did not address it specifically at the moment of Nosotros' founding, such concerns were likely also informed—especially for established actors like him—by subtle but significant shifts in Hollywood's hiring practices in the 1960s. Newer production practices, in tandem with greater emphasis on certain modes of authenticity, meant that a Latina/o actor in 1970 no longer had access to the same diversity of roles that he or she might have had in 1950. Indeed, Anthony Quinn's 1964 nomination for Best Actor in *Zorba* not only would be Quinn's final Academy Award nomination but it would also stand as the last Oscar nomination for an actor of Latina/o or Latin American descent for more than two decades. (Argentinean actress Norma Aleandro would be nominated in 1987 as Best Supporting Actress for *Gaby: A True Story*, and Edward James Olmos would be the next US Latino to be recognized in any category when nominated as Best Actor for 1988's *Stand and Deliver*.)

Just as the Academy Awards did not recognize any actors of Latina/o descent for the twenty years before Thomas Gomez's nomination as Best Supporting Actor in 1947, so, too, would Oscar ignore Latina/o actors for the twenty-plus years after Quinn's nomination for *Zorba the Greek*. Yet, as Montalban and his colleagues were surely aware, six Latina/o actors were nominated eleven times (winning four) between 1947 and 1964. So, while Nosotros's founding was of a piece with other progressive initiatives at the time, its interest in expanding opportunities came at a time of peculiar retrenchment, a moment when the heightening of Latina/o awareness appeared to have a corollary in greater obstacles for Latina/o actors in US popular performance.[79]

When introducing Nosotros to the press, Montalban affirmed, "[W]e are not demanding jobs . . . but we are insisting that we not be excluded from consideration because our surname happens to be Gonzalez, Lopez or even Montalban."[80] Montalban's attention to surnames signals another paradox of the 1960s: emerging Latina/o actors started changing their names. Hollywood histories, both scholarly and popular, typically attribute an actor's name change to a ritual of submission to the marketing imperatives of US commercial entertainment. Other accounts note the shift in the 1960s toward a "new Hollywood," which valued the evident ethnicity of rising stars like Al Pacino, Barbra Streisand, and Dustin Hoffman as highly as the "old Hollywood" had sought to erase it. Yet, for Latina/o actors, the story is not so uniform. While Rita Cansino was radically remade as the "star" Rita Hayworth, Rosita Moreno dropped only a syllable to become Rita Moreno. Throughout the 1950s, jobbing television and film actors like Miriam Colón, Henry Silva, and Carlos Rivas, among others, entered the business and began working without Anglicizing their names. By the mid-1960s, however, that had begun to change.

In perhaps the most oft-told surname story (one mentioned obliquely at the first Nosotros press conference), Henry Delgado—one of Juano Hernandez's students from the University of Puerto Rico and an instructor at his Los Angeles Lyceum—struggled to gain a foothold in Hollywood for nearly a decade. In 1965, after appearing in a successful, widely seen, and well-reviewed Los Angeles production of Ray Bradbury's Latino-themed play *The Wonderful Ice Cream Suit*, Delgado signed with a new agent. After losing two parts in one day because of his name, however, Delgado and his agent agreed to remake Henry Delgado as Henry

Darrow. As Henry Darrow, the actor quickly found that, while he did not necessarily book more work, he did get seen in more auditions with his new name. The paradox came a year or so later when producer David Dortort—who had admired Delgado's performance in *The Wonderful Ice Cream Suit*—tried for months to locate Henry Delgado to test for the principal role in the NBC-TV series *High Chaparral*. Fortified by his insistence that *High Chaparral*'s principal Mexican American roles be cast with Latina/o actors, Dortort persisted, ultimately finding Darrow and signing him to the role of Manolito Montoya, which Darrow would play for the duration of the series (1967–71).

Darrow's near miss only underscored the widespread impression in the mid- to late 1960s, especially among early career actors, that Latina/o-sounding surnames might impede one's career, and Darrow was not alone in making a name change.[81] Some invented stage names, like Bronx-born Raquel Mitrani, who blended a childhood nickname with a variation of her father's first name to become "Shelley Morrison" a year or two before she took the role of the English-impaired Puerto Rican nun Sister Sixto in the television comedy *The Flying Nun* (1967–70). Some dropped incriminating surnames altogether, like Dominican American actor James Victor, a veteran bit player who would go on to appear in the pathbreaking—if short-lived—1976 ABC-TV sitcom *Viva Valdez*. Some Latina actors adopted their married names, even if their first professional credits appeared under their birth names, like Yvonne (Othon) Wilder, likely best remembered as Anita's friend Consuelo ("I know you do!") in the 1961 film version of *West Side Story*. Indeed, for actors still getting their professional start in the mid-1960s—in stark contrast to those like Liz Torres, Gregory Sierra, and Hector Elizondo (all of whom began working in the early 1970s)—secreting one's Latina/o heritage seemed an advantageous strategy.

"Welch" was, after all, Raquel Tejada's married name. Indeed, Raquel Welch's breakout stardom, as well as her status as the era's most prominent "stealth Latina," confirms the peculiar ambivalence with regard to Latina/o visibility in US popular performance in the late 1960s. Just ten years before her star-making role in 1966's *One Million Years B.C.*, Raquel Tejada made her professional debut dancing in the *Pal Joey* chorus at the La Jolla Playhouse, the theatre cofounded by Mel Ferrer.[82] Like the Latina/o stars of a previous era, Welch's ethnicity was neither entirely elided nor especially emphasized by the press. Indeed, nearly every press account of Raquel Welch's burgeoning career is careful to note the actress's Latin-ish heritage, and her ethnicity remained an easily accessed "open secret" during her rise to fame. As *Time* magazine put it in 1969, "[H]er father, Armand, is a Bolivian-born structural engineer; her mother, Josephine, is of English stock."[83] Likewise, most reports included mention of Raquel's birth name, as in a 1968 *Los Angeles Times Magazine* profile, which described "the all-too-human girl who was Raquel Tejada from San Diego's fashionable La Jolla [district]."[84]

For Latina/o audiences and fans, this "open secret" sometimes provided an affirming source of ethnic pride. Celebrated Chicano film director Gregory Nava, best known for his films *Mi Familia* and *Selena* (as well as the television series *American Family*, in which Welch took a featured role in the 2002 season), recalled how Raquel Tejada's early success was a source of pride for Latino San Diego in the 1950s. "She was the prettiest girl in town," Nava remembered. "The whole Latino community was very proud of her."[85] Latinas/os outside Raquel's hometown shared a similar affinity with the rising star. As Chicano film critic and historian Charles Ramírez Berg later observed, "those of us who were Latinos knew that Raquel Welch was a Latina, and we got to enjoy her success all along."[86]

But the "open secret" of Welch's off-white heritage did not operate solely as a source of praise for the rising actress in the late 1960s. Strange insinuations about her ethnoracial heritage imbued many press accounts of her arrival as "a dark heroine to fill the goddess gap."[87] Columnist Army Archerd sneered, "[D]on't believe any of those stories about so-called sex symbol Raquel Welch wanting to change her image.... Raquel courts controversy [and] secrecy ... whatever so-called 'changes' are attributed to her."[88] When queried about 1968's newest sex symbol, one "self-described 'hardened lady reporter' from a news desk" opined that Raquel "used to look like a Mexican waitress from Tijuana! Heavy eyebrows, greasy face—they've done wonders for her.'"[89] Other observers showed a keen interest in the neophyte actress's lack of facility with a Mexican accent for her roles in the films *Bandolero* (1968) and *100 Rifles* (1969). One journalist wagged that Raquel's "accent, like her blouse, keeps slipping,"[90] while another noted that such slippery diction "scotched rumors that Raquel was a crypto-Chicano; her accent was pure Hollywood."[91] (Years later Welch contextualized her notorious "accent issues" by describing her father's adamant assimilationism in postwar California. "He never spoke Spanish in the home," Welch recalled, "so as not to have us have an accent.")[92]

Such a duality—that Latino audiences might seek and find proof of Welch's authentic Latina-ness at the same time that non-Latino audiences could seek and find proof of her inauthenticity—cues both a shift and survival in what I have been calling "stealth Latino" typecasting. While Montalban's, Hernandez's, and Ferrer's "stealth Latino" typecasting rehearsed the limits of Latino raciality at midcentury, Welch's openly secreted Latina heritage practices another "stealth" aspect of Latina/o casting, wherein Latina/o actors "pass" in certain roles and "come out" in others, yet remain legible *as* Latino *to* Latino audiences the whole time. In a more contemporary register, *stealth Latino* codifies what Felix Sanchez, the executive director of the National Hispanic Foundation for the Arts, once described as certain performers' distinct ability "to be ethnically present to the Latino audience and ethnically invisible to a majority audience."[93]

Yet, even though the conventions of casting for Latina/o actors shifted drastically in the mid-1960s, attention to the roles Latina/o actors are actually hired to play continues to document the ways in which emerging and shifting notions of Latina/o raciality are documented by casting. In the 1950s, Latina/o actors were cast interracially, or in roles that enacted the intimate encounters at the outer limits of racial difference, sometimes through the surrogation of "other" ethnic or racial characteristics, sometimes by just being the "other" man. Beginning in the 1960s, we begin to see the cultural, political, and aesthetic pressures that cultivated practices of casting Latina/o actors "intra"racially or in roles that portrayed characters in ways that asked Latina/o actors to rehearse the cross-cultural continuities among disparate Latina/o groups toward a presumptively authentic—yet popularly intelligible—performance of Latinidad.

Although non-Latina/o actors continued to be assigned Latina/o roles, the late 1960s brought heightened popular scrutiny to the acceptability of cross-racial casting practices. On the one hand, this shift meant that, while actors who looked and sounded like Ricardo Montalban would likely be considered for any Latino role (regardless of the character's ethnicity); on the other hand, actors who looked and sounded like Juano Hernandez and Mel Ferrer would only infrequently be so considered, again regardless of the character's ethnicity. Still, careful attention to casting histories continues to offer historical documentation of the ways in which US popular performance rehearses and enacts emerging notions of Latina/o raciality in the contemporary moment.

CHAPTER 3

How The Sharks
Became Puerto Rican

As the Broadway season of 1957–58 came to a close, three musicals absorbed most of the attention of those opining which was the most notable production that year. Critical consensus gathered around Meredith Willson's *The Music Man* (recipient of that year's Tony for Best Musical) as the most exceptionally accomplished. Enthusiasm also attended the year's most popular hit, *Jamaica*, the effervescent calypso musical starring Lena Horne opposite a winning Ricardo Montalban. The greatest mix of opinions circulated around a third musical, certainly the year's most ambitious but also the most divisive among Broadway watchers: *West Side Story*. Indeed, at the end of the season, the consensus seemed to be that *The Music Man* was destined for the canon of great American musicals, with *Jamaica* poised to enter the repertoire as a reliable standard. *West Side Story*'s legacy seemed less certain.[1]

When *West Side Story* closed on Broadway in June 1959, the early consensus of barely a year before had been proven quite wrong. Although *The Music Man* continued triumphantly marching on Broadway, *Jamaica* had just closed, with no plans for a road show to introduce it to audiences beyond New York. *West Side Story*, which played to sold-out houses throughout the last months of its Broadway run, proved a huge critical and popular hit in London (where it opened in 1958). Buzz was strong for the musical's limited tour of major US cities, and negotiations were already under way for a major motion picture, with director-choreographer Jerome Robbins in talks to direct. *West Side Story* remained a point of fascination and curiosity throughout the subsequent year. This compelled producers to break with convention and return the road company to New York, reopening the "original production" on Broadway in April 1960, where it continued to play for another 249 performances. Almost at the same time, shooting for the film began on Manhattan's rapidly changing west side. When the movie *West Side Story* opened in October 1961, it proved an immediate hit. Over the next few months, *West Side Story* broke attendance records in major cities across the United States. The soundtrack album, also released in October 1961, entered the *Billboard* chart as the number-one album, a position it would maintain for more than a year. In early 1962, *West Side Story* was nominated for eleven Academy Awards, and it won Best Picture at the Academy Awards, Golden Globes, and New York Film Critics Circle Awards.

In less than five years, *West Side Story was* transformed from an admirable experiment for the musical stage into one of the most celebrated works in American performance, straddling elite and popular culture as it addressed audiences around the world. Almost immediately after its 1957 premiere, two distinct but parallel interpretive traditions began to guide understandings of the musical's significance. These parallel modes of canonicity emphasized, in turn, either *West Side Story*'s influence as a singular collaboration among some of the twentieth century's most influential musical theatre makers, or the musical's impact as a famously fallacious fiction of Puerto Rican-ness in US popular performance. For scholars, fans, and theatre practitioners inclined to approach *West Side Story* as a canonical American musical, the creative genius evident as early as 1949 when its main creators (director and choreographer Jerome Robbins, composer and part-time lyricist Leonard Bernstein, and librettist Arthur Laurents) set out to reinvent and forever change the American musical. At every juncture in the collaborative process over the eight years during which they developed the musical, these theatre-makers hoped—even planned—for *West Side Story* to become a benchmark of the American musical as an artistic form. Such ambitions, in fact, motivated the project's creative genesis from Robbins's first conception of it in 1949. For the original collaborators—Robbins, Bernstein, and Laurents (lyricist Stephen Sondheim joined the collaboration comparatively late in the process)— the success of *West Side Story*'s original 1957 Broadway production seemed both to verify and to amplify their initial ambitions for the piece.

At the same time, *West Side Story* spurred long-standing cultural debates interrogating the musical's particular contributions to the limiting repertoire of Latina/o depictions in US popular performance. As we shall also see, even the decision to "use" Puerto Ricans in a musical adaptation of Shakespeare's *Romeo and Juliet* appears to have occurred to Robbins, Bernstein, and Laurents as an expeditious afterthought, motivated neither by explicit antipathy toward nor active interest in the lived experience of Puerto Ricans in New York City. Even so, critiques of the musical's representation of Puerto Rican-ness have circulated, often outside conventional circuits of theatrical commentary, since before the musical's first public performance. In the more than half century since the musical's premiere, *West Side Story* has served as a central object for US Latina/o cultural critics as they have sharpened the tools of their trade. As Frances Negrón-Muntaner argues, "*West Side Story* is . . . nothing short of a Puerto Rican *Birth of a Nation* (1915): a blatant, seminal (pun intended), valorized, aestheticized eruption into the (American) national 'consciousness.'"[2]

In the pages that follow, I develop a history of *West Side Story* that explains not only how The Sharks became Puerto Rican but how the musical's development, adaptation, and circulation established as it one of the most emblematic—and problematic—depictions of Latinas/os in US popular performance. My account explicates how *West Side Story*'s incremental success contributed to the contemporary crisis of US popular representation of Puerto Ricans in the years around the musical's 1957 stage premiere. Paying close attention to the musical's theatrical construction and its subsequent adaptation to film, I show how the almost arbitrary decision to make The Sharks Puerto Rican influenced the development of the character of Anita and the collective characterization of The Jets. Further, I demonstrate how the choices made in adapting the show from stage to screen refined the racialization of the Puerto Rican male characters in precise and enduring—although perhaps inadvertent—ways. Finally, I show how the 1960 film version recalibrated the contemporary controversies animating the stage musical—the twin "problems" of juvenile delinquency and Puerto Rican migration to the mainland—which amplified the racializing logic of the piece by offering an inaugural performance of one of the most enduring stock characters in the performance of Latino-ness in twentieth-century US popular performance: the Latino gang member.

How The Sharks Became Puerto Rican

As the legend comes to us, the genesis of *West Side Story* occurred eight years prior to the musical's 1957 premiere, in the first weeks of January 1949.[3] Choreographer Jerome Robbins hit on an idea to set William Shakespeare's *Romeo and Juliet* in contemporary New York City, "at the coincidence of Easter-Passover celebrations," when feelings would be running "high" between Jews and Catholics. Robbins's excitement soon caught the interest of composer Leonard Bernstein, who liked the "bigger idea of making a musical that tells a tragic story in musical-comedy terms, using only musical-comedy techniques."[4] Within the week, playwright Arthur Laurents was onboard, but he soon recognized that— tragedy or not—staging the *Romeo and Juliet* romance on Manhattan's East Side—with a Jewish Juliet and Catholic Romeo—might be little more than "*Abie's Irish Rose* [set] to music."[5] (*Abie's Irish Rose* was a long-running 1920s comedy by Anne Nichols, which explored the marriage troubles of a Jewish boy and a Catholic girl.)[6] But as the 1950s began, the respective careers of Robbins, Bernstein, and Laurents were on the rise, and it would be nearly six years before the "modern Romeo" project would once again occupy their attention.

Flash-forward to August 25, 1954, when Laurents and Bernstein bumped into each other by chance at the Beverly Hills Hotel. Conversation soon turned to the "Romeo project" and a Los Angeles newspaper headline—"Gang Riots on Olvera Street"—about gang fights between Mexican Americans and Anglos. Laurents and Bernstein agreed that the gang warfare in Los Angeles's Mexican American neighborhoods could make the updated Romeo story work. Laurents, however, was loath to drop the New York setting, fearing he might write what he called "movie" Mexicans. "But New York and Harlem," Laurents later recalled, "I knew firsthand, and Puerto Ricans and Negroes and immigrants who had become Americans."[7] Robbins loved the new racial spin on the gang idea,[8] and the working title changed from *East Side Story* to *Gangway!*[9]

For collaborators Robbins, Bernstein, and Laurents, the "modern Romeo" project was first and foremost a formal experiment. As critic Ethan Mordden has observed, the shared endeavor sought "a structure that would flow rather than jerk, whose narrative could move from book into music and then dance without anyone's noticing the joins."[10] In their transfer of the Romeo story from Verona to contemporary New York City, the collaborators trolled for a social context in which the dramatic action could be both powerful and plausible. They soon seized on two hot-button issues of their day—the juvenile gang and Puerto Rican "problems"—to imagine Shakespeare's romantic tragedy amid a blood feud between two rival teen gangs jockeying for dominance in an impoverished Manhattan neighborhood of the 1950s. Within emerging contemporary understandings of youth criminality in the mid-1950s, "juvenile delinquents" were increasingly understood to be individual—usually white—kids gone astray, while "gangs" were ethnically or racially identified groups of kids defending and violating ethnoracial boundaries. Popular media, too, in such emblematic productions as Nicholas Ray's 1955 film *Rebel without a Cause*, depicted juvenile delinquency as endangering "good" (usually white, typically middle class) kids who might go "bad."[11] By the mid-1950s, both the media and public officials had also begun to "discover" youth gangs, especially as racialized street conflicts between groups of urban youths became more commonplace. Experts increasingly characterized the "gang problem" as a (usually) racial conflict among the urban underclass.

Coincidentally, large-scale Puerto Rican migration to the mainland had begun in 1946, accelerated by the postwar economic boom and newly affordable air routes between New York and San Juan. As historian Lorrin Thomas notes, "[T]he postwar boom inspired a migration that nearly doubled [New York City's] Puerto Rican population in two years," with each subsequent year bringing tens of "thousands of new Puerto Rican migrants . . . streaming into New York's ports and airports, lured by abundant industrial jobs and the promise of escape from Puerto Rico's poverty."[12] The "astonishing explosion in Puerto Rican arrivals" beginning in 1946, according to historian Juan Gonzalez, "continued without letup for the next fifteen years."[13] Thus, throughout the 1950s, contemporary social commentators sought the cause of a perceived upsurge in youth criminality, even as they also asked whether the new Puerto Rican migrants might find a place in the ethnic and racial structure that organized a still largely segregated America.

For the creators of *West Side Story*, the popular fascination with juvenile gang violence carved the dramaturgical contours of a world characterized by the constant threat of incipient violence. At the same time, the multicultural realities of 1950s New York made a casual social encounter between a Polish American boy and Puerto Rican girl emphatically plausible for audiences, even as the possibility of such an encounter triggered anxieties about potentially violent intergroup conflict. Arthur Laurents's introduction of the warring groups signaled such anxiety: "Two teen-age gangs, the Jets and the Sharks . . . vital, restless, sardonic; the Sharks are Puerto Ricans, the Jets an anthology of what is called 'American.'"[14] This selection of "Puerto Ricans" as the group to rival the "anthology of what is called 'American'" influentially paired the "social problems" of youth criminality and Puerto Rican migration, which had not previously been connected in the popular imaginary let alone "twinned" as they

would be in *West Side Story*. The pairing also triggered the creative work
necessary to develop the musical. As Bernstein wrote in his log (a revised
version of which was published in the production *Playbill*), I "had a fine
long session with Arthur today, by the pool. . . . We're fired again by the
Romeo notion . . . and have come up with what I think is going to be it:
two teen-age gangs, one the warring Puerto Ricans, the other self-styled
'Americans.' Suddenly it all springs to life. I hear rhythms and pulses,
and—most of all—I can sort of feel the form."[15]

However, and in ways that would have enduring significance for the
musical's circulation, reception, and future adaptation, the creators
approached the social realities of juvenile gangs and Puerto Rican migration as the tethers of plausibility necessary to their primarily artistic
exploration of musical theatrical form. Robbins, in particular, resisted
the idea that he was "documenting" contemporary social formations. "I
went to the territory of the delinquents," Robbins recalled later. "I went
to their social directors, their gang members and leaders. I went to their
dances. Not that I was looking for anything specific, only the key, the one
small thing you discover that opens up larger vistas."[16]

Nonetheless, reviewers and audiences alike lauded *West Side Story*'s
presumed sociological accuracy. The *Daily Mirror* proclaimed *West Side
Story* a "chiller, a thriller, as up-to-the-minute as tomorrow's headlines."[17]
Some reviewers heard the language as authentic, praising Laurents
and Sondheim for "put[ting] an amazing amount of teen-age jargon
onstage without forcing it."[18] In a letter to the *New York Times* arts editor, theatergoers Gary Smith and Barry Frank wondered whether "the
dramatic social significance of [*West Side Story*] might serve some practical purpose. Could special matinees sponsored by the city be given for
high school audiences? Some of our teenagers might benefit from such
a searching, creative and entertaining treatment of their problems."[19]
And this propensity to view *West Side Story* as a sociologically authentic
representation of—or even solution to—New York City's social problems
only increased over time. By 1964 (and thus informed by the hugely
successful 1961 screen version), noted psychoanalyst and social theorist
Bruno Bettelheim saw fit to use *West Side Story* as a case study of ethnic
hostility and group belonging.[20] As one Broadway historian later observed,
"[I]n 1957, the gang warfare and rioting which dominated the show may
have seemed far-fetched to New York theater audiences still unwilling to
admit that such conditions were reality rather than fancy. Ten years later,
however, even the skeptics realized that *West Side Story* could almost be
called a documentary portrayal."[21]

On its opening in 1957, *West Side Story* received reviews that ranged from equivocally positive to overtly hostile. In one of the most favorable early reviews, Brooks Atkinson averred, "[A]lthough the material is horrifying, the workmanship is admirable"—hardly a rave.[22] On the other hand, Walter Kerr warned that *West Side Story* was "almost never emotionally affecting" and cautioned his readers, "[D]on't look for laughter or—for that matter—tears."[23] Still, in the two years that followed, the musical defied its mixed critical reception with a New York run of nearly eight hundred performances, a national tour of major cities, and a return to Broadway in 1959, which was greeted by uniformly positive praise from the New York critics. Each phase of *West Side Story*'s incremental success—in tandem with the celebration of Robbins and Bernstein as American national treasures—seemed proof positive that the musical's formal experiment was a success.

Critiquing West Side Story

That The Sharks are Puerto Rican is one of the simple facts in *West Side Story*, but how and why did it come to pass that the musical would become so significant within US Latina/o popular performance and representation? Indeed, why is *West Side Story* not considered the great "juvenile delinquency musical," when its composition, presentation, and early reception were—as we shall see—shaped as much, if not more, by the contemporary debates about youth criminality? To posit an answer, I submit that *West Side Story*—perhaps inadvertently,, but nonetheless importantly—addressed an uncertainty among the US cultural elite regarding how the new Puerto Rican arrivals in New York should be understood, especially with regard to existing racial structures and hierarchies. Were the Puerto Ricans arriving from the island to the mainland, like previous generations of European immigrants, through the "golden door" of Ellis Island? Or were they dark-skinned migrants like African Americans of the Great Migration from the American South?[24] *West Side Story*'s portrayal of Puerto Ricans, with mostly non-Puerto Rican performers, constructed a compelling illusion, an explanatory yet obfuscating lens through which to see Puerto Ricans, a vision that would soon become an object of belief. In so doing, *West Side Story*—first in the theatrical spectacle and later in its cinematic variation—appeared to resolve the crisis of Puerto Rican representation in US popular culture that had been roiling in the decade prior to its 1957 stage premiere. And along the way *West Side Story* became established as the template for all things Puerto Rican in US popular performance.

As both mark and measure of this phenomenon—beginning even before *West Side Story*'s premiere—US Latina/o and Puerto Rican cultural workers, artists and critics alike, had interrogated the racialized meanings mobilized by the musical and their particular impact on the limiting repertoire of Latina/o depictions in US popular performance. Indeed, since the musical's premiere in 1957, concerns about its performance of Puerto Rican-ness have inspired a rich tradition of critical counterperformance. In print and in person, protesters have lobbied producers, venues, and audiences to criticize *West Side Story*'s performance of Puerto Rican identity and culture.[25] This tradition of critique routes according to three primary—and possibly generational—strategies for reproving *West Side Story*'s unintended but consequential racializing impact: disappointment, disavowal, and disidentification.

Disappointed reactions to *West Side Story*'s racialism began as early as August 1957, during the new musical's out-of-town tryout in Washington, DC. On August 20, 1957, the day of the production's first preview performance, *West Side Story*'s producers received a telephone message from the editors of *La Prensa*, New York City's leading Spanish-language newspaper. Mere hours before curtain, *La Prensa*'s editors threatened to picket the show if it arrived on the New York stage without cuts or alterations to the song "America." Of particular concern was a single lyric, in which the character Anita mocks another character's naive idealization of her homeland. *La Prensa* claimed that Anita's lyric ("Puerto Rico—Island of Tropic Diseases") perpetuated the pejorative view that Puerto Ricans—whether living on the island or in New York City—were public health nuisances. The musical's producers disregarded the paper's request to alter or delete the offending lyric. When *West Side Story* opened a month later at Manhattan's Winter Garden Theatre on September 26, 1957, the threatened picketers from *La Prensa* never materialized. Actress Chita Rivera—herself of Puerto Rican descent—sang the lyric unaltered.

Since its 1957 premiere, complaints about the musical's intransigent inaccuracies have ranged from the offhand dismay of literary scholar Roberto Marquez, who describes being "insulted by the gossamer counterfeit of *West Side Story*,"[26] to those that echo the provocative mix of outrage, annoyance, and disappointment expressed by writer and activist Jesús Colón. Writing in the late 1950s, when *West Side Story* was still a new Broadway sensation, Colón observed that "we Puerto Ricans have . . . been subjected to treatment in . . . a fabulously successful musical show.

But invariably this treatment harps on what is superficial and sentimental, transient and ephemeral, or bizarre and grotesque in Puerto Rican life—and always out of context with the real history, culture and traditions of my people."[27] This "disappointment" mode of critical response would not cease, undergirding most responses to the musical that explicate the myriad inaccuracies and inauthenticities within its depiction of Puerto Rican-ness on stage.

In contrast, the "disavowal" mode of critically reinterpreting *West Side Story* describes a more primal experience of racialized intercultural encounter. Theatre critic and historian Alberto Sandoval-Sánchez details his own experience this way: "*West Side Story* was frequently imposed upon me as a model of/for my Puerto Rican ethnic identity. . . . Over and over again, to make me feel comfortable in their family rooms and to tell me of their knowledge about Puerto Ricans, [Anglo-American acquaintances] would start their conversation with *West Side Story*."[28] Likewise, critical reflections on the phantasm of "Maria" have proven a recurring theme in the poetry and prose of Puerto Rican author Judith Ortiz Cofer, and other Latina scholars and performers have acknowledged the complicated ways in which *West Side Story* has informed their work.[29]

Finally, the "disidentification" phase marks perhaps the most recent node in this tradition of critiquing *West Side Story*'s general significance within US Latina/o cultural production and commentary. In José Esteban Muñoz's influential configuration, disidentification describes the "hermeneutical performance of decoding mass, high, or any other cultural field from the perspective of a minority subject who is disempowered in such a representational hierarchy."[30] Within this category, I might locate critics like David Román, Ernesto Acevedo-Muñoz, Frances Negrón-Muntaner, and myself, alongside cultural workers like Lin-Manuel Miranda and even Jennifer Lopez (both of whom have pointed to the complicated influence of *West Side Story* on their own development as performing artists).[31] In the last half century, pointed explications of *West Side Story*'s racism have balanced awkwardly with reverential accounts of the musical's canonical genius.[32]

Krup You!

For Jerome Robbins, the "modern Romeo" project was guided by two parallel inspirations, each drawn in different but equal measure from his own life. On the one hand, Robbins wanted to use the *Romeo and*

Juliet scenario to tell the story of generational conflict within a broader portrait of Jewish and Italian immigration to New York's Lower East Side. Early treatments of the story are epic, internecine, and in both style and structure presciently anticipate the immigration family sagas that would eventually define the "ethnic revival" of the early 1970s. This is the same period in which Robbins himself revived and reframed his early "East Side Story" inspiration to great success in *Fiddler on the Roof.* Yet, as much as Robbins's passion for his musical adaptation of *Romeo and Juliet* was compelled by his interest in the story of American im/migration, the "modern Romeo" project was also inspired by his drive to develop an emphatically masculine choreographic vocabulary for American dance. Indeed, for Robbins, the hero or protagonist of what became *West Side Story* was never really the star-crossed lover Tony but rather his gang, the emphatically male singing and dancing ensemble that—with the most dialogue, dancing, and songs assigned to it—became in Robbins's conception and staging the conflicted protagonist of *West Side Story.*

West Side Story introduces Robbins's protagonist, The Jets, as an ensemble comprised of idiosyncratic characters who maintain their individuation, even as—through shared movement, motive, and melody—they move as one. In this way (and in ways anticipating *Hair*'s tribe, *A Chorus Line*'s gypsies, and even *Cats'* jellicles), *West Side Story* deploys the musical apparatus to dramatize the simultaneously collective yet individual experience of a previously anonymous caste of characters. While the script and score do invest Riff, Diesel, BabyJohn, and Anybodys with idiosyncratic characterizations, the musical relies on The Jets as an ensemble character to propel the drama of its plot. Indeed, by most measures, The Jets are rightly read as *West Side Story*'s protagonist. Compelled by their conflict with The Sharks, and catalyzed by Tony's betrayal of his identity as a Jet, the crisis over whether and how The Jets will survive this West Side night (with or without Tony) coordinates the musical's every dramatic beat—and also cues how The Jets activate the drama of race within *West Side Story.*

The Jets' songs provide perhaps the clearest map of how *West Side Story* composes its ensemble protagonist. When considered together, the three songs performed only by The Jets comprise a triptych of disparate articulations of the collective interiority of their experience.[33] The first of these ensemble soliloquys—titled, aptly enough, "The Jet Song"—is also the first song to be sung in the musical; it details the nature, purpose, and power of the fraternal bond shared by the gang members. The remaining two Jets' songs bracket the fateful "Rumble," one galvanizing group solidarity in the moments before battle, the other reconstituting the newly leaderless group in the moments after. On stage, "Cool" comes first, describing the strategic reserve of feeling and gesture maintained by the implacable façade of the street kid. "Gee, Officer Krupke" comes after, affirming The Jets' derisive critique of the social welfare apparatus that awaits them. (On screen, "Krupke" comes first, and, as we shall see, this simple switch of dramatic placement notably alters the affect of the song.) Each of the songs articulates a distinct aspect of The Jets' group consciousness, as it also tutors those naive about the rituals of gang life—whether on-stage characters like BabyJohn or members of the audience—into understanding what it means to be "a Jet all the way / From your first cigarette / To your last dyin' day."

"The Jet Song" demonstrates how the ensemble soliloquy works with deceptive simplicity. After two previous opening song attempts to frame The Jets and The Sharks in antagonistic counterpoint (including "Mix," which rhymed its title with a common epithet describing Latinos) were deemed "too fast, too complicated, too canonical,"[34] the collaborators reconceived the show's opening moments, editing toward an aesthetic of simplicity that yielded both the nearly wordless "Prologue" and "The Jet Song."

"The Jet Song" begins as a retort. When planning for that night's council with The Sharks, Riff agitates Action by naming Tony as his second. "Who needs Tony," Action rebuts, "he don't belong any more." Riff's responds with the "The Jet Song" and so reminds Action, The Jets, and the audience of the high stakes of being a Jet. Riff sings, "When you're a Jet, / If the spit hits the fan, / You got brothers around, / You're a family man." Riff's lead inspires an echolalic response from each of The Jets, whose individual vocal turns (like Action's "When you're a Jet, you're the top cat in town") build incrementally toward the ensemble's crescendo, which the gang members sing as one ("Here come The Jets, / Yeah! And we're gonna beat / Every last buggin' gang. . . . / On the whole! / Ever—! / Mother—! / Lovin'—! / Street!"). Within "The Jet Song," individual distinctiveness accretes into collective identity in ways that are typical of the three Jets' songs in the show. This amalgamation of individual within group identity was also anchored by Robbins's distinctive deployment of "method"-style directorial strategies within the show. Drawing on sensibilities ubiquitous in serious playmaking of the 1950s, Robbins sought performances freighted with psychological and behavioral detail from his entire company. To that end, the notoriously volatile director immersed his young cast within the antagonistic emotional

landscape of the show.[35] Cast members were subjected to Robbins's spontaneous interrogations about their characters' backstories. Production
staff posted news clippings about interracial conflict and gang violence
along the back of the stage. On breaks, and even outside rehearsal, Robbins forbade "Jet" and "Shark" performers to mix socially at any time,
with violators publicly berated and tattlers praised.[36] All told, though,
Robbins's unorthodox strategies cultivated an ensemble with legendary
devotion to the director, as well as a strong sense of character—in which
an individual characterization was a facet of an overarching, primary
group identification—that amplified *West Side Story*'s dramatic urgency
and impact.

Whereas "The Jet Song" expresses an ensemble affirmation that gang
affiliation answers all needs, the musical's first solo (sung by Tony, The
Jets' now disaffected cofounder) expresses some doubt: "Something's
coming, I don't know what it is / But it is / Gonna be great!" The two
numbers that bracket "The Jet Song" thereby frame the crisis confronted by The Jets—the physical threat of The Sharks (as enacted by the
choreographic epic encounter between The Jets and The Sharks in the
opening "Prologue") and the ideological threat posed by Tony, a lapsed
leader now disavowing the value of group membership. In "Something's
Coming," as he sings optimistically of portentous change ("The air is
humming / And something great is coming!"), Tony implicitly confirms
Action's earlier suspicions about the group. This cues the audience that
both Action and Tony recognize what Riff does not: The Jets are in crisis,
struggling to hold themselves together while confronting unexpected
challenges, from both within and without.

The Jets' crisis of survival compels *West Side Story*'s dramatic action at
every turn. Even the question of whether The Jets' cofounder, Tony, can
independently pursue the something he sees coming—or whether he
really will remain a Jet to his last dying day—is part of The Jets' defining
struggle as an ensemble character. And at each point of fateful conflict
in the musical's narrative, Jet solidarity—the question of whether a Jet
really is a Jet all the way—routes the musical's tragedy, through both the
rumble and the "taunting" of Anita. Even more, in the moments immediately prior to these narrative junctures, The Jets confirm their group
identity in "Cool" and "Gee, Officer Krupke."

As group soliloquys, and in ways similar to the earlier "Jet Song," both
"Cool" and "Gee, Officer Krupke" discipline the individual voice into a
singular group identity, rehearsing the strength of group solidarity in the
face of looming challenges. In the one, The Jets both release and contain

their excess excitement in anticipation of the rumble; in the other, they rehearse their necessarily sardonic defiance as they ready themselves to rescue a fugitive Tony. On stage in 1957, The Jets got "Cool" before their tragic confrontation with The Sharks and protested "Gee, Officer Krupke" afterwards. On screen a few years later, the songs were switched for the purposes of dramatic economy, so that "Krupke" came before the bloodshed and "Cool" not long after. By excavating the thematic implications of flipping these two numbers, we can see how this seemingly simple trade not only changed the ensemble characterization of The Jets but also amplified the raciality of their conflict with The Sharks.

"Gee, Officer Krupke" was decidedly *West Side Story*'s most commented-upon number when the stage production opened on Broadway in 1957. "Krupke" did not find its way into the script until June 1957,[37] when Bernstein delivered a melody scrapped from *Candide* to lyricist Stephen Sondheim for the song to be sung by The Jets in the moments after the bloody rumble. On this jaunty vaudevillian melody, Sondheim crafted the musical's most elaborate lyric to depict how, in the words of one reviewer, "a so-called juvenile delinquent gets a going-over by all the authorities whose problem he is—the cop, the judge, the social worker, and the psychiatrist."[38] The ironic incongruity between Bernstein's bright melody and Sondheim's mordant lyrics offended some critics, even as it delighted others.[39] On the one hand, the *New York Times*' Brooks Atkinson fretted over the song's "light view of a frightening, . . . painful and baffling problem" and suggested that "the taste of this jeering song is open for question," while the *Journal American*'s John McClain praised the song as "the most hilarious travesty of our times . . . a plaint which should settle the problem of juvenile delinquency forever."[40] The critic for the *New York Post* dismissed it as a "few scornful thrusts at the police and at theories about juvenile delinquency," while another thought it "fun to have delinquents sing and act their notion how idiotic they consider juvenile court judges, psychiatrists, and social workers."[41] One reviewer even wondered at the song's obscenity, questioning whether an expletive might be heard in the final lyric: "Gee, Officer Krupke / *Krup* you!"[42]

"Gee, Officer Krupke" derisively dismissed contemporary common sense regarding the "problem" of juvenile delinquency in ways that were hardly commonplace in 1957. Since the late 1940s, Federal Bureau of Investigation (FBI) director Herbert Hoover had likened youth criminality to "the sulphurous lava, which boils beneath the slumbering volcano."[43] Even as the *New York Times*' celebrated Soviet correspondent Harrison Salisbury opined that "the rapid liquidation of adolescent delinquency [is] becoming a matter of national security," Gallup polls confirmed that popular opinion held the family to blame for adolescent delinquency, even as social service and juridical authorities advocated empathetic intervention. The urgent need for such intervention drove popular culture narratives as well.[44] In the months prior to *West Side Story*'s stage premiere, films as different as Robert Altman's teensploitation melodrama *The Delinquents* and the feel-good farce *The Delicate Delinquent* (starring Jerry Lewis) both narrated the existence of youth criminality as caused by familial neglect and a problem best solved by empathetic yet authoritative adult intervention. Even one of the year's most admired delinquency dramas, *Dino* (an acclaimed 1956 teleplay remade for the big screen in 1957 to capitalize on star Sal Mineo's heartthrob status), followed what one reviewer mocked as "the now traditional screen conflict between the Shaggy-Headed Surly Teenager and the Kind Patient Adult."[45] (*Dino*'s nail-biter tale of a delinquent's last-second redemption also proved especially popular among high school drama teachers, with the 1957 stage play version ranking among those most produced by high schools for the next ten years.)[46]

On stage, "Krupke" satirized this delinquency consensus in ways on which nearly every reviewer of the Broadway production saw fit to comment. Yet the legible impact of "Krupke" should not be mistaken as simply a feature of *West Side Story*'s contemporaneity. Rather, the song's placement in the moments when the newly leaderless Jets must reconsolidate as a group, having scattered after Riff's death at the rumble, also amplifies the acidity of the song's satire. Considered in this dramatic context, "Gee, Officer Krupke" becomes a neo-Brechtian moment of social critique in which The Jets ably demonstrate their sophisticated understanding of the juridical apparatus that fails to understand them. By acerbically underscoring the inadequacies of the very system poised to absorb them should they (or Tony) be caught, in "Gee, Officer Krupke," The Jets fortify their ensemble identity in opposition to what one reviewer called "our era's patented psychology and chromium-plated panaceas [and] the over-educated ignoramuses professing to offer cures for the eroding evils of poverty and racism."[47] Thus, in its dramatic placement in the stage version, "Gee, Officer Krupke" articulates The Jets' peripatetic insight that "the system" poses as great a threat to their ultimate survival as The Sharks do.

On screen, however, "Gee, Officer Krupke" maintains barely a whiff of the satiric sneer it wielded on stage, at least in part because in the film "Krupke" comes in the moments before the rumble, with "Cool" occu-

The Jets in *West Side Story* on stage and screen (1957/1961). (Images of stage and screen productions by permission of *Photofest*)

pying the dramatic juncture held by "Krupke" on stage.[48] This switch was compelled by a few factors, including screenwriter Ernest Lehman's agreement with director Robert Wise's opposition to any "comic interludes after the rumble [that might] break the escalating sense of inevitable tragedy." Although this concern had been expressed for the stage production as well, Jerome Robbins agreed to the change on film, at least in part because the movie's Riff (Russ Tamblyn) did not impress Robbins as a strong enough dancer to handle the demanding choreography of "Cool." Robbins also agreed with Wise that Tamblyn was especially well suited to the comic requirements of "Krupke." Once flipped with "Cool" on screen, however, the dramatic urgency amplifying the ironic gravity of "Gee, Officer Krupke" on stage was drained from the song, and the cinematic "Krupke" became an artfully silly spectacle of boys acting out after a dance, absent the seriously satiric slap at the powers that be that had so enflamed commentators on the occasion of West Side Story's Broadway premiere.

The meaning of "Cool," too, shifted with the switch in its dramatic placement. On stage, "Cool" was the second of The Jets' ensemble soliloquys, in which their leader Riff readied them for their scheduled conference with The Sharks by reminding them how to keep their fury wound tight behind an implacable "cool" appearance. For Cold War audiences, the idea of a cool façade providing a mask for roiling criminality carried special menace, not only for theatregoers who might pass young "toughs" on their way to or from the theatre but also in a more abstract way. Observing The Jets' arrival on Broadway (barely a week after the Soviet Union's launch of Sputnik), Saturday Review commentator Henry Hewes interpreted West Side Story's depiction of the territorial conflict among The Jets and The Sharks as "a capsule Cold War" in which "the growing population of Puerto Ricans in the block demands an all-out attempt to destroy them before they become too powerful." For Hewes, The Jets' "war council" with The Sharks was a metaphor for global relations between the US and Soviet governments.[49]

On stage "Cool" amplified the motif of anticipation guiding the dramatic action of West Side Story's first act, accelerating the emotional momentum toward that act's fatal culmination at the rumble. When placed after Riff and Bernardo have both been killed, though, "Cool" operates less as a canny statement of wily style than as an even more ominous manifesto anticipating the deadly hazards of an unpredictably hostile environment. In this way, the seemingly simple flip of "Cool" and "Krupke" in the screen version also marks an important shift in the ensemble characterization of The Jets. On stage The Jets' songs explained not only the motive ("When you're a Jet") and manner ("Just play it cool, boy") of juvenile delinquency but also its meaning within the greater society ("We're down on our knees / 'Cause no one wants a fella with a social disease"), with each song's particular contribution to the ensemble characterization fortified by its dramatic placement within the broader narrative.

On screen, though, this accretive impact works differently, depicting instead how a gratifying ("The Jet Song") and even fun way of life ("Krupke") is suddenly lost and now requires a newly serious strategy for survival ("Cool") in its place. Where the stage version of "Krupke" satirized society's failures as the final beat in The Jets triptych, the screen version of "Cool" does not target societal structures but rather identifies a changing urban landscape as the group's primary threat. Such subtle, seemingly simple shifts in the placement of The Jets' songs in the screen version of *West Side Story* reorient the stage musical's curiosity about what makes the juvenile delinquent tick toward the ominous threat of racialized gangs in the urban jungle.

The crisis mapped by The Jets' songs also maps the crisis of whiteness at midcentury. No longer simply singing and dancing icons of "juvenile delinquency," The Jets emerge as a cinematic embodiment of whiteness in peril—at once newly consolidated and newly under siege. On stage the crisis faced by The Jets remains primarily one of generational solidarity and survival, with the collapse of its group identity triggered into its tragic tailspin by the disloyalties of forbidden love. On screen, however, The Jets' crisis is realigned within a racialized register. For the movie Jets, their shared crisis is not so much generational as it is racial, with Tony's betrayal anchored by the interraciality of his romance with Maria. On screen the collective characterization of The Jets as a cinematic embodiment of the second generation of urban European ethnics (or "the anthology that is called 'American'") demonstrates the instability of their provisional claims to the security promised by whiteness. Within this cinematic depiction, as Julia Foulkes and others have convincingly demonstrated, The Jets' solidarity becomes the "cool" face guarding an increasingly urbanized color line from those threatening to violate that racialized border: The Sharks.

You Forget I'm in America!

From the outset, Jerome Robbins's vision for what became *West Side Story* was guided by his investment in bringing the emotional experience of

The Jets to vivid physical and musical life on stage.[50] Crafting the world of The Sharks, on the other hand, was for Robbins mostly a means to the end of realizing his "modern Romeo" vision. And it shows. On stage The Sharks (aside from Bernardo and Chino) barely speak and do not sing a song of their own, except in counterpoint in "Quintet." Maria, Anita, and the other Shark girls are dynamic presences—both physically and vocally—but do little (with one notable exception) to compel the action of the story, even as they contribute some of the show's most diverting numbers. As described earlier, this relative imbalance has long earned the suspicion of some observers, especially those wary of *West Side Story*'s elaboration of a musical-theatrical Latin-ness that cues, by turns, spectacle and threat.

The film's heightening of The Sharks' threatening spectacularity—in tandem with its racialization of the gang's conflict with The Jets—enflamed these suspicions. Performance historian David Román summarizes this tradition of suspicion when he writes that *West Side Story*'s "casting of non-Latinos in Latino roles, its perpetuation of Latino stereotypes as criminal and primitive, and its endorsement of American identity over Island loyalty" has carved a unique notoriety for itself: "*West Side Story*—as one of the handful of Latino representations on Broadway—ignites Latino ire."[51] Here Román aptly tags the questions—of casting, of identity, of criminality—that have brought *West Side Story* to the center of myriad inquiries about what it means to "play Latino" in US popular performance.

A brief history of *West Side Story*'s casting for stage and screen—as well as some of the backstories regarding its depiction of Puerto Rican identity and Latina/o criminality—underscores the ways in which its composition, adaptation, and early circulation sit at a historical fault line of practices of performance-making at midcentury. While I would be reluctant to call *West Side Story* a watershed work, there is a legible distance between its before and after. This distance is worth exploring. *West Side Story* stands as an exemplar of how the guiding aesthetics of verisimilitude changed as the 1950s became the 1960s. The piece's mélange of stylized modernism and vérité aspirations stands as but one documentation of the incremental pressures confronting performance-makers to "accurately" reflect (or deftly elide) the cultural diversities defining contemporary life. Even brief historical excavations regarding the musical's approach to casting Latina/o performance, staging Puerto Rican identity, and enacting Latina/o criminality reveal how *West Side Story* rehearsed some of the contemporary changes happening well beyond the theatre or soundstage, even as it was scripted by soon-to-be-antiquated performance practices and techniques.

Casting

West Side Story's approach to casting—especially for the stage—was perhaps as significant a formal breakthrough as the musical's more celebrated "seamless" integration of dance, music, and drama. Indeed, from the earliest days of the actual production process, Jerome Robbins insisted that *West Side Story*'s ensemble include only those who could both sing and dance. Typically, musical productions (like 1953's *Wonderful Town*) would hire distinct singing and dance choruses, deploying each as necessary to fortify the look and sound of the show. In a memo to Laurents and Bernstein, Robbins wrote, "[I]t's easier to rehearse with separate units, but [it's] most beneficial to the unity of the show to have the principals do everything."[52] Robbins also resisted the conventional wisdom that a stage musical should be built around recognizable stars. Instead, he sought an emphatically youthful cast of "unknowns" to bring additional "unity" to the piece. A feature article published in the *New York Times* in the days before *West Side Story*'s out-of-town tryout hyperbolized this effort as a "talent dragnet." In the article, Robbins offered a self-valorizing account of his efforts to scout talent ("from settlement houses and theatrical agents, from high schools and ballet companies, from college choirs and night clubs") in ways that evoke the sort of legendary Hollywood publicity stunt work undertaken in the casting of *Gone with the Wind* (or, a few generations later, *Selena*). While some have doubted Robbins's account of *West Side Story*'s casting "dragnet," call sheets from the Broadway cast auditions confirm that the director-choreographer not only sought young multiskilled performers for all the principal roles (which, with *West Side Story*'s success in subsequent years, ultimately compelled a rising generation of young performers to train to be what would later come to be called a "triple threat") but also actively sought what he somewhat euphemistically noted in his casting materials as the "real thing."[53]

For Robbins the "real thing" referred exclusively to some—but not all—of the Latina/o performers who auditioned during the 1957 casting cycle for the Broadway production. It is worth emphasizing that *West Side Story*'s casting of Latina/o characters (in both its stage and screen versions) was aligned with the normative casting conventions of the period, wherein Latina/o actors enjoyed no special priority for Latina/o roles. Even so, casting records suggest that Robbins did actively seek out Latina/o actors to play principal Latina/o roles for the Broadway production.[54] Audition call sheets confirm that Robbins and his collaborators reviewed Latina/o performers for the principal roles of Maria, Bernardo, Anita, and Chino, beginning as early as December 1956 and continuing through to the finalization of the casting process in May 1957. The name of Cuban-born soprano Maria Teresa Carillo (described as "P.R. Julie Andrews") is seen for the role of Maria more than once, along with nearly a dozen or so other Latinas auditioning variously for Maria, Anita, and the ensemble. The names of Latino actors also appear intermittently on audition rosters, with three different ones (Augie Rodriguez, Elliott Santiago, and Ernesto Gonzales) entering the callback cycle for Bernardo. However, no Latino actors appear to have been considered for roles as members of The Jets. In contrast, non-Latino auditioners are routinely considered for both Jet and Shark parts. (A then unknown Jerry Orbach was noted as a "very good" possibility for either Jet or Shark parts when he first auditioned in in December 1956. By the final stage of casting in May 1957, Orbach was mostly in contention for a Shark role, primarily that of Chino.) The role of Chino ultimately went to Broadway newcomer Jaime Sanchez, whom Robbins's notes describe as "Actor—Singer real P.R. young." Sanchez (whose first name appears variously as Jaime, Jaimie, and Jamie) was born in Rincón, Puerto Rico, and had worked in Puerto Rican theatre before moving to New York just a few years before his *West Side Story* audition.[55]

Chita Rivera is not described as "the real thing" in Robbins's notes (although her name is circled twice, quite emphatically, upon her first audition), nor does the *New York Times*' "Talent Dragnet" article acknowledge Rivera's Puerto Rican heritage when it identifies "Jamie" Sanchez as the only Puerto Rican finally cast. Yet Rivera's placement in the pivotal role of Anita is perhaps the casting decision of the most enduring significance for the musical's long afterlife. Audition records suggest that Rivera's audition resolved a long-standing impasse between Laurents and Robbins about reframing the role. Even as they entered auditions, Robbins retained his early suspicions that Laurents's choice to script Anita as Maria's older, savvier counterpart made her a "typical downbeat blues torch bearing second character (Julie of *Showboat*)."[56] Rivera's audition, though, seems to have resolved the conflict, as Robbins saw few others for the role after it. During the audition process, Robbins also began to reimagine "America" as an all-female showcase, as we shall see.

The impact of Rivera's casting in the role of Anita endures beyond her original performance and her impact on the shape of the show. Indeed, just as *West Side Story*'s casting aesthetic drew on midcentury practices of casting non-Latinos in Latino roles, so, too, did Rivera's casting (in a very stealth Latina way) amplify Anita's confrontation with the powerful pleasures, perils, and problems of the color line. We can see this legacy manifested in the casting processes for subsequent *West Side Story* productions. As the show went first to London and then to Hollywood before returning to New York for the 1964 City Center revival, no comparably aggressive recruitment of Latina/o actors for Shark roles appears to have taken place. But throughout the productions Anita is unique in having been consistently cast with a Latina performer. The London production was delayed to accommodate Rivera's schedule. Rita Moreno was hired for the film, narrowly beating out BarBara Luna, who took on the role at City Center in 1964.[57] (The notable exception perhaps proving this "rule" would be Debbie Allen, who played Anita in the 1980 revival.) As Deborah Paredez has evocatively suggested, these subsequent surrogations cue some of the ways Rivera's casting in the role of Anita helped to script the role as a "Latina" in ways distinct from other roles of the period, and even in ways distinct from other "Latin" roles in *West Side Story*.[58] And few places in this script make this as evident as in "America."

America

Anita leads "America" on both stage and screen, but Broadway's "America" is not at all the same as Hollywood's. The theatrical version of "America" is a diversion, an exuberant and funny interlude that shows Anita and the other Shark girls cutting up after their boyfriends leave for something called a "war council" with The Jets. Though still energetic and entertaining, the movie's "America" is an argument. The Shark girls (as led by Anita) express their knowing enthusiasm for a life away from the island of Puerto Rico; The Sharks themselves parry with assertions of anger and resentment regarding the many hostilities and daily humiliations they face on the mainland. The stage "America" resolves as the women dance together, while the culminating dance in the screen's "America" confirms the intransigence of the conflict between The Sharks and The Jets. As with "Krupke," sustained attention to the changes evident between the stage and screen versions of "America" both reveal and confirm some of the specific ways in which The Sharks' raciality was amplified in *West Side Story*'s adaptation from stage to screen.

On stage "America" is impelled by a satiric squabble that pits Rosalia's naive nostalgia for Puerto Rico against Anita's formidable wit and worldly sophistication. The scene shifts as Bernardo and The Sharks depart to meet The Jets, leaving "their girls" on the rooftop. Described by librettist Arthur Laurents as "not too bright," Rosalia (originally portrayed by non-Latina Marilyn Cooper) then begins to yearn—first in speech and then in song—for "Puerto Rico / You lovely island / Island of tropical breezes," which elicits a scathing rebuke from Anita ("Puerto Rico / You ugly island / Island of tropic diseases"). Anita then asserts her emphatic preference for the mainland ("I like to be in America / Okay by me in America!"), simultaneously celebrating her new home ("Everything free in America") and nodding to its difficulties ("For a small fee in America"). As the ensemble joins Anita, Rosalia's simple suggestions ("I like the city of San Juan") are trumped by Anita's sardonic retorts ("I know a boat you can get on"). In the song's final lyric exchange, Rosalia's vision of an island homecoming ("Everyone there will give a big cheer!") withers under Anita's acid reply ("Everyone there will have moved here"), and the entire ensemble erupts in what the script calls "a joyous dance" until the scene ends.

Upon its Broadway premiere, "America" was uniformly acknowledged as one of *West Side Story*'s most captivating highlights. Still, among the many theatrical reviews that assiduously examined the comedic barbs of "Gee, Officer Krupke," few even noted the redolent commentary in "America." A handful of reviewers did praise "America" simply, like the *Theatre Arts* reviewer, who characterized the song as "a comical commentary on this country from the Puerto Ricans' point of view."[59] More reviewers singled out Rivera's performance, like John Chapman of the *New York Daily News,* who most colorfully exemplified the tenor of such notices. He wrote, "Chita Rivera, as a sinuous and fiery Latin, lights up like a handful of Fourth-of-July sparklers."[60] Only Euphemia Van Rensselaer Wyatt (writing for *Catholic World*) ignored "Gee, Officer Krupke" in her otherwise comprehensive review of the Broadway production, opting instead to scrutinize Tony and Maria's "private pledging of their troth" and to express her disapproval of the "the rather ribald and lively song, 'America,' sung by Rita [*sic*] Rivera."[61] But perhaps the most notable critique of the song came shortly after *West Side Story*'s official New York opening, when Dr. Howard A. Rusk critiqued Sondheim's "island of tropic diseases" lyric in the *New York Times* as "a blow below the belt" and "not based in fact."[62] Attacking the pejorative insinuation that Puerto Rican migrants posed a threat to public health (also the basis of *La Prensa*'s threatened protest of *West Side Story* out of town), Rusk took Sondheim and his cocreators to task for their ignorance of the Puerto Ricans at the center of their new musical. Rusk's critique, however, did not effect any immediate change to the song, and Anita's retort remained to instigate the acerbic dialogic structure of "America."

On screen, however, "America" unlooses The Sharks from the near silence of their theatrical incarnation. Anita (now Rita Moreno) still leads the song, though with some evident changes. Not only is the "tropic diseases" lyric that so offended Dr. Rusk and *La Prensa* nowhere to be heard, but Rosalia's nostalgia no longer introduces the song. Instead, Ernest Lehman's screenplay describes Anita "faking it, dramatically," as she sings the opening verse ("Puerto Rico / My heart's devotion") before expressing "her real meaning" ("Let it sink back in the ocean"). Anita continues, first with lyrics recognizable from the stage version ("Always the hurricanes blowing / Always the population growing/") before introducing lyrics new for the screen ("And the money owing / And the sunlight streaming / And the natives steaming"). Anita finishes the verse as she did on stage ("I like the isle of Manhattan / Smoke on your pipe and put that in"), and the Shark women join in the refrain ("I like to be in America / Okay by me in America"). Anita continues to lead the ensemble ("Everything free in America "), but Bernardo takes over the last rhymed line of the chorus and delivers the lyric's punch line ("For a small fee in America").

Bernardo (George Chakiris) is joined by the rest of The Sharks, and in this instant *West Side Story* constitutes The Sharks onscreen as an ensemble in ways neither seen nor heard on stage. For the rest of the song, "America" escalates its rapid, gendered call-and-response. The women celebrate the mainland, with the men expressing their emphatic preference for the island. These exchanges elaborate the song's dialogic structure with additional lyric exchanges, nearly doubling the length of the song on screen. Finally, instead of culminating in a single exuberant dance, the screen version of the number punctuates each rhymed quatrain of "in America" with what screenwriter Lehman describes as "an interlude of whistling and dancing," all of which culminates with a shared "Olé."

On stage, the men of The Jets have their own cycle of songs (as explicated earlier), and the women of The Sharks have theirs. These songs are those that give collective voice to the separate spheres brought to collision by Tony and Maria's coupling. While Tony is always removed from the ensemble characterization that The Jets triptych articulates, Anita and Maria are presented as being both part of and apart from the group identity they voice in "America" and "I Feel Pretty." On stage, under librettist Arthur Laurents's exacting attention, this balance was carefully maintained. When Jerome Robbins determined that Chita Rivera was his Anita, the earliest version of "America" (which was conceived as a comic dialogue among the men and women of The Sharks)

West Side Story's "America" on stage and screen (1957/1961). (Publicity shot for the stage production by permission of *Photofest*; publicity still for the film in the collection of the author)

was scrapped. Although Peter Gennaro choreographed the number, Robbins reworked "America" to showcase Rivera. As lyricist Stephen Sondheim recalled, "[M]oment by moment [Gennaro's choreography] worked, but something didn't come together. And then Jerry got his hands on it and reshaped it all and—suddenly, the number worked."[63]

Notably, the inverse happened as the screen version of the song was readied for filming. Almost immediately prior to the scheduled shooting of "America," MGM Studios unceremoniously fired Robbins as the film's codirector. Gennaro stepped in to finalize the staging of the new "America" number, under the supervision of the remaining half of the film's directing team, Robert Wise.[64] The result is an "America" that pits *West Side Story*'s Puerto Rican community against itself in a battle of the sexes, one in which the women affirm assimilation's promise of futurity, even as the men confirm the myriad ways in which poverty and racism reveal the falsity of that assurance.

Although the conflict between The Jets and The Sharks contextualizes Tony and Maria's romance in both versions, the stage musical's "America" (performed only by the Shark women) contributes to the show's theatricalization of the distance between Maria's and Tony's worlds as being defined as much by gender as by culture. Put another way, The Sharks that sing and dance so captivatingly on stage are women (like Maria), just as The Jets who do so are men (like Tony). The stage "America" provides a perhaps thrilling glimpse into the homosocial pleasures of Puerto Rican young women talking among themselves, while the screen's "America" delights in the thrills (and threats) of heterosexual conflict, as it also explains The Sharks' reasons for fighting with "their girls" and The Jets.

The screen version of "America" thereby displaces the stage's separate spheres, both to give a voice to The Sharks and to integrate "America" within the central dramatic conflict that compels *West Side Story*. By reframing the song's central disagreement as a gendered conflict, wherein the women want to stay in America while the men want no part of it, the filmmakers also situate The Sharks within a well-rehearsed tradition of racializing US depictions of Latin American masculinity as backward, savage, and almost pathologically rooted in tradition, especially in contrast to Anglo or Euro-American masculinity. In this ideology-laden tradition, Latina figures conventionally depict willingness in the face of Anglo conquest, while Latino figures emblematize irrational, tradition-bound, nostalgia-impaired obstacles to Anglo modernization.[65] In these ways, even seemingly simple emendations in *West Side Story*'s adaptation from the stage to the screen restage the story's coordinating romance as a racial narrative of erotic contact. On screen Tony and Maria emerge from their first encounter not simply as romantics naively traversing their homosocially and culturally separate spheres of experience (as they did on stage) but as familiar cinematic figures: the Anglo adventurer caught in and by the embrace of a Latin lover. The tragic collision wrought by their love on screen, therefore, becomes a more explicitly racial cautionary tale of the perils of interracial, heterosexual contact.

For it is in "America" that The Sharks—*West Side Story*'s few Puerto Rican male characters—are invested with musical voice. By giving The Sharks a collective, articulate voice, the filmmakers elaborated The Sharks as characters, and in so doing, they created a template for the Latino gang member as a stock character in US popular performance—a character, in this case, named "Chino."

Chino's Last Stand

The theatrical version of *West Side Story* twinned the "problems" of juvenile delinquency and the Puerto Rican situation with an almost simplistic economy. On stage, The Jets theatricalized "juvenile delinquency," while Maria, Anita, and the Shark women performed the "Puerto Rican situation" in exotic, feminized isolation (leaving The Sharks, for better or worse, nearly inarticulate on stage). *West Side Story*'s film adaptation, however, mashed up these theatrically separate "social problem" spheres by giving The Sharks additional lines, scenes, and—most significantly—a song, incorporating the Shark men into "America." Yet there is one Shark who stands apart as Maria's betrothed and Bernardo's lieutenant—Chino—who is perhaps the most transformed character in *West Side Story*'s adaptation to film. Indeed, Chino's cinematic fate underscores how *West Side Story*'s defining "problems" (juvenile delinquency, Puerto Rican migration) were distilled on screen into a "new" stock character: the criminalized Latino youth.

Chino is unique among The Sharks. Introduced in Arthur Laurents's libretto as "a shy, gentle, sweet-faced boy," Chino is not only one of Bernardo's "lieutenants" but also Bernardo's chosen husband for his sister Maria. Chino is also the only Shark other than Bernardo to have scripted spoken lines that clearly individuate him as a distinct character. (Remember that each named member of The Jets, in contrast, gets a scripted line of speech, song, or both.) Chino was originally performed by Puerto

Chino and The Sharks on stage (1957). Jaime Sanchez as Chino is second from the left, and Ken Le Roy as Bernardo is second from the right. (Image by permission of *Photofest*)

Rican–born actor Jaime Sanchez, making him the only original Broadway Shark to be (in Robbins's shorthand) "the real thing." (Hollywood's Chino was Jose de la Vega, an actor-dancer of Filipino and Colombian descent.) But just as Chino is the only one among The Sharks to defend Maria's choice to dance with Tony at the gym, Chino is also the first among The Sharks to discover the true nature of Maria's feelings for her brother's killer. Thus, as defender of both Bernardo's and Maria's honor, Chino also becomes The Shark whose proclaimed pursuit of vengeance against Tony creates the current of tension that compels *West Side Story*'s final arc of dramatic action, both on stage and on film. It is Chino that The Jets try to find "before he finds Tony." It is Chino that Anita implicates after The Jets assault her ("Tell the murderer that Maria's never going to meet him! Tell him Chino found out and—shot her!"). It is Chino who a grief-stricken Tony seeks when he steps from hiding ("Chino, I'm calling for you, Chino! Hurry! . . . There's nobody but me. . . .

Will you, please . . .". And it is Chino's single shot that takes Tony's life in the moments after he and Maria are reunited—however briefly—in an embrace.

Chino's gunshot brings The Jets and The Sharks to the scene for Maria's penultimate speech, in which she first silently demands the surrender of Chino's handgun ("How do you fire this gun, Chino? Just by pulling this little trigger?") before pointing the gun, in turn, on Chino, The Jets, The Sharks, the adults, and finally herself ("How many can I kill, Chino? How many—and still have one bullet left for me?"). Maria then allows Chino to join The Jets and The Sharks and assist in removing Tony's lifeless body from the playground, before leading the impromptu funereal procession that visually reconciles the rival groups. On stage, this procession evacuated nearly the entire company from the stage, leaving only the adults—Doc, Schrank, Krupke, and GladHand (the ineffectual supervisor of "The Dance at the Gym")—who are, according to Laurents's stage direction, "bowed, alone, useless." Screenwriter Ernest Lehman suggested that the ensemble "appear, for the moment, to have found understanding, in tragedy." The actual concluding image of the film tells a different story, however, one apparently scripted by neither Laurents nor Lehman. In director Wise's framing of the film's final moment, the funereal procession moves from the playground, and Maria, along with Doc, follows behind. Individual Jets and Sharks hold back before dispersing in opposite directions. Finally, Chino is led away by Lieutenant Schrank and Officer Krupke, thereby composing the film's concluding dramatic action: a Latino gang member being taken into custody.

Thus, in the film's final dramatic gesture, Chino is once again differentiated from the rest of The Sharks, but this time his difference cues shifts beyond the narrative frame of *West Side Story*. On stage, Chino's transformation—innocent turned murderer—is of a piece with *West Side Story*'s many accidental devastations (Maria learning to hate, the rumble turning deadly, and Anita's assault), which anchors Chino's reintegration into the musical's overall generational portrait of disaffected uncertainty. Wise's film, however, scripts a specific future for Chino. We don't know what's going to happen to any of the other characters. We don't even know where Anita is. But we know one thing for sure: Chino is going to jail.

Wise's addition of a clearly criminal future for Chino in his film adaptation of *West Side Story* garnered no special attention from either his collaborators or the film's many commentators, either at the time of its the film's release or in the half century since. To be sure, Chino's implied incarceration is a tiny detail that comes in only the very last moments of a long and complex film. Even so, the fact that Chino's impending incarceration is rendered so simply signals not only the historical distance between the stage musical's premiere in 1957 and the film's success in 1961 but also *West Side Story*'s perhaps inadvertent influence on depictions of Puerto Rican youth in US popular performance in those intervening years.

As noted earlier, *West Side Story*'s depiction of Puerto Ricans in New York was almost immediately misrecognized as a documentary account. In addition, *West Side Story*'s Puerto Rican character types and narrative templates began to appear in other genres almost immediately after the musical's premiere. In 1959 Irving Shulman's popular potboiler novel of 1949, *Cry Tough*, finally arrived on the screen, with one notable (and, by this time, familiar) change. In the novel, the Jewish protagonist, Mitchell Wolf (a former delinquent who must resist the pressures of his old gang when he is paroled from prison), is reimagined as Puerto Rican Miguel Antonio Enrico Francisco Estrada. Comparably, in 1960, in the last film role she would perform before Anita, Rita Moreno starred in the teen soaper, *Rebel Breed*, in which she plays Lola Montalvo, a Latina of ambiguous heritage whose torrid romance with an Anglo boy tosses her Los Angeles high school into a tumult. But perhaps the most striking elaboration of *West Side Story*'s narrative themes arrived even earlier, in the spring of 1958, with the "Fiesta at Midnight" episode of the television crime drama *Decoy*.

Shot in vérité style with handheld cameras, and using the streets of New York for exteriors, *Decoy* was the first television crime drama to follow a woman police officer, Casey Jones (Beverly Garland), as she worked cases purportedly inspired by those handled by New York City's "Bureau of Policewomen." *Decoy*'s first syndicated episode aired in the fall of 1957, within weeks of *West Side Story*'s opening on Broadway. *Decoy*'s "Fiesta at Midnight" was scripted and shot within weeks of the 1958 Tony Awards, where *West Side Story* was nominated for, but lost, Best Musical honors to *The Music Man*. "Fiesta at Midnight" (scripted by Jerome Coopersmith) tells the story of "Juan Ortega, age 21." "For a young immigrant from Puerto Rico," Garland's voice-over informs us, "music is the closest link to home." We see Juan (played by Cuban American actor Tomas Milian) buying admission to the Guardarraya Social Club, as the voice-over observes, "Before long Juan would see other parts of our city *and* a door that leads to the electric chair." The episode follows Officer Casey Jones as she works to verify that Juan, arrested that night under suspicion of theft, has not been wrongly accused ("someone steals an apple from a fruit cart and they're ready to lynch anybody by the name of José or Pablo . . . or Juan"). Casey's quest for the only witness Juan claims can confirm his actual whereabouts at the time of the robbery (a young woman Juan knows only as Maria) leads the policewoman to the apartment of Maria's cousin, Anita (portrayed by Broadway actress Gloria Marlowe). Anita soon realizes—and Casey soon suspects—that Anita's suave husband Raoul committed the crime for which Juan is presently jailed. Casey's clever detecting, in tandem with Anita's guilt-torn ambivalence, leads Casey to Maria (played by the now legendary Puerto Rican actress Miriam Colón), who confirms Juan's innocence.

Decoy's "Fiesta at Midnight" is noteworthy not simply because its worldly yet conflicted Anita and sheltered and pure Maria characters also happen to be Puerto Ricans living in New York City but also because *Decoy*'s characters chart a comparably gendered gauntlet wherein a shy, gentle Puerto Rican man's actual innocence is no protection from an inevitable encounter with the criminal justice system. Indeed, *Decoy*'s "Fiesta at Midnight" (which aired nationally three years before *West Side Story*'s film premiere and entered rerun syndication after the series' cancellation in the summer of 1958) confirms how readily *West Side Story*'s characters and scenarios were adopted and adapted within narratives of Puerto Rican experience in an array of US popular performance genres.

West Side Story also emerges as a ready narrative template for nonfiction accounts of the threat of criminality posed by (and posed to) Puerto Rican youth in New York, especially after the notorious "Cape Man" killings of the summer of 1959. Shortly before midnight on August 29, 1959 (barely two months after *West Side Story* had closed on Broadway to begin a ten-city national tour), a small group of Puerto Rican teenagers ventured to a concrete lot in Manhattan's Hell's Kitchen, and in the words of historian Eric C. Schneider, "in a matter of minutes, two boys were dead and one was seriously injured, all because of mistaken identity, ethnic tension and rumors of a rumble."[66] The New York tabloid press seized on the story—especially the alleged killer, Salvador Agron, or the "Cape Man"—for a flurry of stories about Puerto Rican gangs in New York City that proliferated in the following months. Although explicit references to *West Side Story* are few, most accounts are haunted by the symbols and tropes of Puerto Rican disaffection widely rehearsed both on stage in *West Side Story* and in accounts of the musical's theatrical success.

In the weeks immediately after the incident, the tabloid *New York Her-*

THE
REAL
WEST
SIDE
STORY

There's nothing romantic
about our slums—only the
reality of an uneven fight

José Rivera's laugh, like his sudden urge to run or wrestle, reflects an explosive and, as yet, uncommitted spirit.

José Rivera and "The Real West Side Story" in *LOOK*, February 1960. (Detail of magazine layout, courtesy of *LOOK* Magazine Photograph Collection, Prints and Photographs Division, Library of Congress)

ald Tribune assiduously profiled Agron and the other suspects. The tabloid took particular care to capture and publish candid photos, apparently snapped during or after their arraignment, of each of the Puerto Rican teens implicated in the incident, "where death struck in the playground," captioning each photograph with the boy's name and age (e.g., "Ruben Aguirre, sixteen, gestures toward cameraman").[67] In a *New York Times Magazine* story published a month later, writer Dan Wakefield offered a more abstract portrait of "The Other Puerto Ricans," providing a historical and sociological explanation for youth criminality as a special challenge within "the fight that most [Puerto Ricans] must make a against slum living and intolerance." In both the *New York Times* and the *New York Herald Tribune*, Puerto Rican youth criminality confirms, in Wakefield's words, "the gulf between parents and children [exposed] almost every time a Puerto Rican boy gets into trouble in New York."[68]

LOOK magazine's "The Real West Side Story" feature, published in February 1960, offers an even more detailed portrait of the perils of Puerto Rican boyhood. In a by turns sensational and sensitive photoessay ("a story of brutal reality and incipient tragedy"), *LOOK* followed fourteen-year-old José Rivera through a typical day on Manhattan's West Side to document how "the struggle between two sets of values—the social vs. the antisocial—for the future of José Rivera is the real story of the West Side."[69] These "real West Side Story" accounts ratify Broadway's more stylized imaginings in a peculiar oscillation, the lurid details of the one amplifying the emotional context of the other (and vice versa). Yet, throughout, the portrait of Puerto Rican youth criminality remains emphatically masculine. Readers might only see Maria or Anita on the stage, but these journalistic accounts remind them not only that a boy like Bernardo might have died on the street last night but also that a boy like Chino (or José or Salvador) might be seeking vengeance right now.

More than lovers on a balcony or dancers on a rooftop, the hand-cuffed Puerto Rican boy Chino emblematizes the racialized conclusions about Latino-ness that *West Side Story* both rehearsed and brought to life in popular performance. Robert Wise's composition of the movie's final scene indelibly inscribes Chino as a distillation of the social problems that the musical theatrically twinned in gendered separate spheres. Chino's cinematic recharacterization, in tandem with other narratives charting the entry of Puerto Rican boys into criminal lives, emerges as perhaps the inaugural appearance of one of the most enduring stock characters in subsequent depictions of Latino masculinity in US popular performance: the Latino gang member. The film *West Side Story* thereby invests Chino's singular form with both "juvenile delinquency" and "the Puerto Rican problem," while also installing the "Latin gang member" as a racialized stock character in American popular performance. It is to this question of stereotype that my next chapter turns.

CHAPTER 4

Executing the Stereotype

Rita Moreno began her sustained critique of ethnic typecasting during the press junket for *West Side Story*. For about two years, beginning after she finished *West Side Story* in 1960 and continuing through the film's initial critical and box office success in 1962, Moreno posed her own critique of the "spitfire" roles so frequently offered her. "Why oh why do Latin girls on the screen always have to be tempestuous sexpots?" Moreno wondered in a 1960 *Newsday* profile ("Latin Beauty Wonders Why Her Type Is Always Type Cast"), in which she also observed that *West Side Story*'s Anita marked "the first time I've played a real woman."[1] In a column published the following summer (for which Moreno herself held the byline), she explained, "Until [*West Side Story*] I [had] never seen a reasonable attempt to present Puerto Ricans—or Latins, in general— with any accuracy in a motion picture."[2]

A few months later, Moreno elaborated her critique for television columnist Dick Kleiner: "For eleven years, I've always been the Mexican spitfire or the Indian girl. . . . I know I'm not Mary College. But I'd like to have some parts which say something." Kleiner's column drew connections between Moreno's Puerto Rican birth and childhood migration to New York to explain how her *West Side Story* role was different: "Of course, she's still a Latin-blooded spitfire—Puerto Rican this time— but she doesn't mind." Newspapers across the country ran Kleiner's syndicated column in October 1961, as *West Side Story* began its first New York screenings. Most of these papers added headlines that highlighted either the feelings behind Moreno's critique ("Moreno Says She's Tired of 'Spitfire' Roles" from a paper in southern Texas) or its force ("Rita Moreno Blasts TV Typecasting" from one in central California), with only a few ratifying her typecasting claims ("Pretty Mexican Spitfire Gets Opportunity to Act" from northern Utah).[3] With few exceptions, Moreno's prerelease press for *West Side Story* highlighted the tensions caused by typecasting. One United Press International (UPI) reporter confessed, "[T]his reporter expected . . . a 'sexpot' [but] was surprised and pleased [that] Rita Moreno is what . . . some people would call a 100 percent American girl."[4]

Despite Moreno's preventive advance work, most reviews of *West Side Story* celebrated her performance as Anita in "spitfire" terms. The *Chicago Daily Tribune*'s Mae Tinee singled out her "fiery performance as the sexy spunky Anita," while Marjory Adams of the *Boston Globe* declared, "Rita Moreno practically sears the screen with her blazing dances." Bosley Crowther of the *New York Times* wagged simply, "Rita Moreno is a spitfire."[5] Being so praised only sharpened Moreno's critique. In a *Los Angeles Times* profile, Moreno offered "sharp comment" on her growing resentment of "such terms as spitfire and sexpot." Asked whether *West Side Story* heralded new career opportunities, Moreno averred, "[T]hey still call me spitfire. That's the trouble. . . . Besides, what is a spitfire?"[6] A decade or so later, Moreno crafted a role that would provide a forceful answer to her own question: Googie Gomez.

As Googie Gomez, the character she cocreated with playwright Terrence McNally for his 1975 play *The Ritz*, Moreno enacted a camp satire of the fiery sexpot character she had so often played. By her own account (one oft-recalled in both scholarly and popular surveys of her career), Moreno developed the persona of "the worst Hispanic cabaret singer of all time" as a joke to amuse herself and her colleagues "in a hundred 'idle' houses in dressing rooms and at laid back parties with showbiz friends."[7] A singer-dancer who can neither sing nor dance—and whose conspicuously thick accent renders her comedically prone to mispronunciation—Googie Gomez is a character foiled by her own aspirations (and wardrobe malfunctions) because she is, in Moreno's words, "someone who's bigger than life and who adores herself."[8] After encountering what Moreno called her "crazy shtick" at a mutual friend's birthday party, playwright McNally adapted Moreno's party trick into a scripted character that Moreno herself went on to play in McNally's Broadway production, for which the actress was recognized with a Drama Desk nomination and Tony Award for Best Featured Actress in a Play.

Rita Moreno as Googie Gomez in *The Ritz* (1976). (Publicity still, collection of the author)

At the time, Moreno celebrated her success with Googie as a "thumb-ing my nose" rebuke of "all those Hollywood writers responsible for lines like 'You Yankee peeg, you rape my seester, I keel you!'"[9] In the years since, scholars and critics have appreciated Moreno's Googie Gomez as a satiric disruption of stereotype's conventions. For Frances Negrón-Mutaner, "Moreno radically refashions the shame of her Hollywood career" through Googie Gomez, and Mary Beltrán notes Moreno's coau-thorship of Googie as marking a moment when "Moreno finally had a voice" with which to comment "on [her] former spitfire roles with humor and a wink."[10] While Rachel Lee Rubin and Jeffrey Paul Melnick see Googie as Moreno's chance to "gain revenge" on her professional past, Priscilla Peña Ovalle views the "grotesque" Googie more ambivalently, though still noting Moreno's use of "biting humor to maintain control of her persona [as] Latina mythology was shifting in the 1970s."[11]

For contemporary critics, Moreno's Googie commented not only on hypersexual spitfires of entertainments past but also on one of the most visible entertainers of the mid-1970s. As the *New York Times* contributor Shaun Considine observed (in the same feature article that first intro-duced Moreno's Googie genesis tale), "Googie is a wild burlesque of every Latin cliché and performer, from Lupe Vélez to Charo."[12] Reviewers of the film version of *The Ritz* (released in the late summer of 1976) also made the connection between Moreno's Googie and Charo, with one critic for a national wire service characterizing Googie as "an aspiring, second-string Charo" and another (writing for a paper in upstate New York) calling her "a road show Charo."[13] By the mid-1970s, Charo's broadly comedic persona, revealing outfits, and *cuchi-cuchi* catchphrase had established the Spanish-born, classically trained guitarist as one of the most reliable and recognizable "guest star" presences on television throughout the 1970s.[14] (One columnist quipped that commercial television's many variety and talk shows existed, in part, "to kee[p] Charo off unemployment.")[15] Mentored by her much older husband (1940s bandleader Xavier Cugat), Charo's persona deftly evoked those fast-talking, malaprop-prone Latin icons of previous generations (like Vélez, Carmen Miranda, and Desi Arnaz), while also updating their familiar shtick with emphatically contemporary costumes (hip-hugging bellbottoms, revealing halter tops, giant wigs with elaborate falls) and naively suggestive malapropisms ("Please don't misconscrew me when I am saying . . ."). So it is perhaps not surprising that contemporary observers noted the connections between Charo's persona and Moreno's Googie Gomez character.

In the mid-1970s, both Moreno and Charo expertly worked the same thickly accented line of business—the sexually provocative Latina naif—to great success. Moreno garnered awards and acclaim for her stage performance, and, two weeks after the film of *The Ritz* hit theatres in August 1976, Charo made her acting debut in the television movie *Charo and the Sergeant*, which the veteran performer followed with recurring principal roles on television series (such as *Chico and the Man* and *The Love Boat*) and small parts in major motion pictures (such as *The Concorde . . . Airport '79*). Considered together, Googie's and Charo's simultaneous successes might be rightly understood as simple historical coincidence—or as an example of camp pleasures bridging the presumed gap between high and low cultural forms. Still, where Moreno's crafting of Googie has been widely understood (then and now) as clever critique, Charo's sustained enactment of her persona has most typically been regarded as a craven (or camp) exploitation of a most extreme cliché.[16] Both characters are comedic personas crafted by veteran, multitalented performers that, once repurposed within familiar entertainment genres, amused audiences with a comparably garbled mix of skin, sequins, and Spanglish. Both are exemplary of the limited and limiting roles available to Latinas in commercial entertainments in the 1970s. Both are very funny—and just a little bit frightening.

So what's so different about Googie and Charo? The unsubtle answer is, of course, that Moreno's Googie enacts a critique of the very cliché that Charo embodies. It is a distinction carefully drawn by Moreno herself, by Googie's contemporary observers, and by subsequent generations of commentators. For her part, Charo (whose half century in the public eye has garnered scant scholarly attention) typically dodges questions about her persona, opting instead to remind interlocutors of both her recognition as a classical musician and the peculiarity of her US celebrity. "Around the world I am known as a great musician," Charo is wont to say, "but in America I am known as the *cuchi-cuchi* girl. That's okay because *cuchi-cuchi* has taken me all the way to the bank."[17] On one level, then, it seems clear: Moreno's Googie character and Charo's onstage persona demonstrate how two very different performers can skillfully work the same line of business toward clearly different ends.

This chapter examines how the satiric surrogation of familiar "types" has emerged as a signal strategy for Latinas/os authoring critically engaged performance (whether as writers, actors, or some combination of both). My account examines how activist Latina/o playwrights and performers, especially since the 1960s, have refined particular strategies for playing with and against received stereotypes and how this constellation of strategies emerged as a signal convention for Latina/o artists authoring performance. As I revisit the particular significance of counterstereotyping as a strategy within the early Chicano movement (especially as a mechanism for protesting culturally embedded ignorance, insensitivity, and bigotry), I offer a loose genealogy of how the discourse of stereotype emerged within US scholarly, popular, and activist literatures, evincing the critical limits of that discourse's main thematics. Next I chart the parallel tradition of theorizing the stereotype through performance that is discernible in the on-stage work crafted by Latina/o writers and performers in the 1960s, 1970s, and 1980s. As a demonstration, I first assess the early work of Luis Valdez (from the *actos* to *Zoot Suit*) as one exemplar of the tactic I term "executing the stereotype," wherein received stereotypes are enacted, eviscerated, and entombed as part of a dramaturgic ritual of representational renewal. I then provide a selective overview of how subsequent Latina/o writers and performers also "executed the stereotype" as expansive archetypes or talismanic effigies. I conclude by offering my own theoretical intervention into the discourse of stereotype by returning to the historical moment of Googie Gomez and Charo, and by offering an extended reading of Dolores Prida's 1977 musical play *Beautiful Señoritas*.

Why Stereotype

In late 1968, Chicanos organized against media stereotypes in a big way, particularly targeting the "Frito Bandito." First introduced on children's television as a character that, with a mix of humor and menace, threatened to steal the consumer's prized snack chip, the ad concept proved to be a quick success for the Frito-Lay company. The character of the Frito Bandito was soon a regular feature in print and television advertising for the product. Over the next few years, Chicana/o and Mexican American advocacy groups led an organized protest of the character, demanding federal intervention to remove such racially pejorative stereotypes from the nation's airwaves. In 1971, Frito-Lay succumbed to pressure from consumers, columnists, and Congress, dropping the Frito Bandito from future advertisements. As media historian Chon Noriega notes, the successful campaign against the Frito Bandito campaign confirmed the importance of stereotypes as "a major site of struggle for the Chicano [movement], as media representation *of* the community and media use and control *by* the community began to be seen as directly related to social causes." As scholars like Noriega, Charles Ramírez Berg, Mary Beltrán, and others have documented, stereotypes have, since the beginning of the film industry, served as the primary vehicle through which Latinos have been introduced to US audiences. Noriega writes, "[T]he fact of [Latino] racial diversity rarely enters the picture, except through stereotypes. For Latinos, the fact of stereotypes is matched by the general paucity of either good or bad Latino roles."[18]

Additionally, resistance against the "fact of stereotypes" informs the centrality of what Ramírez Berg has called "the counter-stereotyping rationale" that has long guided Chicano film practice and theory. By 1968 this rationale had emerged as a core tactic within the early Chicano *teatro* movement, perhaps most evidently in the *actos* developed by Luis Valdez and El Teatro Campesino. Though not reaching as broad an audience as the Frito Bandito protests, the work of Latina/o performance-makers like Valdez had also identified the fact of stereotype as a special site for activist creativity, modeling what would become, by the time of Googie Gomez's Broadway debut in 1975, a core strategy of critical, creative, and political intervention by Latina/o performance-makers.

These satiric surrogations stood in contrast to the targeted media activism of the campaign against the Frito Bandito and also to more "accommodationist" groups like Nosotros (the industry group founded by Ricardo Montalban in 1969 to advocate for better and broader employment opportunities for Latinas/os working in the entertainment industry). While the Frito Bandito protest announced new strategies for Chicana/o media activism—strategies that connected the Chicana/o grassroots to broader systems of economic and political power controlled by Hollywood, Madison Avenue, and Washington—Nosotros adapted long-standing models of advocacy (rehearsed in earlier eras by such groups as the NAACP and ad hoc committees within the Screen Actors Guild and Actors Equity) specifically to address the limited opportunities open to Latina/o actors. Put another way, the Frito Bandito campaign attacked the crafters of stereotypes from outside the system of production, while Nosotros sought change from within. Yet, as this chapter demonstrates, at the same time Latina/o performers were developing a third strategy: executing the stereotype through a complex, conscious process of strategic (and often satiric) surrogation.

Because all three of these distinct and disparate strategies engage "the fact of stereotype," some attention to the historical genealogy of the notion of stereotype—or the discourse of stereotype—seems warranted.

The Discourse of Stereotype

In its commonplace usage in the United States, "stereotype" describes the act of making judgments and assigning negative qualities to individuals or groups.[19] Although the word had been used in the United States and Europe since at least the early 1800s, American political essayist and newspaper columnist Walter Lippman's 1922 book *Public Opinion* "introduced the term *stereotype* into the social, cultural, and psychological vocabulary of contemporary life."[20] As cultural historians Elizabeth and Stewart Ewen note, "[T]he term had been used before, but never in quite the same way."[21] In *Public Opinion*, Lippman sought to understand mass media's role in escalating the nationalist fervors in that led to World War I, and he studied the ways in which mass media encouraged individuals to develop passionate feelings about nations, regions, and peoples far removed from their daily lives. Lippman was especially intrigued by the formation of what he called the "pictures in our heads," or "the way in which the world is imagined" as "not necessarily the world we should like it to be [but] simply the kind of world we expect it to be."[22]

Employed as a newspaperman, Lippman retrieved a nearly archaic printer's term to give this cognitive interplay a name: *stereotype*. (Since the early 1700s, traditional printing presses had used a specially cast metal printing plate—a stereotype—in order to replicate a particular graphic element or sequence of type.) In *Public Opinion*, Lippman thus redeployed *stereotype* as a metaphor to describe how mass media—especially the emerging and seemingly transparent authority of photography— recalibrated the imaginative space between "the world outside and the pictures in our heads."[23] For Lippman a mass-mediated stereotype ratified one's preconceptions, confirming what one already thought one knew: "If what we are looking at corresponds successfully with what we anticipated, the stereotype is reinforced for the future."[24] For Lippman, the stereotype's appeal lay in the "charm" born of its self-ratifying familiarity,[25] which neither required nor abided complexity when delivering satisfying stories. Lippman's analysis thus explained both the stereotype, as "easily consumable, industrially generated substitute for intimate knowledge,"[26] and its apparent necessity within the rapidly changing social landscape of the early twentieth century.

In the years following World War II, the social psychologist Gordon W. Allport incrementally elaborated Lippman's notion of stereotype in his influential theorization of intergroup prejudice. Beginning with his 1948 pamphlet *ABC's of Scapegoating*, Allport saw stereotypes reducing people, groups, and events to "a few clear cut traits,"[27] thereby confirming feelings of difference between social groups (especially those without direct experiential knowledge of one another). This understanding of stereotype proved foundational for Allport's "contact theory" of intergroup prejudice, which holds that intergroup attitudes are directly determined by the degree of interaction among groups of people societally distinguished as different from one another. For Allport *stereotype* described the "exaggerated belief associated with a category, and its function is to justify conduct in relation to that category."[28] Building on Lippman's idea that stereotypes resolved the gap between "the world outside and the pictures in our heads," Allport suggested that stereotypes also helped create that cognitive gap, especially with regard to racial and ethnic distinctions.

Allport shared Lippman's concern about the replicative force of mass media, writing as early as 1948 that the "effect of any single motion picture, play, or pageant is likely to be quite small. However, when the same type of emphasis is found repeatedly, the screen can become a powerful tool in the formation of stereotypes."[29] Throughout the 1950s, Allport's contact theory and its depiction of the corrosive impact of mediatized stereotypes on intergroup relations infused political, legal, and scholarly discussions about the influence of popular culture and performance on modern society.[30] Such influences ranged from the House Un-American Activities Committee's (HUAC's) concerns about Hollywood communists to the Supreme Court's evidentiary interest in the role of popular culture in determining the self-esteem of young black children in *Brown v. Board of Education*).[31]

By the 1960s and 1970s, the social scientific discourse of stereotype would prove foundational to emerging academic disciplines (such as communications and media and cinema studies), with each field developing a variety of methods with which to assess the impact of mediatized stereotypes. Some methods cultivated a critical literacy regarding stereotype conventions, which promised to equip the active spectator to recognize stereotypes as "cues" to the ideological operation of power within media, while other methods evinced the operation of stereotype as part of the grammar of cinema in order to demonstrate stereotype's long history of depicting minoritized groups.[32] These approaches elicited an array of comprehensive taxonomies cataloging the stereotyped depictions of specific groups. Foundational works like Donald Bogle's *Toms, Coons, Mulattoes, Mammies, and Bucks: An Interpretive History of Blacks in American Film* (1973), Raymond William Stedman's *Shadows of the Indian: Stereotypes in American Culture* (1982), Molly Haskell's *From Reverence to Rape: The Treatment of Women in the Movies* (1974), and Vito Russo's *The Celluloid Closet: Homosexuality in the Movies* (1981) indexed the recurrence of stereotypes as documentation of bias against racial and sexual minorities in US entertainments.[33] Alongside works by such authors as Robert G. Lee, Clara Rodriguez, Charles Ramírez Berg, and Jack G. Shaheen, among others, comprehensive stereotype taxonomy emerged as the dominant scholarly genre for critical discussions of the ideological construction of social identities in US popular performance.[34] Whether in the format of an essay, monograph, or documentary film, these indexical assemblages both displayed and disavowed what Lee describes as the power of the (especially racial) stereotype "to survive, mutate, and reproduce."[35] Often, as Chon Noriega and others have demonstrated, these stereotype taxonomies enacted a form of critical and creative "consciousness raising" that encouraged both spectators and cultural workers to intervene in the media's depiction of minoritized groups.[36]

In 1972 the Chinese American author, activist, and playwright Frank Chin (with Jeffery Paul Chan) wrote, "The ideal racial stereotype is a low maintenance engine of white supremacy whose efficiency increases with age, as it [becomes] 'authenticated' and 'verified.'"[37] This engine evokes both the functionalism of Lippman and Allport and the simultaneously scholarly and popular indexical tradition of stereotype taxonomies that has evolved over the last half century. At the same time, the analytic framed by Chin and Chan also cues the more theoretical routes charted within the discourse of stereotype in the 1970s and 1980s, produced by such writers as Richard Dyer, Stuart Hall, and Homi Bhabha. Taken together, these thinkers open questions about whether stereotypes tell a story (Dyer), enforce power relations (Hall), or tell the story of power (Bhabha).

A founding figure of what has come to be called British cultural studies, Richard Dyer, premised his 1972 analysis of stereotype squarely within the basic definitions and precepts offered by Walter Lippman fifty years prior. Influenced significantly by Ernst H. Gombrich's prescient theorizations of visual culture,[38] Dyer emphasized stereotype's "aesthetic function as a mode of characterization in fiction."[39] For Dyer stereotypes are an "aesthetic as well as social construct," which not only impose (typically disparaging) social meanings but also instigate specific narrative modes of characterization. Dyer argued that, as "a particular sub-category of a broader category of fictional characters, the type," the social type is distinct from the stereotype because "stereotypes always carry within their very representation an implicit narrative" and they repeat "an identical plot function."[40]

Dyer's theorization of stereotype (as a binding agent between a narrative's aesthetic and political meanings) was developed perhaps most fully through the work of one of his most influential interpreters, Stuart Hall, and Hall's pathbreaking theorization of "encoded" meanings.[41] Hall's work emphasized stereotype's actions—its operation as a "representational practice"—rather than its social forms or aesthetic functions. For Hall stereotypes "get a hold of the few simple, vivid, memorable, easily grasped and widely recognized characteristics about a person, reduce everything about that person to those traits, exaggerate and simplify them, and fix them without change or development to eternity."[42] In Hall's elegantly algebraic formulation, the stereotype symbolically reduc-

es difference and excludes complexity to reinforce existing power ineq-
uities. Hall aimed not to analyze the stereotype but to develop "different
strategies aligned to intervene in the field of representation, to contest
'negative' images and transform representational practices around 'race'
in a more 'positive' direction."[43]

A decade or so after Dyer and Hall, Homi Bhabha distilled a theorization of stereotype that—in refuting Lippman's and Allport's core
conceits—also clarified Chin and Chan's evocative formulation. For Bhabha stereotype is "not the setting up of a false image which becomes the
scapegoat of discriminatory practice" but "an ambivalent mode of knowledge and power" that serves as "the major discursive strategy" of colonialism.[44] So by approaching stereotype as a discursive hallmark of modernity,
Bhabha affirmed its ambivalence (or what Sander L. Gilman identified as
its "protean" aspects),[45] and so rebuked the corrective presumption that
stereotypes are necessarily and inevitably wrong. For Bhabha the stereotype is always already an "impossible object," a sign for "knowledge that
is arrested and fetishistic and circulates through colonial discourse as [a]
limited form of otherness," and a ubiquitous discursive means of preserv-
ing and protecting existing structures of cultural power.[46]

Yet throughout the work of all the contributors to the discourse
of stereotype—Lippman, Allport, Chin and Chan, Dyer, Hall, and
Bhabha, among others—a curious continuity emerges. The stereotype
itself remains an indefatigable obstacle, an unyielding antagonist in a
sustained battle over the discursive features of representational truth.
Indeed, whether the intention is to explicate racialist constructions in
cultural representation or to propose a postcolonial psychoanalytic perspective or to instigate political interventions into apparatuses of cultural production, critics, scholars, and artists inevitably encounter this
curious critical impasse within the discourse of stereotype. Put simply,
stereotypes seem to be impervious to all efforts to extinguish them—
always winning, somehow surviving, ever ready to manifest another day.

Indeed, specific historical stereotypes—like the "mammy" or the
"Madame Butterfly" or the "Latin lover" or the "sheik"—have withstood
all kinds of astute artistic creations, confounding the best deconstruc-
tionist efforts and the most skilled political interventions. Even as Richard Dyer's famed 1979 assertion ("stereotype today is almost always a
term of abuse") remains as true as ever, it is just as true that stereotypes
seem never to have gone out of style.[47] In the words of Charles Ramírez
Berg, stereotypes "do not so much evolve as simply alter their guise at
the denotative surface, while keeping all the stereotype's connotations

intact."[48] Even more, the racialized types so often isolated as stereotypes have accrued their own complex genealogies, wherein the contours of the character type morph and adapt to the culture's shifting tastes and needs. And perhaps most confounding of all, as scholars and artists continue expertly to parse the stereotype's mechanics, catalog its myriad appearances, and explicate its ideological implications, the discourse of stereotype continues to, perhaps inadvertently, reinscribe the stereotype itself as a fetishized object, somehow outside the particularities of historical time and the practicalities of cultural production. As Mireille Rosello has provocatively noted, stereotypes are "very easy to identify, quote and denounce, and yet they are impossible to eliminate. More disturbingly, those who loudly oppose stereotypes may be their best allies."[49] So, in startlingly viral ways—especially within the scholarly discourse of stereotype—stereotypes have remained insidious scene stealers, pulling focus in nearly every critical discussion of race and ethnicity in US popular performance.

Executing the Stereotype

For the last fifty years, US Latina/o dramatists and performers have executed the stereotype. They have enacted the stereotype so that they might eviscerate the stereotype, even as they ready themselves to—ultimately, inevitably—entomb the stereotype as an effigy of cultural memory. In Joseph Roach's configuration, the effigy is "a means to evoke an absence, to body something forth, especially something from the distant past."[50] This section demonstrates how Chicana/o and Latina/o performance-makers have deployed stereotypes as effigies, both to herald the absence of authentic Chicana/o and Latina/o depictions within US popular performance and to hold open what Roach calls "a place in cultural memory into which many people may step depending on circumstances and occasions."[51] Within Latina/o drama and performance, each act of the stereotype's execution—enacting, eviscerating, entombing—is a political and politicizing gesture that signals the most distinctive and important contributions of Latina/o performances in the last half century. As Latina/o dramatists and performers execute the stereotypes inherited from disparaging mass mediations of Latina/o experience, and especially as they repurpose these stereotypes as effigies, these writers and performers have staged a searching conversation about form, culture, and performance spanning five decades of Latina/o experience. Yet this performative vocabulary of political intervention (which Latina/o dramatists and performers have rehearsed with particular verve, creativity, and stamina since the 1960s) has not yet been fully appreciated as a foundational theoretical contribution within either the critical theorization of stereotype or the disparate tradition of Latino/o cultural studies.

By way of explanation, I will begin, as so many do, with Luis Valdez and his now canonical *acto*, *Los Vendidos* (1967). I begin with Valdez and El Teatro Campesino not to imply that they are the font from which all Latina/o drama flows but instead to underscore how effectively Valdez and El Teatro Campesino animated the strategy I am calling "executing the stereotype" among the diverse writers, artists, and performers working the cultural front of the Chicano movement. Read in this context, *Los Vendidos* emerges as an emblem of what I call "executing the stereotype"—enacting the stereotype in order to eviscerate and entomb it—which rehearses a core theatrical vocabulary to guide artists in their confrontation with received stereotypes.

Founded in California in 1965, El Teatro Campesino was, in the words of Jorge Huerta, "spawned from the very birth pangs of the California farmworkers' unionizing efforts" to become a theatre dedicated "to expos[ing] the injustices in the fields and to urg[ing] other farmworkers to join the Union." With a distinctive style that merged European theatrical techniques from commedia dell'arte and Brecht with *mexicano* cultural styles from *carpa* to Cantinflas, El Teatro Campesino's work in the fields soon expanded to college campuses and community centers around the country. Under the leadership of Luis Valdez, the troupe began to explore other themes relevant to the broader Mexican American and immigrant communities, including "the assimilationist, the educational system, the Chicano Movement and the War in Vietnam."[52] The 1971 publication of the company's first anthology of *actos* (brief agitprop-style plays) introduced El Teatro Campesino's techniques to Chicana/o student and community groups throughout the US Southwest and beyond, directly and indirectly instigating community-based *teatro* work around the country.

Los Vendidos (1967)—which literally translates to "The Sell-Outs" or "The Sold Ones"—was among the most popular of those early *actos*. Valdez sets the action at "Honest Sancho's Used Mexican Lot." An assimilated government worker arrives from "Governor Reagan's office" to acquire what she calls "a Mexican type for the administration." The proprietor, Honest Sancho, greets his customer, Miss Jimenez, with enthusiasm ("Well, you come to the right place, lady") and surveys his inventory ("This is Honest Sancho's Used Mexican Lot, and we got all types here").[53] Each of Honest Sancho's available Mexican "types"—a farmworker, a *pachuco,* and a revolutionary—proves to be inadequate to the government's needs, until Sancho introduces Eric Garcia ("The Mexican American Model"). Miss Jimenez is thrilled by the "clean shaven, middle class type in a business suit, with glasses," but before long a "malfunction" causes Eric Garcia to spout revolutionary sentiments in Spanish, which activates the other models into a collective rebellion that sends Miss Jimenez screaming from the stage.[54] In the play's final moments, Honest Sancho is himself revealed to be a robot, a tool used by the assembled "types" in their shared *movimiento* for social transformation. By utilizing such recognizable cultural types, as theatre scholar Harry Elam Jr. notes, the play "parod[ies] popular culture icons and subvert[s] stereotypes," and it acts as a "cultural correctiv[e] as the parodied subject is held up to ridicule, revised and critiqued."[55] Honest Sancho and Miss Jimenez—the self-aggrandizing inauthentic "sell-outs" of the play's title—ultimately emerge as the play's true bad guys, who are easily, triumphantly, and deliciously vanquished as the campesino, the *pachuco,* and the revolutionary unite in a common struggle to herald the heroic arrival of the "authentic" Chicano.

Los Vendidos is thus an exemplar of "executing the stereotype," wherein the effective enactment of a particular stereotype (or constellation of stereotypes) eviscerates the apparatus of the stereotype's construction, thereby revealing how the charismatic familiarity of the stereotype works in service of a particular cultural mind-set. As if to sharpen my point, "Honest Sancho's Used Mexican Lot" presents these readily recognizable types as robots, or machines capable of carrying out sequential tasks in a humanoid way. With each automaton's animation, the enactors reveal (to paraphrase Frank Chin) the gears of anti-Chicano sentiment at work. Eric Garcia's ultimate "malfunction" mobilizes what is, in effect, a work stoppage, as the various "Used Mexicans" refuse to work in the manner for which they have been designed. In the play's conclusion, the "good" representation of *chicanismo* dethrones the "bad." Broad stereotypes received from US popular culture (the farmworker, the *pachuco,* the revolutionary, the Mexican American) are no longer operational and can now be discarded as vestiges of a previous representational regime. The new, authentic theatrical manifestation of Chicano collective self-determination might, thanks to the intervention of *Los Vendidos,* now have its reign on the stage. And the play—as a ritual of representational renewal—is complete.

In *Los Vendidos*, Valdez and his enactors both catalog and critique a particular repertoire of Chicano stereotypes in a primal scene of theatrical transformation in which the dramatic apparatus reframes social possibility. The *acto*'s execution of the stereotype is simultaneously a pedagogic and purgative act, with the enactor's able manipulation of the stereotype in performance rehearsing the auditor to recognize, index, and extract the stereotype's component parts, presumably to prevent that stereotype's uninterrogated operation in the future. *Los Vendidos* resolves the drama in the promise of transformation. A decade or so later, however, Valdez will script the alchemy of a charismatic stereotype's renewal in *Zoot Suit* in a more explicit and legible way.

Luis Valdez's 1978 musical drama *Zoot Suit* retold the story of the Sleepy Lagoon murder trial and the so-called Zoot Suit riots. *Zoot Suit* repurposed Brechtian and neocinematic staging techniques to theatricalize the hidden history of discrimination, violence, and injustice experienced by Mexican Americans in Los Angeles during the 1940s, as distilled within the actions of two parallel protagonists.[56] At the play's center, Henry Reyna stands as the Chicano everyman. *Zoot Suit*'s forthright narrative action follows Reyna as he maneuvers the societal stations defining the Chicano experience (family, community, culture, society, police, media). Ghosting Henry's every move and decision is El Pachuco, a figure who steps beyond the play's narrative frame to function as both Henry's and the audience's interlocutor. Although Reyna's story guides *Zoot Suit*'s narrative action, it is El Pachuco who directs the audience's attention and experience to, between, and within the play's many scenes and settings.

With El Pachuco, Valdez appointed as *Zoot Suit*'s emcee one of the most ambivalent icons of Mexican and Mexican American experience within the United States. As Catherine Ramírez and others have expertly demonstrated, throughout the mid-twentieth century, the *pachuco* was as reviled as he was revered. In 1978, as Valdez workshopped his new musical play, few Chicano "types" could efficiently evoke so many contradictory implications—both within and beyond the Mexican American community—as the *pachuco*. Deftly exploiting this context, Valdez (in collaboration with the role's original interpreter, Edward James Olmos) crafted El Pachuco as a mercurial manifestation of the charged multivalence surrounding "the *pachuco*" stereotype. On stage, El Pachuco revels in eviscerating the comforting if contradictory simplicities of "the *pachuco*" stereotype. Throughout *Zoot Suit*, Valdez confirms as undeniable the complexity of "the *pachuco*," even as he affirms El Pachuco's charismatic singularity. Indeed, with El Pachuco, Valdez and *Zoot Suit* can play type both ways—good and bad, positive and negative, angel and devil, rightful and criminal, perverse and moral.

Throughout *Zoot Suit*, El Pachuco is neither a hero nor an antihero. (Such is Henry Reyna's less compelling task.) Instead, and in ways that anticipate theorizations of stereotype by Gilman, Ramírez Berg, and Bhabha, El Pachuco emerges as neither good nor bad but always already both. Indeed, Valdez offers El Pachuco as the perfect enactment of stereotype's charismatic ambivalence. While Henry wrestles with his own all-too-human contradictions, El Pachuco is glib, mercurial, and much more entertaining. This polarity is what invests Valdez's entombment of El Pachuco with its alchemical force.

At the play's climactic moment, when the Chicano Zoot Suiters are scapegoated for all that is wrong in Los Angeles, a group of sailors and marines (goaded by a character known simply as "The Press") assaults El Pachuco, and with a switchblade they strip him bare. El Pachuco rises, his exposed flesh rendering him newly visible as an essential spirit of Chicanidad ("He turns and looks at Henry, with mystic intensity. . . . An Aztec conch blows, and he slowly exits backward with powerful calm into his shadows"). Visibly denuded of "his elegant drapes,"[57] the actor loosens his singular hold on the character El Pachuco, and as the play moves inexorably toward its own ambivalent resolution, the spirit or essence of El Pachuco is dispersed, perhaps residing within Henry Reyna, but perhaps not. Indeed, as Henry's narrative is resolved ("He died of the trauma of his life in 1972"), El Pachuco reroutes the narrative ("That's the way you see it, *ese.* But there's another way to end this story.") as the ensemble envoices a multivalent invocation of Henry as a Chicano everyman ("Henry Reyna, the born leader . . . the social victim . . . *el carnal de aquellas*"), a conjuring that reaches beyond the limits of biographical time to affirm that "Henry Reyna . . . El Pachuco . . . The man . . . the myth . . . still lives."

In *Zoot Suit*'s final moments, Valdez recasts both the *pachuco* and El Pachuco as effigies, in the sense that Joseph Roach defines the term, as "a means to evoke an absence, to body something forth, especially something from the distant past."[58] Valdez's El Pachuco—and his use of stereotype more generally—heralds the absence of authentic Chicana/o and Latina/o depictions within US popular performance, even as the character also—especially in the final moments of the play—holds open the space of cultural memory. El Pachuco's symbolic and Henry's all-too-human destruction liberate the stage community. In this moment, "the *pachuco*" is offered not as stereotype but as a talismanic effigy—one that calls forth those stories not yet rightly told (whether on the stage or beyond it) as it unloosens the past toward the promise of transformation in the present.

Valdez's *Los Vendidos* and *Zoot Suit* serve as important reminders that Latina/o dramatists and performers have, for decades, executed the stereotype to "embody forth" cultural memory. Indeed, even as I offer Valdez's oeuvre as an exemplar of this operation, Valdez's execution of the stereotype is hardly unique within the body of US Latina/o drama and performance of the period. Indeed, enacting the stereotype so as to eviscerate it and thereby reconstitute it as effigy emerges as a signal feature in works by Latina/o playwrights and performers beginning in the 1970s. Rita Moreno does it a few years before *Zoot Suit* with Googie Gomez, as does (as we shall see) Dolores Prida in her play *Beautiful Señoritas* (performed the same years as *Zoot Suit*). Carlos Morton's *Rancho Hollywood* (1980) explores similar strategies, staging an encounter between actual Latinas/os and the stereotypes that threaten to impinge on their full humanity.

Executing the stereotype was not just a 1970s phenomenon. Over subsequent decades, this particular performance strategy evolved in ways that comprised both a signal dramaturgical tradition within US Latina/o performance and a largely unacknowledged contribution to the critical theorization of stereotype in the same period.[59] By way of a brief demonstration, a cursory (and by no means comprehensive) summary of how the conventions of executing the stereotype have been refined in Latina/o drama and performance might prove useful. From the strident, scorched-earth enactments of the 1960s and 1970s to the eviscerations from within in the 1980s and the conspicuous effigy display of the 1990s, these conventions have continued to guide Latina/o dramatists and performers as a theory of practice for the theatrical interrogation of the politics of representation on the US stage.

With the emergence of feminist voices, alongside performers devising work for a broad array of venues, the familiarity of existing types was eviscerated—evacuated and remade from within—in a variety of ways. For example, in 1986's *Roosters* (one of the most widely produced Latina/o plays of the era), Milcha Sanchez-Scott populates her simultaneously magical and realist account of a young Chicana's coming of age by infusing gendered types with an excess of humanity to recraft received stereotypes as expansive archetypes. Other playwrights (like Sanchez-Scott) emerging from the legendary International Arts Relations (INTAR) workshops, guided by Maria Irene Fornés (whose practice and pedagogy were comparatively unconcerned with the politics of stereotype, especially compared to those of Valdez), filled their stages with hitherto unseen and unheard "types." To name-check only a few: Cherríe Moraga's erotic outlaws, from *Shadow of a Man*'s Rocky to *Heroes and Saints*' Cerezita, whose corporeally felt passions conjure new structures for both family and community; the women toiling in the economic shadows in Josefina López's *Real Women Have Curves*; and Migdalia Cruz's fierce young women, confined by the cruelties of circumstance (*Fur*) and convention (*The Have-Little*), who appear to "have-little" until they unleash the transformative poetry of their dreams. On less conventional stages, too, the comedic work of John Leguizamo, Culture Clash, Rick Najera, and Carmelita Tropicana satirically surrogated familiar "Latin types" and through charismatic quick-change alchemies deployed humor to confirm the banal artifice of familiar stereotypes and scenarios and show how much bigger, stranger, and funnier real Latinas/os are by comparison.

Reflecting on the "crossover" success of Latina/o playwrights, Jorge Huerta worried about the skills required to enact Latina/o-authored plays and characters before non-Chicana/o audiences. In a 1994 essay, he writes, "[T]he characters are not stereotypes—they are real—but in the hands of the wrong director or producers, the plays can be a devastating portrayal of Chicano culture." John Leguizamo notes the anxieties animating critical responses to his first one-man show in 1991, *Mambo Mouth*, when he writes that the performance "is a combination cathartic purge of popular Latin media-types and my own personal take on street prototypes and wannabes. Some reviewers and members of the press insinuated that I was perpetuating stereotypes rather than lambasting them."[60]

In 1999 the Tomás Rívera Policy Institute (TRPI), an academic research center headquartered at the University of Southern California, identified stereotypes of Latinos in mainstream US entertainments as the primary "obstacle" to Latino actors seeking employment. In a two-part, comprehensive study of Latinos and the US entertainment industry commissioned by the Screen Actors Guild (SAG), more than two-thirds of TRPI's survey respondents (one thousand Latina/o SAG members) agreed that "Latinos must fit a particular stereotype in order to be cast as Latinos. . . . Latinos who do not fit this stereotype do not receive Latino roles."[61] Indeed, throughout the 1990s, writers and performers deployed an array of verbs prefixed to denote a reversal, expulsion, or erasure of the stereotype's offending action. Scholars and artists alike were forever "dismantling" and "debunking," always "demystifying" and "decentering," as we forever endeavor to "disable," "dismember," and "dispel" the stereotype itself.[62]

Yet, at the same time, writers and performers in the 1990s also revealed stereotype's manifest destiny as effigy, or as a device to hold open spaces for surrogations that might embody forth cultural memory in striking ways. In 1992 Coco Fusco and Guillermo Gomez-Pena staged *The Couple in the Cage,* a live art surrogation of museum practices devised to enact an embodied critique of the colonialist heritages of institutional knowledge. The complex performance phenomena that attended the presentation of *The Couple in the Cage* (in which the installation was not infrequently interpreted by museum auditors as an "actual" exhibit) made explicit the power of stereotype to persist, even in the context of expertly rendered critique.

Perhaps comparably, literary critic William Anthony Nericcio—possibly his generation's most energetic explicator of stereotype—enacted a literal evisceration of a stuffed effigy of the animated character Speedy Gonzales, first in an essay and then in a digital media performance. As Nericcio has argued, "[S]tereotypes may be read as the bloodstains of cultural conflict . . . born from some sort of violence, some form of fracture, some type of antagonism."[63] In *Autopsy of a Rat,* Nericcio, clad in surgical garb, enacts his critical dissection by rendering Speedy's stuffed surrogate limb from limb. Fusco, Gomez-Pena, and Nericcio exemplify the many performance-makers since 1990 who, on encountering the stereotype as a persistent obstacle, have recognized stereotype's stubborn persistence, even amid enactment and evisceration, and engaged the stereotype's trappings as an effigy capable of hailing an absence through which living histories might yet be spoken.

As I have charted the bold-stroke contours of the critical performance tradition I call "executing the stereotype," I have emphasized some of the most prominent voices and works by US Latina/o performance-makers of the last half century. This is not by accident. Rather, my brisk summary offers a broad overview of a long conversation about cultural form, aesthetic function, and political purposes staged by and among US Latina/o writers and performers. Their diverse routes have nonetheless charted a surprisingly coherent engagement with the task of "executing the stereotype" as an expressive, conceptual, and political act. This shared heritage and genealogy also underscores the ways in which these very different Latina/o dramatists and performers evoke the work of scores of other "wrighters" (to borrow Jon D. Rossini's productive formulation) of performances that embody forth Latina/o cultural memory.

When we attend to the precise ways in which Latina/o writers and performers have wrangled stereotypes all this time, when we apprehend the ways in which Latina/o performance-makers have made their art by enacting, eviscerating, entombing—by executing—cultural stereotypes, we see how their work has performed, in Rossini's words, "not merely act[s] of writing, of giving voice to issues, or of righting, of correcting assumptions and revising limited models of identity and history." Theirs are acts of "wrighting, of creating something new in the process of correction and revision that moves beyond cultural assumptions" of and about Latinidad.[64] Not only have Latina/o dramatists and performers contributed a valuable theorization of how stereotypes operate in contemporary life, but Latina/o dramatists and performers also know, perhaps better than anyone, just how to execute the stereotype.

Chita-Rita, Chita-Charo

In 1977, while promoting her new nightclub act, Chita Rivera reflected on being mistaken for other prominent Latina stage performers: "I still get people telling me they loved me in *The Ritz* and now and then, someone comes up and says '*cuchi-cuchi.*'" Rivera punctuated her comment by sounding out the names of her colleagues alongside her own: "Chita-Rita, Chita-Charo." She continued, "[T]hese things don't make me angry. I just don't understand them. Can people possibly think that every Latin performer is the same person?"[65] Not only does Rivera's rhetorical question—how does being a legibly "Latin" performer elide one's individuated personhood?—align with the "stereotype threats" and "blind spots" that have guided recent cognitive theorizations of stereotype,[66] but her homonymic "Chita-Rita, Chita-Charo" riff also presses on the ways that stereotype has, and has not, been theorized within performance studies. In the pages that follow, I resolve this chapter's discussion of "executing the stereotype" as a strategy of countertheorization within Latina/o drama and performance by adding two additional threads to my discussion of stereotype's tangle. First, I offer a brief distillation of my theorization of stereotype's operation in performance practice, and, second, I rehearse how Dolores Prida's 1977 play *Beautiful Señoritas* demonstrates Latina/o performance-makers' long, complex tradition of "doing things with stereotypes."

Stereotype in performance conjures scriptive effigies that behold openings in cultural memory, within and through which performers can (and sometimes do) offer analytic acts of embodied resistance.[67]

When Rivera describes the "Chita-Rita, Chita-Charo" confusions that occasionally greet her, she also hails stereotype's mnemonic function, or theatre director and theorist Anne Bogart's evocative suggestion that every stereotype "is a container of memory . . . containers for meaning which embody the memory of all the other times they have been done."[68] "These things," as Rivera refers to such instances, wrangle three very different women—Rita Moreno, Charo, and Chita Rivera—into a single "type" that conjures, as interchangeable, three of the most prominent and acclaimed "Latin" women performers on the musical variety stage in 1977. So conjured, the idea of this Chita-Rita-Charo type prompts presumptions that specific behaviors will be performed—perhaps an accent or a dance or an outfit or some combination thereof—in an anticipated repetition, not so much of an action already encountered as of a repertoire of behaviors prompted by the type itself.

This operation of "type" is, then, not unlike what Robin Bernstein has termed "a scriptive thing," or "an object of material culture that prompts meaningful bodily behaviors." For Bernstein, the prompts offered by a scriptive thing neither constitute nor reveal a performance ("because individuals commonly resist, revise, or ignore instructions"). Yet such prompts do "reveal a script for a performance," which Bernstein submits can rightly be understood as a historical artifact capable of communicating knowledge about the past. To be sure, the conjuration of a "type" does not make it a "thing" in the material culture sense, but the type's onstage manifestation—often aided by masks, costumes, wigs, props, and physical shtick—cues the restoration of performance behaviors in ways that are perhaps more "scriptive" than prescriptive.[69]

As a scriptive effigy, then, the stereotype's force derives not simply from the representational mechanics of its recognizable replication but also from the ways in which that stereotype scripts the legibility of particular gestural and behavioral repetitions. Even if you have never before encountered (for example) Googie Gomez's particular "type," or line of business, Rita Moreno's effective enactment of the fast-talking, thickly accented, possibly talented bathhouse singer relies on Googie's legibility as both type and character. To perform a character like Googie, an actress must—to crib from Richard Schechner's instantiating notion of "restored behavior" or "twice-behaved" behavior—put on Googie's "type" in the manner that "a mask or costume is," with a "shape [that] can be seen from the outside and changed." In a scriptive sense, the stereotype prompts its enactment according to what playwright Frank Chin has called "a model of behavior."[70] Comparably, Roach aligns his effigy with "stock characters" (such as those familiar from popular performance traditions like commedia dell'arte, minstrelsy, or the Mexican *carpa*), suggesting that such characters "serve as conduits of memory for social performances . . . within which improvisatory variations may be staged."[71]

Just as Roach emphasizes that the effigy is a vessel for improvisation, however, Bernstein also reminds us that a scriptive thing's prompt—its call, if you will—does not guarantee its response. Conjuring stereotype in performance animates effigies scripted for particular enactments, but the encounter between the performer and the stereotype is, to follow Fred Moten, a "catalytic" moment of beholding, wherein the performer might opt to "mess up or mess with the beholder."[72] The enactor's decision—to be or not "to be for the beholder"—instantiates the stereotype's action in performance. Sometimes a performer like Charo may follow the stereotype's prompt with expert ratifying virtuosity. Some (like Rita Moreno's Googie) might improvise opposition within and against the scriptive prompts, resisting the stereotype's objectification by performing analytic acts of embodied resistance. Others might disidentify from the stereotype's operation by sounding their resistance ("Chita-Rita, Chita-Charo"). And still others might behold the space in cultural memory opened by the scriptive effigy and seize it as their chance to just act the hell out of the stereotype, with neither virtuosity nor critique, mobilizing all the stereotype's hegemonic cruelties for fun, for profit, or for proof of the performer's privilege. In each instance, the stereotype prompts but does not perform. What we observe is the enactors' interpretive agency—how they surrogate the stereotype as a scriptive effigy and how they decide to respond to the prompting calls scripted within it. To deploy a stereotype in performance is to animate the ideological power scripted within that stereotype, potentially routing that force in precise and particular ways, but only for the duration of a given performance, neither containing nor controlling the potency beyond the performance itself. As scriptive effigies, stereotypes in performance carry the talismanic power to unleash the forces of cultural memory within and through their surrogation; it becomes a matter of execution whether that talismanic power is used for good or evil.

My rendering of stereotype's force in performance, however, is no new discovery. We can see this understanding of stereotype's complicated force rehearsed in a single, self-consciously activist Latina play of the 1970s: Dolores Prida's *Beautiful Señoritas* (1977). The emotional architecture of this Cuban American playwright's first full-length script for performance is a genre-defying dramatic comedy with music originally produced by New York City's Duo Theater in 1977. The script stages the life journey of a Latina girl, "who grows up before our eyes," as she maneuvers the racialized and gendered ideologies that will attempt to define and confine her experience of self, from the moment of her birth through her maturity. Although the playwright clearly situates the girl at the center of *Beautiful Señoritas*' theatrical scenario, Prida disaggregates her play's putative protagonist by populating the stage with four other Latina performers, each of whom surrogates a variety of iconic Latina "types," in contradistinction to—and often in antagonistic conflict with—"The Man," the single Latino actor who inhabits every male role in the piece.

Prida's play begins with the birth of "The Girl," whose journey from childhood to maturity comprises the narrative action of *Beautiful Señoritas*. The Girl's birth, attended by The Midwife, is bemoaned by the child's father, who cries on seeing The Girl for the first time, "*¡Cómo puede pasarme esto a mí?* The first child that will bear my name it is a . . . girl! ¡Una chancleta! ¡Carajo!" As The Girl (played, as per Prida's instructions, by a young woman) arrives on the stage "look[ing] at everything as if seeing the world for the first time," The Midwife, having observed this primal scene of paternal rejection, observes that "he's off to drown his disappointment in rum, because another woman is born into this world. The same woman another man's son will covet and try to rape at the first opportunity." The Midwife's subsequent monologue details the fraught contradictions of race, ethnicity, and gender that mark the path unfolding before The Girl. "She'll be put on a pedestal and trampled upon at the same time," The Midwife intones, "she will be made a saint and a whore, crowned a queen and exploited and adored."[73]

The Midwife's grim litany of cultural expectations immediately faced by The Girl on her birth also serves as the vamp preceding the play's first exuberant musical production number, "The Beautiful Señoritas Song." As its title might suggest, this raucous song introduces four Latina performers "dressed as Carmen Miranda, Iris Chacón, Charo, and María la O." The Beautiful Señoritas sing and dance a lyrically simple song, with each of the song's seven verses first introducing the ensemble ("We Beautiful Señoritas / With maracas in our souls") before offering an ironic commentary on the expected social role of Latinas in the United States—as well as in US Latino culture ("*Cuchi cuchi bombas* / Always ready for amor").[74] The opening scene of *Beautiful Señoritas* thus presents a stark juxtaposition of two ostensibly incongruous theatrical styles, the nearly allegorical depiction of the birth of the Latina girl child jangling against the gaudy, comic, and hypertheatrical introduction of some of the most notorious icons of Latina-ness in 1970s popular performance. In so doing, Prida also immediately establishes the dramatic dialectic—the collision between Latina individual experience and the overweening cultural expectations of Latina-ness—that will script the core tension within the entire play.

This dialectic between personal experience and cultural expectation also undergirds the central staged action of *Beautiful Señoritas*: a beauty pageant. In this pageant, The Beautiful Señoritas compete in a startling array of categories for an (as yet) unnamed crown. At the same time, The Girl gazes intently but wordlessly on their every move. In the sequence of competition categories that follows the first production number, each of The Beautiful Señoritas is asked to embody the cultural expectations of Latina womanhood in the United States. First, they are asked to embody the exotic beauty of their respective homelands of origin (Cuba, Mexico, Puerto Rico, and "South America") before being challenged to display their expertise in "how to catch a man." Their able demonstration of seduction techniques instigates the final competition of Act One, in which each of The Beautiful Señoritas must dramatically atone for her sin of independent erotic desire. Act Two begins with a musical trapeze act designed to convey the exquisite anxiety of falling in love. The high-flying exuberance of the act's first number is followed immediately by a mournful dirge, entitled "The Wedding Song, or Where Have All the Women Gone." A stark series of ostensibly comic monologues detailing the banalities of domestic violence comes next. Another rousing production number ensues, in which the singers echo the melodies of *West Side Story* as they detail the crassly sexist hypocrisies of Latino cultural activist movements: "We say okay / We will fight not clean / But they say go dear / And type the speech."[75] The Beautiful Señoritas then gather to hear the emcee announce that The Girl has been chosen to wear the crown for which they have all been competing: Miss Señorita Mañana.

> The GIRL enters . . . wearing all the items she has picked from previ-
> ous scenes: the tinsel crown, the flowers, a mantilla, etc. Her face is
> made up as a clown. The WOMEN turn around to look. The GIRL
> looks upset, restless with all the manipulation she has endured. The
> WOMEN are distressed by what they see. They surround the GIRL.[76]

On seeing The Girl, one of the Señoritas quips, "I think we goofed. She's a mess." Then the women surround The Girl and "take off, one by one, all the various items, clean her face, etc.," as they begin to speak directly to The Girl—instead of performing for her—about their lived experiences as women. Finally, The Beautiful Señoritas "look at each other as images on a mirror, discovering themselves in each other. The Girl is now one of them." At this point, The Girl steps forward to sing— for the first time sharing her audible voice within the world of the play— the final song of *Beautiful Señoritas*, a feminist anthem entitled "Don't Deny Us the Music."[77] The concluding gesture of the play—when all The Beautiful Señoritas gather with The Girl to affirm the beginnings of a new vision of Latina personhood—is at once purgative and triumphant. In the play's concluding moments, The Girl and The Beautiful Señoritas stand, stripped of the shackles of received cultural expectations, as The Girl sings forth an unapologetically feminist invocation of radically new possibility. "I am just a woman breaking / The links of a chain," The Girl sings, "a Latin woman with the music inside."[78]

A decade after *Beautiful Señoritas* premiered, Dolores Prida reflected on her first play, which she called a "spoof" of the "stereotypes about Latin woman." Calling the piece "a feminist play, a very early feminist play," Prida noted, "I use all these characters, the Carmen Miranda types with bananas on the head, the Latin bombshell, *la madre sufrida*, and all of them go through a process where they take away all this superficiality and dig inside themselves, to find who they are. It's *búsqueda*, a search."[79] These women—"The Beautiful Señoritas," as they are named in the *dramatis personae*, along with The Girl, who observes them throughout the action of the play but only joins them for the show's final musical number—collectively constitute the play's construction of Latina consciousness. These characters, at once individuated and collective, are dually defined by the stereotypes imposed on them by Anglo racism and patriarchal misogyny. Prida theatrically organizes the play's action so that it emanates from the very existence of this multiply embodied Latina consciousness.

As Prida constructs the female characters in *Beautiful Señoritas*, she draws on what Shawn Michelle Smith describes as "the powerful critical vision that is the 'gift' of double consciousness," through which "a newly racialized self can begin to be reenvisioned."[80] Prida's work stands as a significant early theatrical and Latina articulation of what has come to be described as intersectional feminism.[81] As such, Prida's play deserves to be considered in critical, historical conversation with such foundational feminist texts as *This Bridge Called My Back: Radical Writings by Women of Color* (1981), as well as theatrical pieces such as Beah E. Richards's *Black Woman Speaks* (1950) and Ntzoke Shange's *For Colored Girls Who Have Considered Suicide When the Rainbow Is Enuf* (1975).[82] The pleasures (and analysis) derived from a racial spoof like *Beautiful Señoritas* are inherent in the ambiguous thrills of the battle, not so much in the singularity of the victory. *Beautiful Señoritas* dodges the premises of mimesis (in which the vanquishing performance of authentic Latina-ness might supplant the reductive racism/sexism signaled by the on-stage stereotypes) in ways that sustain the resistant pleasures and analytics of the act of satiric surrogation. The Latina performer's deft maneuvers among these myriad scriptive "types"—authentic and inauthentic, stereotypes and antistereotypes—enacts what it means to sound one's own resistance to the "Chita-Rita, Chita-Charo" logics that objectify every Latina performer as the same person.

CHAPTER 5

Carlos Comes Out

Gay Latin/o Lovers in the AIDS Era

———— ❧ ————

In February 1998, Carlos came out at the New York International Gift Fair. A thirteen-inch "fashion" doll, Carlos was introduced as "The World's First Out and Proud Boyfriend" for Billy ("The World's First Out and Proud Doll"), an "anatomically complete" doll, which had been released with great fanfare by marketer Totem International at the same event a year before. Since its release, more than seventy thousand Billy dolls had been sold, and the blond, blue-eyed, bull-necked, and (according to the London *Observer*) "hung like my My Little Pony" Billy enjoyed endless variations in the world of fashion, with a half dozen changes of outfit.[1] But the appearance of Carlos confirmed that Billy had it all. As the New York gay nightlife magazine *H/X* mused, "[Billy's] got the physique. He's got the huge tool. He's got a hot Latino boyfriend, Carlos."[2] In *Latina* magazine, Ernie Glam warned, "[I]f Barbie wants to date this plastic *papi*, she can forget about it," noting that Carlos "is the boyfriend of Billy" and that the pair "has since made TV appearances on *Saturday Night Live* and Telemundo."[3] In a brief feature article in *Genre* (a lifestyle and entertainment magazine aimed at gay men), "*Hola*, Gorgeous!," Max Harrold wagged. "Carlos is the ying [*sic*] for Billy's yang, the *frijoles negros* to Billy's *arroz blanca* . . . . Stay tuned as the toothsome twosome cut a devastating social swath from South Beach to West Hollywood."[4] Carlos's coming out (and his coming together with Billy) in the spring of 1998 even inspired *the New York Times* to run an April Sunday feature on "doll couples" entitled "Put Your Tiny Hand in Mine." The article observed that "ever since Billy . . . was given a partner, Carlos, early this year, the doll couple has kicked up a stir. . . . But Billy and Carlos are hardly the only doll couple."[5] Indeed, in the spring of 1998, Billy and Carlos may have been among the most prominent gay male couples on the US popular culture map.

Yet, throughout this brief burst of interest in Totem International's introduction of Carlos as the "first out and proud boyfriend" of the "first out and proud gay doll," Billy, the decision to pair uber-Anglo Billy with a Latino boyfriend received little notice from contemporary commentators. Sure, Carlos's Latin-ness elicited copy like *Genre*'s winking Spanish-ish flourishes, or more typically *H/X*'s pairing of the words *hot* and *Latino* as one phrase. To be sure, *Latina*'s Ernie Glam nodded to Carlos's evocation of "sexual stereotypes common [in the] gay community," a point distilled by cultural critic Donald Suggs in *TimeOut New York*: "Carlos is simply a glossily packaged racial stereotype."[6] But few seriously questioned why the first couple in BillyWorld would be half Latino.

During the five or so years before Carlos came out in 1998, gay Latinos—both as public figures and as characters in popular performance—had enjoyed a peculiar prominence in rapidly proliferating accounts of gay life in the United States. Though largely pressed to the margins of invisibility only a few years earlier, the presence of gay Latino characters could be seen across the popular performance horizon throughout the mid-1990s—in films like *Philadelphia* (1993) and *To Wong Foo Thanks for Everything Julie Newmar* (1995), on stage in Broadway productions like *Love! Valour! Compassion* (1994) and *Rent* (1996), and in critically acclaimed television series like *My So-Called Life* (1994–95) and the seventh season of *Seinfeld* (1997–98). During these five years, even outside scripted entertainments seemed to feature gay Latinos anywhere the question of gay civil rights was raised. Consider, for example, two of the most visible gay activists of 1994: Pedro Zamora and José Zuniga.

In the summer of 1994, twenty-two-year-old Cuban American Pedro Zamora became perhaps the first openly gay (and openly HIV-positive) AIDS educator to be featured on a weekly television series, specifically MTV's third installment of its breakout, genre-defining, documentary soap opera *The Real World*. Over sixteen episodes, Zamora savvily exploited the conventions of "reality television" to offer the national audience a glimpse into "what a gay man of color living with AIDS [was] really like."[7] His life included speaking at colleges, participating in rallies, confronting intolerant housemates, dating—and in the series' penultimate episode marrying—another HIV-positive man of color. Zamora's death on November 11, 1994 (the day after *The Real World*'s finale), and his impact as a "televisual activist" (to borrow José Esteban Muñoz's apt formulation),[8] was memorialized in *People* magazine, in an MTV special, and by the president of the United States, Bill Clinton, who observed that Pedro "taught all of us that AIDS is a disease with a human face."[9]

On April 24, 1994—just two months before the first episode of *Real World: San Francisco* aired—twenty-three-year-old Mexican American José Zuniga, a decorated Army medic who had served with distinction during operations Desert Storm and Desert Freedom, stood in dress uniform before a gathering of reporters and announced that he was gay. Zuniga, who a month or so earlier had been named as the Sixth Army's 1992 US Soldier of the Year, declared, "[T]he military teaches that you should have honor and integrity. But I can't live honorably with this secret. I'm gay. I'm proud of it. The Army should accept that."[10] Zuniga hoped his coming out would "put another face on gays in the military" and have an impact on the congressional hearings then under way to thwart efforts to lift the formal ban on gays and lesbians in the military.[11] Within the week, the US military began discharge proceedings against Zuniga, as he began an aggressive media tour in support of lifting the ban.[12]

In a 2011 retrospective profile in *OutServe* magazine, Sue Fulton (one of the first women to graduate from West Point) observed, "[A]t a pivotal time, Zuniga was able to put a face to the issue—the face of a decorated soldier. Through 1993 and into 1994, especially with the publication of his book *Soldier of the Year*, [Zuniga] traveled around the country speaking to audiences about his experiences."[13] Although few contemporary observers in the gay civil rights movement noted it at the time, the high visibility of both Zamora's fight for life and Zuniga's struggle to serve his country made 1994 a year in which young gay Latinos were among the most prominent "new faces" of lesbian, gay, bisexual, transgender (LGBT) activism in the United States.

Thus, at a specific historical moment in the mid-1990s, Zamora and Zuniga became the faces of two of the three separate fronts on which LGBT activists were quickly focusing their energies. Zamora was an emblem of the ongoing agitation both to prevent the spread of HIV/AIDS and to expand life-sustaining medical interventions for those living with the disease. Zuniga became an early representative of the effort to "lift the ban" on military service by LGBT people, both before and after the implementation of what was eventually dubbed "Don't Ask Don't Tell" (a troubled compromise brokered in 1994 that permitted the service of LGBT military personnel but forbade open acknowledgment of their sexual orientation). Indeed, while Zamora became a poster boy for the pursuit of gay life in the midst of the AIDS epidemic, and Zuniga became one for the pursuit of the freedom to serve, so, too, did gay Latinos become prominent on the third main front of 1990s LGBT activism: marriage equality.

As this chapter examines, gay Latin/o lovers became prominent in this period not necessarily to rehearse gay marriage but to perform as partners in a new proliferation of depictions of gay male couplehood in US popular performance. In such disparate productions as *Philadelphia*, *Rent*, and *Seinfeld*, the stock character of the gay Latin/o lover (with some mix of sexiness, sassiness, and swarthiness) cued a measure of difference within the sameness of the same-sex partnership that rendered a gay male pairing as more legibly erotic, romantic, and legitimate. Thus, Carlos's arrival on the scene in 1998 might be read historically as both the end of a peculiar moment of visibility for gay Latinos in US popular performance—the vogue for gay Latin/o lovers would pass as swiftly as it began—and also as a prompt to consider, in the words of one Carlos critic, how "[t]he questions provoked by these dolls are broader than the act of attaching political meanings to a fantasy world."[14]

This chapter historicizes the arrival of the Carlos doll by considering the peculiar proliferation of such "gay Latin/o lovers" appearing within popular performances depicting gay male culture and life in the 1990s. These "gay Latin/o lovers" deploy stylized "Latin" tropes within depictions of ostensibly authentic Latino characters, who are typically defined by their emotional, romantic, or erotic companionship with non-Latino characters. In ways parallel to Ann Pellegrini's assessment of how "the interracial couple [became] virtually the cinematic face of lesbianism" in the films of the same period, the uncertain raciality of these gay Latin/o lovers helps to render gay male couplehood newly legible to mainstream audiences. The presence of the "gay Latin/o lover" amplifies an aspect of difference within the same-sex partnership—or, as Pellegrini argues, "bears the burden of making difference within the same visible"—and thereby renders the gay male couple legible within both minority rights discourses and the emerging diversity rhetorics of the early 1990s.[15] This brief proliferation of spectacular "gay Latin/o lovers" thus must be understood not singly as a fetishistic resurgence of retrograde stereotype but also as an inaugural episode in the "normalization" of the legibly (and homonormatively) gay male couple within US popular performance.[16]

My account begins with a brief prehistory of the gay(ish) Latin(ish) characters that appeared in popular performances after the 1969 Stonewall uprising but prior to the early 1980s AIDS emergency. I then pause to offer an extended reflection on Puerto Rican actor Michael Carmine's appearance as Alberto in the pivotal 1990 AIDS drama *Longtime Companion*, before turning my attention to the accumulation of Broadway and Hollywood productions that integrated gay Latino characters as boyfriends of non-Latino characters between 1992 and 1997. As I explicate the appearance of gay Latin/o lovers in such productions as *Philadelphia, Love! Valor! Compassion!*, and *Rent* (all of which premiered in the five years or so before the introduction of the so-called HIV cocktail, which radically recalibrated the way HIV/AIDS was narrated in both popular and medical discourses), my account pays close attention to how these gay Latin/o lovers recast the narrative conventions of gay male couplehood in popular performance. I then return to the 1997 introduction and subsequent circulation of the Carlos doll and explicate how Carlos distilled the way such gay Latin/o lovers rehearsed an ascending minoritized, homonormative mode of gay male visibility that would come to coordinate LGBT activism in the coming decades.

Gay Latin/o Presence

When Totem International's Carlos doll arrived on the gay scene in 1997 to do "his" part for LGBT awareness, designer John McKitterick may or may not have been aware of the half-century-long tradition of highly visible Latinas/os contributing, in very different ways, to the galvanization of the contemporary LGBT movement even before the Stonewall uprising in New York City in June 1969. Indeed, figures like José Sarria, Sylvia Rivera, John Rechy, and Mario Montez—individuals we might today rightly recognize as Latina/o, as queer, and as performers—had been confronting the artistic, cultural, and political assumptions of their intersecting communities since the 1950s and 1960s. In those decades, for example, nightclub performer José Sarria savvily mixed high drag and San Francisco city politics not only to stand as the nation's first openly gay candidate for elected office in 1961 but also to use the niche of the gay bar to pioneer alternative organizational structures of resistance and community within San Francisco's queer community.[17] In 1960s New

York, Puerto Rican Rene Rivera crafted the high-concept drag persona Mario Montez, becoming one of the first underground icons and sometimes antagonistic muse to such disparate avant-garde forces as Charles Ludlam, Jack Smith, and Andy Warhol.[18] Mexican American writer John Rechy became an underground icon of a different sort during this same period, not only with the success of his genre-defying book *City of Night* but also through his notoriously stylized public persona, which eluded easy categorization of either race or region as it also rehearsed a hypermasculine mode of outlaw sexuality.[19] Another important figure, Sylvia Rivera, stood among the rioters at Stonewall in 1969 and soon became a reliably vocal advocate for gender and racial equity within the emerging LGBT movement, as well as a queer activist presence within the Young Lords,[20] a social movement "committed to articulating a new radical Puerto Rican identity aimed at the [social, economic, and political] betterment of the Puerto Rican people."[21]

To be sure, in the 1960s and early 1970s, the influence of Sarria, Montez, Rechy, Rivera, and other Latina/o queers were likely most visible within and through the cultural and activist avant-garde of the period. Even so, gay Latin/o characters did make some notable appearances on the cinematic, televisual, and theatrical stages of mainstream popular performance throughout the 1970s and early 1980s. Perhaps unsurprisingly, most of these gay(ish) Latin(ish) figures were legible according to conventions well rehearsed in US mainstream popular performance—in Latin numbers, as stealth Latinos, and as characters in serious Broadway spectacles.

Though conspicuously "Latin" musical numbers were all the rage in television variety shows of the 1970s, the clearest gay Latin/o throwbacks to the Hollywood styles of the 1940s and 1950s typically arrived in campy spoofs of the Latin numbers of the past. In Terrence McNally's *The Ritz*, for example, the climactic bathhouse chase sequence is underscored not by a Googie Gomez extravaganza but rather by a haphazard drag cover of a hit "latune" from the 1940s ("We're three *caballeros*! Three gay *caballeros*!"). Indeed, the erotic excesses of Hollywood's high Latin style prompted a few such queerly satiric surrogates. For example, 1981's *Zorro, the Gay Blade* offers a broadly comedic parody of the Californio western as a style and genre. Don Diego (George Hamilton) is rendered unable to continue fighting for good as the swashbuckling Zorro, so he calls in his twin brother Ramon (also played by Hamilton) for aid. Ramon, who now also goes by the name Bunny Wiggelsworth, takes over the fight for good with swishy flourish, finally saving the day. *Zorro, the Gay Blade* directly parodies the "limp-wristed antics and mincing manner" of the Zorro figure, as introduced by Douglas Fairbanks and Tyrone Power (in which Zorro's disguise is not actually his mask and cape but his public pretense of effeminacy).[22] Through a series of elaborately choreographed fight sequences, Hamilton's dual performance delights in the excessive trappings of both hyperbolic masculinity and stylized effeminacy, simultaneously confirming Diego's erotic virility and eliding Bunny's potential sexual agency.

A more musical gay spoof can be seen in a recurring and pivotal musical sequence from 1982's gender-crossing comedy film *Victor/Victoria*. Appearing in three variations over the course of the film, "The Shady Dame from Seville" is a staged musical number that—from its art direction to vocal trills to chorus-boy choreography—appears to draw on Ginny Simms's performance of "Amor" in 1944's *Broadway Rhythm* (as discussed in chapter 1) as a primary referent. In 1944 the bolero scene framing Simms's performance of "Amor" amplified the peculiarly illicit thrills of ethnic surrogation. In 1982 *Victor/Victoria* staged the number—first in rehearsal and then in performance—both to confirm and to display the myriad competencies required of Victoria (Julie Andrews), a woman pretending to be a man who makes his living as a female impersonator, before offering a final rendering of the number (with Robert Preston surrogating Victoria's part) as the film's final burlesque twist. In this way, *The Ritz, Zorro, the Gay Blade,* and *Victor/Victoria*'s "The Shady Dame from Seville" all deploy the frame of the conspicuously "Latin" musical number (and the twined thrills of gayness and Latin-ness) to animate the promise of an unconventional, boundary-disrupting, and possibly erotic encounter, repurposing the interethnic thrills of the 1940s and 1950s toward the perilously ambisexual pleasures of the 1970s disco era.

Disco's heat also brought one of the era's most prominent stealth (gay) Latinos to the stages of US popular performance: Felipe Rose, an original member of the musical group the Village People. Rose's on-stage "Indian" persona, which appeared to draw inspiration both from Hollywood and from college sports half-time shows, both elided and exploited his actual mixed Puerto Rican and Lakota ancestry. Rose's on-stage persona as "the Indian" effaced the particulars of his actual ethnicity to delight in the surrogative play of fantasy, much in the same way that the Village People played coy with the gay male subcultural inspirations for the particular constellation of fetishized icons of masculinity that comprised its ensemble.[23] (Perhaps ironically, Totem International fabricated outfits that made it possible to dress Carlos as a cop, a cowboy, a military man, and a leather man, but—as *Weekly World News'* Ed Anger noted—"the only thing they're missing is Indian Chief. . . . [T]hen you'd have the Village People.")[24]

In ways distinct yet comparable, Puerto Rican and Trinidadian actor Antonio Fargas played a range of queer roles in 1976, ranging from the depressed gay neighbor Bernstein in *Next Stop, Greenwich Village* to *Car Wash*'s fierce Lindy (who utters the now legendary quip "I'm more man than you'll ever be, and more woman than you'll ever get").[25] In ways not unlike Juano Hernandez (as discussed in chapter 2), Fargas became best known for portraying characters standing at the threshold of two ostensibly separate worlds of experience, roles that included not only Bernstein and Lindy but also the ambitious but drug-addled Link in *Foxy Brown* (1974), the all-seeing brothel pianist professor in *Pretty Baby* (1978), and the flashy informant Huggy Bear (Fargas's most iconic role) on television's *Starsky and Hutch* (1975–79). Yet, even putting aside the queer surrogations scripted by both Rose's and Fargas's work in this period, we can see how their performances—as elaborations of stealth (gay) Latino casting practices—rehearse the way uncertainty regarding ethnoracial legibility emerged as a signal feature of the urban landscape in the 1970s.

While these Latin numbers and stealth gay Latinos mostly just hint at the possibility of gay Latinos, at least two of the most celebrated Broadway productions of the mid-1970s did introduce Latino characters maneuvering the queerer intersection of masculinity and sexuality—*Short Eyes* and *A Chorus Line*. In the neorealist prison drama *Short Eyes*, playwright Miguel Piñero tells the dramatic story of a single day in "the House of Detention." Although the dramatic structure of *Short Eyes* is propelled by the disruptive arrival of a particular inmate charged with child molestation, a parallel conflict—whether the new arrival Julio (a.k.a. "Cupcakes") will be "turned out" by the predatory Paco—also underwrites the play's emotional drama. Disregarding ascendant identity-based understandings of male-male sexual intimacy, *Short Eyes* queries not whether Cupcakes will be turned gay but whether he will be transformed by the interplay of sexuality and violence that punctuates prison life. Originally presented at the Riverside Church in January 1974, *Short Eyes* was quickly transferred to Joseph Papp's Public Theater in March, before moving to Broadway in May, where it played through the summer, ultimately earning an array of awards, including a Tony nomination for Best Play. The script was adapted for film in 1977.[26]

The next year, another Joseph Papp production would follow a simi-
larly brisk route to Broadway, and it also featured a dramatically pivotal
Latino character encountering the complexities of homoerotic desire.
Created by Michael Bennett, *A Chorus Line* gathers a group of dancers
vying for a job in the chorus when they are confronted with a director
who is more interested in hearing their stories than assessing their singing and dancing skills. In a series of ensemble montages and chorally
interpolated monologues, a collective identity develops among the disparate dancers, even as the musical's composite portrait of the "gypsy
dancer" also comes into focus. Shortly after the midpoint in the piece,
the ensemble leaves the stage, and, in turn, two single characters step
forward, the second of which is Paul, a gay Puerto Rican dancer who
has participated only reluctantly in the group. Alone on stage, in an
emotionally drenched monologue often listed as a musical number in
the program, Paul relates how his coming out coincided with his professional dance debut as a female impersonator. *A Chorus Line* opened at
the Public Theater in May 1975 and was transferred a month later to
Broadway's Shubert Theatre (where it played for next fifteen years), winning nearly every major award along the way.

Considered together, *Short Eyes'* Cupcakes and *A Chorus Line's* Paul
emerge as Latino characters who animate complex narratives of sex and
ethnicity that tacitly interrogate identity-bound notions of queer desire.
(Just as Paul may or may not be trans-identified, Cupcakes's sexual practices may or may not inform his identity.) At the same time, both plays—
each a phenomenon in its own way—use Latino characters to embody
the complexities of homoerotic desire on the Broadway stage. Moreover,
both productions tacitly relied on the autobiographical authority of
their credited authors (Miguel Piñero and Nicholas Dante, respectively)
to ratify the authenticity of their particular subcultural accounts.[27] In so
doing, then, and alongside *West Side Story's* Sharks of a generation prior
and *Zoot Suit's* *pachucos* of just a few years later, *Short Eyes* and *A Chorus
Line* animated an alternately fierce and fearsome mode of staging Latino
sexuality on Broadway, which would both haunt and guide the introduction of Latino gay characters for the next several decades.

This is not to say that Paul and Cupcakes led a parade of queer Latinos
to the stages of US popular performance. On the contrary, during the
remainder of the 1970s and throughout the 1980s, most film and theatrical productions set within or against contemporary gay male culture
remained emphatically white. While spoofy comedies like *Zorro, the Gay
Blade; Victor/Victoria;* and *The Ritz* might wink nostalgically at past Latin

styles, serious commercial dramas like *Cruising* (1980) and *Making Love* (1982) flirted with the dangers of the gay urban subculture, often relying on the ethnicity-eliding uniformity of the contemporary gay "clone" style as visual shorthand. Within gay male subcultural performances of the period, the "clone" (or the "gay everyman" whose "very uniform . . . be it denim, leather, or Lacoste . . . announce[d] a gay man's attraction to, identification with, and desire for other gay men") was only the most prominent example of an urban gay erotic economy that commodified ethnic, cultural, and economic diversity as fetish, both in "everyday" life and in more formalized erotic enactments on film and elsewhere.[28] Even as the offerings of Spanish-language cinema began to include candid and even erotic depictions of same-sex encounters (especially the crowd-pleasing 1985 Mexican feature *Dona Herlinda and Her Son*, which enjoyed a lengthy cycle on the US art house circuit, and the work of Spanish filmmaker Pedro Almodóvar, whose films began to receive broad US distribution in 1988), conventionally tragic queer narratives of isolated self-abnegation also received acclaim, like Hector Babenco's *Kiss of the Spider Woman*, featuring William Hurt in his Oscar-winning performance as the window dresser Molina.

Gay Latin/o characters were conspicuously absent from AIDS dramas on stage, screen, and television beginning in the mid-1980s. Most (if not all) of these performances contemplated the ways in which the arrival of AIDS destabilized the relative comfort, safety, and privilege of white gay male relationships and communities. In the most seen AIDS dramas of the period, the stigma of AIDS presented an opportunity to confront the stigma of gayness. On Broadway, William Hoffman's Tony-nominated *As Is* (1985) retooled the conventions of the "coming-out" story to accommodate the additional obstacles to self-love and self-acceptance introduced by the disease. On television that same year, *An Early Frost* told the story of a gay man living with AIDS coming out so that he might come home to die, his arrival driving a narrative arc toward intrafamilial acceptance and reconciliation. The urgent need for acceptance, tolerance, and reconciliation was amplified by gay narratives on television and Broadway addressing similar themes of "coming out" and "coming home" during this same period—ranging from television's *Consenting Adult* (1985) to Broadway's *La Cage Aux Folles* (1984) and the film version of *Torch Song Trilogy* (1988)—even without overt reference to AIDS.

Among some of the lesser-seen AIDS dramas, narratives of acceptance and reconciliation show characters exploiting their racial, gender, and economic privilege as tools both to sustain community and to plot new structures and strategies for societal change. Both Robert Sherwood's 1985 gay indie film *Parting Glances* and Robert Chesley's notorious Off Broadway two-hander *Jerker* (1986) dramatized the life-sustaining necessity of "nontraditional" gay kinship structures. Originally airing in early October 1987, the "Killing All the Right People" episode of television's *Designing Women* deployed the conventional features of the 1980s sitcom (zippy one-liners, A-plot/B-plot story structure, "very special episode" thematics) to advocate for both sensible sex education and nondiscriminatory end-of-life protocols. Opening at the Public Theater in 1985, Larry Kramer's *The Normal Heart* offered a searing indictment of governmental nonresponse to the epidemic in its earliest years, even as it both documented and modeled the core strategies (informed medical advocacy, independent crisis intervention, and direct rageful confrontation) that would guide AIDS activism for the next ten years.

By the later 1980s, the emerging genre of the AIDS drama seemed to have little use for gay Latin/o characters. Gay Latin/o presence, typically scarce, might be silly or sexy—fierce or fearsome—but it seemed to have no place in the AIDS dramas of the 1980s. In the 1990s, however, all that would change. In 1993 Spanish heartthrob Antonio Banderas would play Tom Hanks's lover in the Oscar-winning Jonathan Demme film *Philadelphia*, in 1994 the sexy dancer Ramon would threaten and thrill the ensemble in Terrence McNally's elegiac comedy *Love! Valour! Compassion!*, and in 1996 Angel would mend and break hearts in Jonathan Larson's *Rent* on Broadway. In the meantime, John Leguizamo's ChiChi Rodriguez discovered love in the heartland in *To Wong Foo* (1995), Hank Azaria's Agador tried to keep things clean in *The Birdcage* (1996), and Kramer fatefully encountered Yul Vazquez's Bob on *Seinfeld* (1995). And, of course, Carlos came out in 1997. But why did gay Latin/o characters in depictions of gay male life and culture go from being almost invisible to nearly ubiquitous in the span of a decade? To venture an explanation for this peculiar and precise Latin boom, it is necessary to pause to reflect on a single actor's presence in a single scene of a pathbreaking but rarely revisited film from 1990: Michael Carmine's performance as Alberto in Craig Lucas and Norman René's *Longtime Companion*.

Alberto

Michael Carmine was thirty years old when he died on October 14, 1989.[29] A heart attack was reported as cause of death, though many among the actor's colleagues and friends understood his heart's failure to be a complication from AIDS.[30] A New York native of Puerto Rican descent, Carmine began acting at New York City's High School for the Performing Arts. A reliably jobbing actor since his late teens, Carmine's work in theatre, film, and television through the mid-1980s earned him increasing attention and prominence. In New York, between 1984 and 1987, Carmine created roles for Maria Irene Fornés at INTAR, for Cándido Tirado at the African Caribbean Poetry Theatre, and for Reinaldo Povod at the Public Theater and also on Broadway. (Carmine appeared in the original casts of Povod's *Cuba and His Teddy Bear* and *La Puta Vida*, earning consistently strong reviews for both.) During the same period, his performances in two different featured roles on television's *Miami Vice* led to film roles in a variety of genre pictures, including 1985's *Band of the Hand* and the 1987 box office hit *Batteries Not Included*. In April 1988, Carmine spoke optimistically about the direction of his career: "To keep my life fresh, I've got to explore other areas, maybe someday I'll write or direct or maybe have a business outside of show business in case the going gets rough. But I see myself involved in show business for the rest of my life."[31] Only eighteen months later, the same week in which his final film, *Longtime Companion*, received its first screening before an industry audience in New York, Michael Carmine died.

Longtime Companion (in which Michael Carmine appears in a single scene late in the film) follows a group of seven friends, living in New York City from 1981 to 1989, and offers an intimate ensemble portrait of the first decade of the AIDS era. Written by playwright Craig Lucas and directed by his frequent collaborator Norman René, each of *Longtime Companion*'s nine episodes takes place on a single day in a different year, with brief scenes intercut to depict the escalating impact of AIDS on the daily lives of each of the eight principal characters (seven gay men and one straight woman—all white). As one of the earliest narrative feature films to be specifically "about" AIDS, *Longtime Companion* first struggled to find financing and then to secure a cast. Backing from the public television series *American Playhouse* greenlighted the production in early 1989, and a cast of mostly "unknown" New York theatre actors (including Michael Carmine) was assembled by late April of the same year. Shooting took place in and around New York City over thirty-five days in August and September, with a scheduled October screening at the Independent Film Project (IFP) Market serving as the film's de facto delivery date. In the first months of 1990, *Longtime Companion* was screened as an "Un Certain Regard" selection at Cannes, and the film won the Audience Award at the Sundance Film Festival. There, the film's producers brokered a deal with a major distributor.[32]

Released in May 1990, *Longtime Companion* earned generally affirmative reviews, with near raves from *Time* and *Entertainment Weekly* and thumbs up from both Siskel and Ebert. Yet the overall admiration for the film's sensitivity and craftsmanship was tempered by a hesitance about the lack of economic and racial diversity among its cast of characters. *New York*'s David Denby appreciated that the film seemed to intend "not to aggravate fear but to show people making the best of an inconceivable situation," even as he wondered whether the actors might have been "constrained by their exemplary roles," noting the movie's "tepidity."[33] Vincent Canby, writing one of the few outright pans for the *New York Times*, faulted the film's "emphasis exclusively on the toll being taken [by AIDS] within the white gay community," noting, "*Longtime Companion* appears to be as self-absorbed as its characters."[34] Still, over the summer and fall of 1990, *Longtime Companion* proved a modest commercial success, with its nearly five-million-dollar box office take establishing it as one of the most financially successful independent gay films of the 1990s.[35]

Throughout 1991, *Longtime Companion* remained in ready circulation. An aggressive home video release made the film a minor hit on the rental charts, actor Bruce Davison's Academy Award nomination as Best Supporting Actor kept stories about the film in the press, and the film's broadcast as the season opener for Public Broadcasting's *American Playhouse* series in September delivered it directly to homes across the country. Yet throughout *Longtime Companion*'s incremental success, and even as early hesitancy about the film's overwhelming whiteness festered into outright hostility,[36] neither Michael Carmine's performance (as the only actor of color to have a significant secondary role) nor his status as the only member of the cast to have died prior to the film's release garnered more than the occasional, glancing reference.[37]

Michael Carmine's appearance as Alberto comes in *Longtime Companion*'s penultimate episode (which the title card identifies as "September 10, 1988") and arrives immediately following two episodes confirming the deaths of three of the seven principal characters. The hermetic privilege documented in the film's first four episodes (1981–84)—a contentedly insular world of moneyed white men enjoying good jobs, well-appointed Manhattan apartments, and casual vacations—is shattered by the realities and losses wrought by the epidemic in the next few years (1985–87), with the final two episodes confirming the transformation in each of the survivors' lives. The penultimate episode shows the four sur-

Michael Carmine as Alberto in *Longtime Companion* (1990). (Screenshot)

viving members of the film's original seven-person ensemble, each deeply
involved in a distinct yet typical mode of AIDS volunteer work, circa 1988.
The episode opens with Fuzzy (Steven Caffrey) and Lisa (Mary-Louise
Parker) working differently specialized hotlines at New York's Gay Men's
Health Crisis (GMHC) and closes with Howard (Patrick Cassidy) hosting
a benefit performance at a small downtown venue. The emotional focus
of the episode, however, comes in between, as Willy (Campbell Scott, who
serves, arguably, as both the film's protagonist and the audience's surrogate) visits his "buddy" Alberto. The AIDS buddy system was a volunteer
program, pioneered by GMHC and widely adopted internationally thereafter, which offered what Tom Roach has called an open-ended "quasi-
institutionalization" of friendship designed to ensure that a person living
with AIDS would be guaranteed "functional support in her or his everyday life," with the volunteer buddy performing variously as "a caregiver, a
home health aide, an errand runner, [and] a friend."[38]

As Alberto's scene begins, a newly mustached Willy, dressed in khakis
and a periwinkle blue sweater, carries a laundry bag down a sunny street
and into an apartment building with a heavy metal door. As he passes,
a half dozen young people of color (all apparently teens or preteens)
give Willy the side-eye. Willy enters Alberto's modest studio apartment
through the kitchen ("Got your laundry!") to find Alberto reclined and
playing solitaire on a foldout bed. In Alberto's apartment, images of old
movie stars such as Marilyn Monroe and Merle Oberon are taped to the

wall, and a collection of vintage "lady head" vases peek from nearly every visible shelf. A small hand drum hangs above Alberto's daybed, and a shekere-style maraca seems carefully placed on the sideboard. A plastic bead curtain hangs at the threshold of the kitchen, and an aquarium sits in in the open space above the sink, each separating the kitchen from the main living area. The conversation that follows is halting and tense, with Willy making a great effort to cheerfully check on Alberto's lost Medicare card and general well-being ("Getting any exercise? Still feeling wobbly?"). Alberto mostly just nods or shrugs, until Willy indicates that he'll be on his way. Seemingly somewhat alarmed, Carmine's Alberto makes a request: "Could you straighten up a little in the kitchen?" Scott's Willy replies, "Sure. You want to help?" When Alberto shakes his head no, Willy presses, "Your legs bothering you now? Well, you should get up." A confrontation of sorts follows ("I don't think I'll be needing you anymore, Willy. Thank you.") As Carmine's Alberto fires Willy ("You can just leave the keys. You're fired, you got it?"), Scott's Willy rejects Alberto's dismissal ("I'm a volunteer; I don't get paid; you can't fire me") before pressing Alberto again ("I think you're really, really pissed, and I don't blame you, but if you allow yourself to waste away . . .") The two men regard each other in a long moment before both look down. Scott's Willy continues, "I know I'm not one of your friends. Or your family. But . . ." After another long moment, Alberto returns his keys to Willy and stands, alone in the film's frame, as the scene ends.

Michael Carmine's single, two-and-a-half-minute appearance as Alberto in *Longtime Companion* is discomfiting, at once intense and incongruous, neither especially clear nor at all pleasant. Not only is Alberto the film's only character who is a person of color (aside from a handful of medical and other caregivers whose presence and dialogue are mostly expository), but Willy's visit to Alberto is the film's first scene in which any of the principal characters engages emotionally with someone beyond his or her personal or professional circle.[39] Even more, Willy and Alberto's relationship is among the few in the film left completely unresolved, in either subsequent dialogue or the concluding dream reunion on the beach at Fire Island. Most references to Carmine's presence in film reviews note the scene's incongruity. The *New York Times'* Canby misunderstood the "buddy" relationship between Carmine's Alberto and Scott's Willy, and he sneered at the scene as one "in which a white character makes a mercy call on a Hispanic AIDS victim."[40]

For Farrah Anwar, writing for the British Film Institute's *Monthly Film Bulletin*, Alberto's evident Latino-ness reads as cinematic shorthand for "the film's attitudes to drug users," which "culminat[es] in Willy's stern lecture to an indifferent Puerto Rican addict."[41] (Nothing in the film's diegesis specifically suggests that Alberto is an addict.) David Elliott, movie critic for the *San Diego Union*, suspected that the scene ("briefly showing an ill, angry Latino") was "a sop to AIDS demographics." At the same time, Elliott was also one of the few commentators on the Alberto scene specifically to acknowledge Carmine's contribution, noting that the scene "is acted all-out by Michael Carmine, who died after the filming."[42]

Even so, the seemingly incongruous presence of Michael Carmine as Alberto in *Longtime Companion* bears ready diegetic justification. On a character level, Willy's relative ease interacting with a person living with AIDS confirms how much he has changed since the earlier scenes when he was afraid to touch even his most beloved friends as they became ill. Plus, he's a personal trainer, so he's used to giving orders. On a narrative level, the charged encounter provides the emotional center of the constellation of scenes comprising the 1988 episode, while also depicting "buddy" work as a core volunteer intervention within the response to the epidemic.

On a political level, the choice to present this uncertain, awkward, and tense encounter between Carmine's Alberto and Scott's Willy (in his best gay cliché drag) seems to be neither a stern "mercy call" nor a cynical demographic sop but rather a conscious gesture toward the actual confrontations with privilege and difference that were both guiding and defining AIDS activism in the early years of ACT-UP (the AIDS Coalition To Unleash Power). Moreover, Craig Lucas and Norman René's choice not only to script the role of Willy's buddy as a new character (rather than, say, an already-introduced presence, like the distinctive-looking waiter who haunts the edges of the film's narrative) but also to cast a legibly Latino actor in the role also draws on an emerging representational habit (identified by cultural historian David Román as "tropical fruit") in activist literary expressions of the period. As Román notes, for "writers committed to social change" in the late 1980s, the narrative presence of a Latino or Caribbean gay man functioned not only as "a means to comment on the revolution at hand" but also as a "reminder" of the necessity of structural changes within existing "social institutions and policies in order to accommodate and affirm the various differences between and among" the fiction's implied community of interpreters.[43]

Not only does Michael Carmine's Alberto perform this "tropical fruit" function, but his presence in *Longtime Companion* also augurs the particular roles gay Latino character would play within popular performances depicting gay male lives in the coming decade. In productions like *Philadelphia* and *Love! Valour! Compassion!*, the gay 1990s revolution looked toward not just life and liberty but also the pursuit of happiness, in the particular form of gay male couplehood—preferably with a fierce Latino boyfriend.

Dancing with Miguel, Ramon, and Angel

Philadelphia took a different tack in telling the AIDS story than did its most immediate predecessor, *Longtime Companion*. Perhaps chastened by the backlash against *Longtime Companion* (especially the perceived homogeneity and privilege of the film's all-white ensemble cast), direc- tor Jonathan Demme and screenwriter Ron Nyswaner took evident pains to frame *Philadelphia*'s story explicitly within a legibly racial framework of civil rights discourse. In the film, Tom Hanks plays Andy Beckett, a heretofore successful attorney in one of Philadephia's most prestigious law firms, who has been recently fired, he believes, because he has AIDS. Hanks's Beckett struggles to obtain legal representation for a planned discrimination suit (no one in town is willing to take on his powerhouse firm), which leads him to personal injury attorney Joe Miller (Denzel Washington). Joe's antipathy toward gays—along with fears regarding his possible exposure to Andy's illness—initially compels him to refuse the case. However, after a chance encounter with Andy in the law library (during which Andy's visibly escalating illness evinces biased treatment from the library's patrons and personnel), Joe recognizes the merits— both juridical and financial—of Andy's case, and he agrees to serve as his attorney. As the two men build and execute their (ultimately successful) case, they become friends. When Andy dies in the film's penultimate sequence, Joe's presence in the concluding circle of Andy's family and friends confirms the film's guiding interest in what the *New York Times'* Janet Maslin called the "hope and frustration [of] the promise of broth- erly love."[44]

Critical responses to *Philadelphia* marked a similar balance of hope and frustration. "*Philadelphia* breaks no new dramatic ground," observed film critic Roger Ebert. "Instead, it relies on the safe formula of the court- room drama to add suspense and resolution [and] uses the chemistry of popular stars in a reliable genre to sidestep what looks like controversy." While Ebert praised *Philadelphia*'s "righteous heart," *Entertainment Week- ly*'s Owen Gleiberman expressed frustration with the film's use of the "stuff of vintage courtroom films (and buddy flicks)" to craft a "liberal message movie" that both turns Andy's "legal battle into a stop-and-shop instructional tour of AIDS, homophobia, and American gay life" and "ends up asking us to care about homosexuals because they're dying, as if the fact that they're living weren't reason enough."[45] Most reviewers noted *Philadelphia*'s strategic deployment of Hollywood shorthand ("two major Hollywood stars—one black, one white—team up to fight AIDS") to effect a deft narrative alignment of the discrimination against gay men, whether on the basis of their sexual orientation or their presumptive "high risk" for HIV/AIDS, within a conventional cinematic rhetoric of civil rights. (Notably, Ebert compared *Philadelphia* to the 1967 drama about interracial marriage, *Guess Who's Coming to Dinner.*)

Fewer reviewers noted the ways in which Demme and Nyswaner also deployed this narrative within a familial emotional frame (already conventional within AIDS dramas on television), wherein coming out as a gay man with AIDS was also an act of coming home. Indeed, through the courtroom drama that drives *Philadelphia*'s narrative action, *Philadelphia*'s emotional arc enacts a story of familial reintegration, in which Andy Beckett's identity as a gay man, his couplehood with his "longtime companion" Miguel (portrayed by Antonio Banderas), and his gay community are all meticulously integrated within the Beckett family by the film's conclusion. Only a few reviews mentioned Antonio Banderas's featured presence and supporting performance as Andy's lover Miguel.

An established Spanish actor, previously known mostly for his central (and often highly sexual) roles in films by Pedro Almodóvar, Banderas's turn as Andy's lover marked only his second major role in a US film. Whereas critics took little note of Banderas's presence in the film, Tom Hanks made much of it. When confronted with boilerplate questions about what it was like for him as a straight actor to play a gay man, Hanks routinely deflected them with invocations of Banderas's exceptional good looks and sexual charisma. In *Newsweek* magazine, Hanks declaimed, "[I]t's bold for me to what? To play a man who goes to sleep in Antonio Banderas's arms? Who has sexual intercourse with him? . . . I look at Andy and Miguel together and I just think they're adorable. When they're dancing in their little sailor suits, I thought that was just the coolest thing."[46] To a syndicated columnist, he joked, "[L]et me tell you, to be able to dance with Antonio Banderas, I am the envy of, I understand 96 percent of the women in the world and, what, about 22 percent of the men?"[47]

Hanks refined this formulation when accepting that year's Golden

Globe for Best Actor in a Drama ("To be in love with Antonio Banderas—I'm the envy of men and women all over the world"), and he offered a more intimate variation when accepting the Oscar a few months later ("[Antonio Banderas], second to my lover, is the only person I would trade for"). Hanks's many rehearsals of Banderas's undeniable desirability elaborated director Jonathan Demme's rationale for casting Banderas in the first place. In a feature story in *The Advocate*, Demme affirmed that Banderas's charisma ("his appeal cuts across all preferences") would "make the chemistry [between Andy and Miguel] acceptable to a straight audience." The director explained, "I knew the women would adore seeing him . . . that gay males would adore seeing him. I was even confident that he's the kind of cool, cool guy that somehow even heteros could go 'He's handsome but I don't feel threatened.'"[48]

Banderas's casting did not rescript Andy's lover as Latin/o, however. As screenwriter Ron Nyswaner explained, "Miguel was written as a Hispanic for one simple reason: That's my sexual fantasy."[49] Nyswaner's frankness on this point confirms not only that the choice to make Andy's lover Latin/o was a foundational one, and not a "mere" happenstance of casting, but also that *Philadelphia*'s Miguel was meant to animate desire. Indeed, the consciousness of this choice—to script and cast an idealized gay Latin/o lover for *Philadelphia*'s white gay everyman—suggests that Banderas's Miguel is more central to the film than reviewers first apprehended. *Philadelphia* recasts Andy's privilege (a white man of substantive social, economic, and educational standing) as difference through his intimacies with men of color. The film's dramatic structure charts the developing professional relationship shared by Hanks's Andy and Washington's Joe, as the two—in a strategic and scrappy display of analytic competence—become partners in their pursuit of justice for Andy. Meanwhile, Banderas's Miguel offers charismatic confirmation of the fact that Hanks's Andy and Washington's Joe share a professional partnership, not the "other" kind. On the one hand, Andy's nonsexual intimacies with Joe ratify the righteousness of his aggressive pursuit of his own civil rights; on the other, Andy's tacitly sexual intimacies with Miguel amplify his difference as a sexual minority. Together, these intimate interracial relationships triangulate Andy's conspicuous privilege and recast it, making his queer difference legible within the particular optics of US multiculturalism in the 1990s.

But where *Philadelphia* uses Denzel Washington's Joe to see that Tom Hanks's Andy is fighting for his rights, it uses Antonio Banderas's Miguel to render gay male couplehood visible, as rooted in both desire and difference. Andy and Miguel may look "adorable," recalling Hanks's words, "when they're dancing in their little sailor suits," but they do not look the same. In this way, *Philadelphia* efficiently rehearses a core set of conventions for making gay couplehood legible, wherein the erotic charisma of the idealized gay Latin/o lover marks an on-stage same-sex pairing as a gay couple. As other scholars have asserted, the "Latin lover" is defined by an excess of both masculinity and femininity. His thrilling, romantic, flouncing flourish conceals the threat of the rapacious, forceful libido. But just as the Latin lover is both too macho and too feminine, so does he possess a bit too much ethnicity to be simply white.

The idealized gay Latin/o lovers of the early 1990s embody these excesses of both race and gender in ways that make gay couplehood newly legible for mainstream audiences. In some instances, like Banderas's Miguel in *Philadelphia* or (as we shall see) Yul Vazquez's Bob on the television show *Seinfeld*, the idealized gay Latin/o lover simply embodies the glancing thrill (or threat) of homosexual intimacy to confirm the fact that two male characters are in fact a gay couple. In other instances, like the character of Ramon in *Love! Valour! Compassion!* or Angel in *Rent*, an idealized gay Latin/o lover catalyzes the possibilities of and for gay male coupling in transformative ways.

Terrence McNally's play *Love! Valour! Compassion!* opened at the New York Theatre Workshop in the fall of 1994. The play, which was successfully transferred to Broadway for a two-year run (during which it won the Tony for Best Play), presents a poignant, comedic portrait of gay male intimate life in the AIDS era. In an ensemble of eight characters (whose lives and lifestyles bear hallmarks of privilege similar to those of the *Longtime Companion* ensemble of five years prior), Ramon's character stands somewhat apart. Ramon (who the *New York Times*' Vincent Canby characterized as "tough-talking, proudly gay . . . [an] aggressive Puerto Rican dancer on his way up," and who Michael Musto called "a raw pile of libido") stood out, not just as the only man of color but also as one of only two characters in their twenties.[50] As David Román has noted, Ramon bears the "mark of difference," in terms of his Latino ethnicity but also in terms of his age, which sets him up as a stage "representativ[e] of a generation who have come out into a gay public world already informed by AIDS."[51]

With extended sequences of scripted nudity and erotic encounter, Ramon's difference—in age, in ethnicity, in worldview—catalyzes conflicts within the play's constellation of friends, lovers, and fuck buddies. McNally uses Ramon both to embody and inspire carnality and to instigate the play's interrogation of what compels and contains the unruly erotics of gay male sexuality. As Santiago Castillanos has argued, Ramon functions as the play's (and subsequent 1997 film adaptation's) primary device "to construct and delimit boundaries around gay (homo) normativities."[52] For José Esteban Muñoz, Ramon evokes "the racist aura that envelopes the Latino body in the dominant white gay cultural imagination." Even more, though, the character of Ramon (as played by non-Latino actor Randy Becker, both on stage and on film) animates McNally's interrogation of which mode of gay male intimacy—friend or lover—might withstand the threat of mortality.[53] In *Love! Valour! Compassion!*, Ramon's myriad couplings unsettle the play's vision of gay male couplehood. As the play's resident gay Latin/o lover, Ramon's presence becomes the catalyst for some of its most searching questions about gay male intimacy.

A little more than a year later, another gay Latin/o lover took the stage at the New York Theatre Workshop to inspire a distinctively different vision of couplehood. Whereas *Love! Valour! Compassion!*'s Ramon called gay male couplehood into question, Angel Schunard called queer couplehood into being in Jonathan Larson's *Rent*. Originally presented in a limited three-week run at the New York Theatre Workshop, the musical soon became a phenomenon, quickly moving to Broadway—where it would play for more than a decade—and earning a raft of awards, including Tonys both for Best Musical and for Wilson Jermaine Heredia as Best Featured Actor in a Musical. Not unlike Ramon, Angel is a catalytic presence in *Rent*. Unlike Ramon, Angel is a gay Latino drag queen, living among a comparably destitute cohort of artists and activists on New York's Lower East Side. Early in the first act of the musical, Angel encounters Collins, who has just been assaulted. While tending to Collins's injuries, the two discover their shared HIV-positive status, as well as their immediate chemistry. This connection between Angel and Collins inaugurates the first of two ascending stories of new love (a third story details a couple's difficulty sustaining their relationship), which together provide the emotional through lines for *Rent*'s looping narrative arc. Throughout *Rent*, Angel walks between worlds, providing needed introductions, interventions, and infusions of much-needed cash. Angel's unexpected death is the event that impels both the disintegration of the ensemble's community and its subsequent reconstitution in the musical's final moments. But it is Angel and Collins's couplehood that recurrently reorients the musical's emotional certainty, and it is their love that contributes the musical's soaring love duet, "I'll Cover You."

Miguel, Ramon, and Angel—each in his own distinct way—catalyze performance narratives querying the importance of gay male couplehood.[54] In their varied ensembles, Miguel's, Ramon's, and Angel's Latinness contributes the legibility of their respective couplings with non-Latino partners, amplifying the differences among these male bodies in ways that clarify their legibility as erotic or romantic partnerships, not platonic ones. True, each characterization traffics in hoary stereotypes of the fierce and fearsome aspects of Latino masculinity, and yes, each relies on the familiar racializing conventions that film scholar David Van Leer has described as "cutting off" lesbians and gays of color "from all visible markers of communal experience or social environment," so that they might function as "deracinated images of white gay tolerance."[55] In all these ways, these idealized gay Latin/o lovers rehearse and ready the popular performance stage for Carlos, whose entrance in 1998 as Billy's favorite accessory promises to "celebrate diversity" and "put a little humour in the gay debate."[56]

The Brief Wondrous Life of Carlos the Doll

Though Carlos proved more popular, Billy was the first to "come out," which he did at the New York International Gift Fair in early 1997. Celebrated by Billy's creator and British fashion designer John McKitterick as "a crossover product with a lot of humor,"[57] the thirteen-inch fashion doll's debut was the product of more than three years of planning by McKitterick and a group of investors known as the "Friends of Billy" for the "successful marketing of the first truly gay product into the mainstream resulting in further gay visibility."[58] But McKitterick's grand ambitions and Billy's fifty-dollar recommended retail price were not the only sizable aspects of Billy's debut that gave spectators pause. A prominent "21 and over" sticker on the doll's packaging confirmed that the Billy was—in Totem International's phrasing—"anatomically complete." If his anatomical completeness made him the biggest boy on the boy-doll block, Billy had a platform to match. His creator's ambitions and the doll's attributes were concisely crafted into a single-sentence mission statement: Billy would "celebrate individuality, diversity, and at the same time getting a little bit of gay visibility onto the high street and into the media."

Totem International's intriguing media hook proved successful. Under a headline that read "When G.I. Joe Just Won't Do," *Newsweek* ran a photo of Billy (captioned "Sorry, Barbie") and opined, "There've been rumors about Ken for years, but Billy is being billed as the first openly gay doll."[59] *The Advocate* headlined its story "A Friend for Ken," and the Associated Press took a similar tack with "Move over, Ken, there's a new man on the block. But he's not going after Barbie."[60] Meanwhile, Knight-Ridder invoked yet another doll comparison as it observed, "Billy won't be a doll you'll find at the mass retailers. It seems they aren't exactly clamoring to be the first on the block to carry the world's first 'out and proud' gay doll. Not that Billy isn't politically correct. He exudes diversity. . . . What's equally amazing [is] that Billy is almost giving Tickle Me Elmo a run for the money."[61] By the end of the New York International Gift Fair, Billy, "The World's First Out and Proud Gay Doll," had indeed emerged as one of the influential trade show's biggest breakout stars, with the first five thousand dolls having sold within days of their delivery to stores. Totem International quickly prepared another twenty thousand Billys for the holiday season, which stirred another wave of hype. "Christmas sales of this sick new doll are already through the roof," ranted Ed Anger (a.k.a. Rafe Klinger), the longtime "My America" columnist for the reliably sensational tabloid *Weekly World News*: "Just what America's children need right now. A gay boy doll with an erection."[62]

But Billy was no overnight success. Conceived originally by fashion designer McKitterick "by chance" in 1992, Billy's bulging brawn was initially a two-dimensional template drawing, the fashion figure on which McKitterick would sketch various outfits. Before the end of 1993, McKitterick had sculpted his two-dimensional drawing into the first Billy doll, a one-of-a-kind creation that was auctioned for $275 at a London AIDS benefit in November 1994. In 1995 a group of investors (the "Friends of Billy") formed and commissioned a limited run of twelve more Billy dolls, each in its own handmade ensemble (all of which were quickly sold for several hundred dollars each).[63] Hoping that the doll might "provide a positive example of an out and proud gay man," Friends of Billy (in partnership with the US-based marketing company Totem International) sought a toy manufacturer able and willing to mass-produce an anatomically complete and gay-identified doll.[64] In 1996, after no stateside fabricator could be found, Totem International identified a European manufacturer capable of both producing and hand finishing the doll. In January 1997, McKitterick and his partner, Juan Antonio Andres, secured a copyright for the doll's design,[65] formed a new company called Totem International, and made final preparations for Billy's debut before "an unsuspecting but positively receptive American public" at the 1997 New York International Gift Fair. Throughout, designer

McKitterick celebrated Billy's ability to both introduce "a little humour into the gay debate" and "be a political tool," noting, "[Billy] can say a lot of things that people can't."[66]

At his debut, Billy wore the outfit that would be marketed as "San Francisco Billy"—cutoff jean shorts and an armless flannel shirt worn over a white Billy tee, with a string of freedom rings around his neck and the requisite red "AIDS ribbon" pinned to his chest. Billy fondly reflected on his "official 'coming out' outfit" as part of the "In the Closet" feature on the 1997 BillyWorld website, in which a naked Billy "answered" the question "What shall we wear today?" with unattributed first-person descriptions of each of his available-for-purchase outfits. His "San Francisco Billy" ensemble offered a "special tribute to . . . a beautiful city with an amazing attitude toward individuality and liberal thinking." Each of Billy's other marketed ensembles received similar descriptions. His "Master Billy" ensemble was an "outfit to play in," while his "Cowboy Billy" and "Sailor Billy" outfits were "all about fantasy and [making] me feel free and wanting fun. It's very liberating."[67]

Each of these ensembles outfit Billy in the "gay macho" tradition of gay masculine performance (codified in the 1970s as "clone" style), which, as Martin P. Levine has argued, enacts "a delicate interplay between straight imitation and variation," wherein gay men aspired to assure that "others would know they were not only real men, but real *gay* men."[68] Such an impulse to outfit one's outness with carefully queered accessories aligned neatly with the commercial imperatives of the boutiques and bookshops where Billy would soon be on display. By the end of 1997, these would include more than 170 merchandisers in thirty-five states, the District of Columbia, and eastern Canada. (In Alaska, Hawaii, Utah, or any of the other twelve states without an official Billy merchandiser, national mail-order retailers like the Tzabaco Catalog would answer the toll-free calls of would-be Billy buyers.)[69] Even as Brunet Billy, introduced in August 1997, Billy's apparent change of physical appearance is presented as just another accessory, explained in promotional language: "Billy has been known to dabble in the dye pot and is available either as a platinum blond or a brunet."[70] Perhaps unsurprisingly, Brunet Billy was introduced wearing a new outfit (sold separately as "Miami Billy," with a tank top, athletic shorts with "Billy" emblazoned on one leg, and slides), alongside "Billy Clothing" boxed sets featuring the four previously available costumes.

Roughly one year and seventy thousand Billys later, the first material testament to Billy's commitment to "diversity"—Carlos—appeared in gay and lesbian bookstores, gift stores, catalogs, on-line services, and fine erotic boutiques everywhere. Carlos was also thirteen inches tall and comparably complete. Totem International's reprinted publicity literature introduced Carlos with enthusiastic aplomb.

> FOR IMMEDIATE RELEASE: Stop burning up the phone, fax, and modem lines. The word is out and you read it here first. Billy has a new lover: a Latino named Carlos. The boys met back in May while on vacation in South Beach. When the two realized that they both live in New York, they exchanged numbers and got together when they got home. They've been inseparable ever since (although they've both kept their own apartments). Carlos is a native of Puerto Rico. He takes just as much care of his body as Billy. And he is every bit as endowed, with one slight cultural variation. What a difference.[71]

What a difference indeed. Billy is "The World's First Out and Proud Gay Doll"; Carlos is "The World's First Out and Proud Boyfriend."

Designer John McKitterick explained that the idea for Carlos came from the many Billy doll fans who "really wanted" the blond and blue-eyed Billy to have a Latino lover.[72] (That the Spanish entrepreneur Juan Antonio Andres was McKitterick's primary partner in the design and launch of BillyWorld remained a detail assiduously elided in McKitterick's promotional strategy.)[73] Instead, McKitterick and Totem International crafted Carlos's origin narrative as an affirmative action to confirm Billy's "politics," or BillyWorld's commodified celebration of diversity and inclusivity. Yet, while Billy was built and rebuilt over a period of approximately five years, Carlos went from idea to introduction in about one year. Additionally, while the celebration of diversity was central to Totem International's marketing of Billy from the outset, with Billy's own difference instantiating the idealized gay world of Billy, Carlos's bodily "difference" was sculpted within the doll's design.

Totem International's 1998 introduction of Carlos as "The World's First Out and Proud Boyfriend" codified the exotic erotics of Carlos's presence as a gay Latin/o lover for Billy. He was, as José Quiroga has noted, "that Latino guy endowed with a narrative as clear as his well-defined pecs."[74] Moreover, as constructed by Totem International, the 1998 Carlos doll wore the markings of Latino difference, through both his name (Carlos) and his "slight cultural variation" (found both in his foreskin and in his browner skin tone). Thus, even aside from its official narrative, Totem sculpted the doll to prompt perception of Carlos's

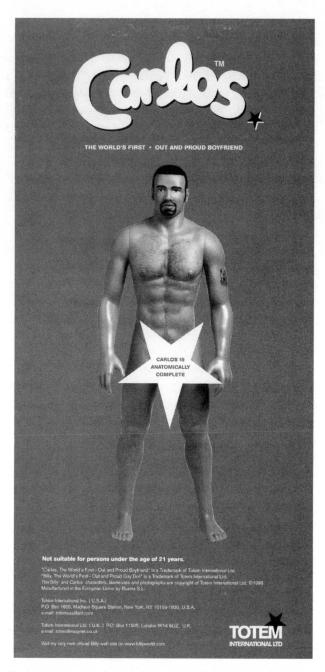

Carlos doll product insert, circa 1997. (Collection of the author)

Latino-ness within a matrix of subcultural visual codes readily circulated within sexually explicit gay male popular cultures of the 1990s.

Carlos's "one slight cultural variation," in particular, invokes the fetishization of the uncircumcised penis within US gay male sexual cultures since at least the 1970s. Cultural commentator Daniel Harris has argued that the foreskin became "a sacrosanct part of the penis" when "the faux prole" (or white gay "clone" of the 1970s) began to fetishize the foreskin "as a distinctive feature of lower class American men," presumptively as a result of the abrupt shift toward routine circumcision of male children born in US hospitals after World War II.[75] In addition to such cross-class fetishization, however, this particular erotic enthusiasm had, by the 1990s, developed a distinctively ethnic hue, especially as visual verification of Latino masculine authenticity. In a 1997 letter to the editor of *Hombres Latinos* magazine, "George from Springfield, Illinois," threatened to cancel his subscription because, "nearly all the models [in a recent issue] were not intact (i.e. cut). That makes them look like Anglos instead of Latinos." In their published response, *Hombres Latinos'* editors wrote, "[W]hile it's true that most Latino men are uncut, their ethnicity isn't a guarantee that they are uncircumcised and this by itself has not been an exclusionary factor for" the magazine.[76] Totem's design of Carlos's "slight cultural variation" confirmed that Carlos was literally cast from a different mold than Billy, while also invoking a particularly visual vocabulary to eroticize that difference. This set of choices compelled the editors of *QV* (a Los Angeles–based quarterly that became in 1997 the first nationally distributed magazine by, for, and about gay Latinos) to wonder whether "Carlos's uncircumcision is just another stereotype linked to (our) his cultural heritage. . . . Maybe it would have been fun to surprise us with each individual doll."[77]

Carlos wore his difference from Billy not only in his penile "cultural variation" but also in his skin tone. As cultural critic Donald Suggs noted, "[W]hile Barbie is best known for her costume changes, Billy's favorite accessory is his new boyfriend Carlos, a darker, slimmer, even better-selling (3 to 1) version of himself."[78] The fetishization of the Latino skin tone had more recently been formalized within the pornographic vernaculars of gay male popular performance. As one of the most successful gay videographers in the 1990s, Kristen Bjorn recalled, "[W]hen I started out there were very few Latin videos on the market. . . . So, it was assumed that everyone wanted to see blond models from California and nothing else. But I knew that I liked different kinds of guys and was interested in exotic locations. Luckily, as it turns out, other people liked that too."[79]

Bjorn's early still photographic work featuring nude South American models initially encountered resistance from American porn distributors. In Bjorn's account, distributors "thought that black or white was all right but what they didn't like were all the shades in between . . . [for] they felt that Americans were used to blacks and they were used to whites not to these other things that couldn't be categorized as either."[80] Bjorn's first full-length videos—all of which featured casts comprised of a diversity of Latin American and Latino performers and bore titles like *Carnaval in Rio* (1989), *Caribbean Heat* (1991), and *Manhattan Latin* (1992)—proved immediately successful and augured a new trend toward high production values in gay adult video. Even more, "Bjorn broke decisively with [gay erotica's] convention" of "racially segregated" casts, as Joe A. Thomas has argued, and he became known for "mixing attractive men of various races and ethnicities, and especially multiracial performers."[81] Bjorn's success spawned imitators, clarifying enthusiasm for what one gay adult video reviewer described as "guys with such perfect creme-caramel flesh tones that . . . is aesthetically pleasing as well as sexy."[82] In skin tone and sculpted detail, Carlos stimulated what Eduardo Contreras has critiqued as the depoliticized "color-crazed fascination" among white gay men.[83]

Carlos's thirteen-inch plastic frame thus confirms the sculpted contours of the fantasies that molded him. And, for Carlos, that fantasy world is called "BillyWorld." As José Quiroga affirms, "Carlos is always the one trying to assimilate into Billy's lifestyle."[84] Donald Suggs hails this construction in pointed detail: "[Carlos is] supposed to deliver the goods—in this case a goatee, painted-on chest hair, and a disproportionately large uncut cock—without having any real identity of his own."[85] Billy's world widens at the same pace as his wardrobe; when Carlos appears, he appears adjacent to Billy, as another accessory in Billy's open closet. Indeed, Vacation Carlos's t-shirt reads "no one knows my boyfriend is gay," while San Francisco Billy's t-shirt reads only "Billy." When attired in his "leather" outfit, Carlos was never sold as "Master Carlos" but always as "Leather Carlos" or "New York Carlos," with his studded armband consistently wrapped around his right bicep. (Meanwhile, the armband worn by "Master Billy" or "Leather Billy" was always wrapped around Billy's left, thus, subtly and subculturally cueing Carlos's position in service to Billy.)

On Carlos's introduction, Totem introduced a variety of matching ensembles for both Carlos and Billy. The dynamic duo appeared as firemen and cops (though Totem gave Carlos his badge long after Billy first appeared on the beat), as wrestlers and Santas (though Carlos's packaging labels him as "Feliz Navidad Carlos"), and as baseball players who share the same evocative jersey number ("69"), their pairing on the diamond "inspired by the international success [of] Mark McGwire and Sammy Sosa. . . . [But] don't ask who is the pitcher and who is the catcher."[86] Yet Wall Street Billy found no Wall Street Carlos, and Totem sent Billy, not Carlos, to the 1998 Gay Games. Also, notably, there is an inscription of Billy's name inside the tattooed heart on Carlos's bicep. About this, the *QV* editors wondered, "Wow, is that true commitment? [Or is] Carlos falling into a stereotype of being Billy's Latino 'Boy Toy'?"

The racial hegemony of Billy's world becomes not unlike what Erica Rand has described as Barbie's hegemonic whiteness, in which "diversity comes into play only when it does not entail significantly displacing white, blond Barbie." (Mattell's first Puerto Rican Barbie was introduced mere months before Carlos came out.)[87] Ann DuCille reminds us of the "difficulties and dangers of treating race and gender as biological stigmata that can be fixed in plastic and mass-reproduced" when such difference "is antimatter that continues to matter tremendously, especially for those whose bodies bear its visible markings and carry its material consequences."[88] So, even with a penis as thick as his own wrist (and longer than his own foot), Carlos wore his cultural variation in a way that appeared to naturalize his primary utility as Billy's gay Latin/o lover, confirming Billy's evident tolerance, while also securing Carlos's identity in relation only to Billy's. Within BillyWorld, Carlos existed for Billy, enriching Billy's landscape of erotic *and* cultural possibility, while also anchoring Billy's centrality as an idealization of a necessarily white gay everyman.

The year in which Billy got Carlos he also got the starring role in the first of what would be three elaborations of BillyWorld in distinct genres of gay male cultural production between 1998 and 2001. Released in the fall of 1998, the adult erotic feature film *Billy 2000: Billy Goes to Hollywood* staged what one reviewer called "an amusing series of vignettes in which various dolls come to life and have decidedly undoll-like sex."[89] *Billy 2000* adopted a conventional porn narrative structure, wherein an overarching fantasy scenario links five distinct, sexually explicit scenes. Throughout the eighty-five-minute film, the Billy and Carlos dolls function as talismanic objects of desire. In each sequence, a clerk in an adult bookstore sells a variety of Billy dolls to different white male customers. When a customer takes his Billy doll home, either Billy comes to life to actualize the customer's deepest erotic fantasy or the customer imagines himself manifesting as Billy. "The plot device," one reviewer noted, "has been done a hundred times before. . . . We see the doll, then we see a person wearing the same clothing as the doll, and then we see two guys having sex."[90] Only in the third of the video's five scenes does this plot vary: two customers (one white man and one man of color) enter the store, and the sales clerk's own idle fantasy transforms them into Master Billy and Leather Carlos, enacting an elaborate dominance-submission fantasy (and, remember, it's Master Billy). In *Billy 2000*, the pornographic fantasy of Billy exists for *either* identification or objectification, with Carlos manifesting literally (and explicitly) in service to Billy.

In contrast perhaps, the erotic picture book *Big Fun with Billy* (published in the summer of 2001) emphasized how Carlos enhanced Billy's world. Fine art photographer Dianora Niccolini's images contribute the pictographic novella's visual structure, with playwright David Leddick's rhymed verse providing its narrative. Deftly integrating Billy's appearance in each of his many ensembles, Leddick's text and Niccolini's images together depict BillyWorld's idealized landscape in which masculine, muscular beauty elides racial, cultural, and class distinctions. In Leddick's narrative, "Doll" becomes Billy's surname, and one day, Billy Doll takes off early from his Wall Street job and by chance meets Carlos ("We met at the gym / I know it's a cliché / But the moment I saw him / He blew me away"). The two return to Carlos's loft for an afternoon romp depicted in Niccolini's photographs ("'This thing I'd like to do . . . / I hope you are willing . . .' / 'I never bottom,' said Carlos, / 'But I bet you'd be filling"). The two neglect to exchange numbers, but Billy remains smitten with Carlos and determined to find him. When the two reconnect, Billy Doll changes everything "so Carlos won't escape" ("Once in love with Carlos I made a whole new plan / I quit my job, moved in with him, and became a New York fireman"). The pair then begins a buff, beautiful life in the big city. Even Tyson—the African American doll introduced in 1999 by Totem as "The World's First Out and Proud Best Friend—appears. With Tyson, ("We've made a new friend of the cop that walks our beat / A great-looking guy named Tyson—He really is quite neat"), Carlos and Billy start an erotic male revue ("The Masters"), which permits Niccolini to stage a variety of photographs of Tyson being platonically nude with his new "best friends." [91] Still, *Big Fun with Billy*'s narrative resolves with a visual montage of Billy and Carlos, posed in all the sexual positions two unjointed dolls might accomplish as Billy finally "submits" to Carlos ("You know love always changes—you're on top and then you're not / However it goes, we plan to love each other a lot").

The 112-page picture book concludes with Billy and Carlos in loving embrace, presumably commencing a life of happily ever after.[92]

With the 1999 debut of "Out and Proud Best Friend" Tyson, Totem International's third (and final) doll introduced another aspect of diversity into the BillyWorld pantheon. As the first African American doll to arrive in BillyWorld,[93] Tyson was introduced wearing two ensembles (Leather and Military). His presence in BillyWorld stirred some uncertainties. One newspaper account mused, "Collectors of the dolls are wondering whether Tyson—a TV reporter who dresses in leather on the weekends—will come between Billy and Carlos."[94] Likewise, Tyson's blackness also invoked the tradition of Barbie's black "friends" (such as Francie and Shani), as well as the queer reminder that the military man had been one of the two black Village People. More than his narrative, however, Tyson's name, in tandem with his shaved head and goatee, evoked two iconic black celebrities of the late 1990s: boxer Mike Tyson and model Tyson Beckford. When lawyers for both the boxer and the model confirmed that they were reviewing whether Totem's Tyson might infringe on the name and image of their respective clients, McKitterick denied that either had inspired the name of Billy's new best friend, asserting, "We wanted something that was African-American-sounding, but without being stereotypical."[95] Few other narrative elaborations of Tyson's presence in BillyWorld emerged. Media interest in Billy's novelty had definitely waned by late 1999. In *Big Fun with Billy*, which appeared a year or so after Tyson's introduction, Leddick does include a Tyson subplot, described above, thereby permitting Niccolini's photographs of Tyson being nude with his "best friends."[96]

Though Tyson's 1999 introduction promised to broaden BillyWorld's celebration of diversity even further, Totem International's apparent struggles in the early 2000s got in the way. Ambitious plans to launch BillyWorld.com as a retail lifestyle hub (featuring e-mail, shopping, and news platforms) seemed to stop abruptly with the burst of the "dot-com" bubble in early 2000. Although the threatened lawsuits over Tyson's name never materialized, Totem's release of "BPS Billy"—which featured Billy, Carlos, and Tyson delivering Totem packages while wearing brown uniforms with gold "BPS" insignia—elicited a forceful infringement challenge from United Parcel Service (UPS). In early 2002, Totem conceded the violation and stopped both production and distribution of "BPS Billy" and related products.[97] Totem International would not release another Billy product or tie-in after the 2001 release of "BPS Billy" and *Big Fun with Billy*.

At the same time, in the fall of 1999, other "adult" gay dolls entered the marketplace, including "amusing low-rent drag-queen" dolls launched by a start-up called Arsenic and Apple Pie (and arriving to market at the same time—but at half the price—as the drag versions of "Dolly Billy" and "Cha Cha Carlos").[98] By the time Tom of Finland's "Rebel" action figure hit the market in 2003 (boasting comparably prominent anatomical completeness but with more than fifteen points of articulation in contrast to Billy's five moving joints),[99] BillyWorld itself seemed frozen in time, with few updates to the company website from 2002 until the page lapsed entirely in 2005. Also, around 2002, John McKitterick ceased being Billy's human spokesperson, returning to his "day job" as head of the Fashion Design program at London's Kingston University, a position he would hold until (in the words of one observer) "vanish[ing] from the Internet" after the summer of 2004. Although online retailers and resellers continued to market the more than 250,000 total Billy items (dolls and accessories) released by Totem International between 1997 and 2001, the original UK copyrights for the dolls were allowed to lapse in 2007.[100] In the early 2010s, the BillyWorld.com domain was acquired by an Oregon-based company and relaunched as a men's shopping website "dedicated to all things manly."[101]

The history of the Carlos doll is reminiscent—in ways both straightforward and strange—of the longer parallel traditions of gay racial erotics and politics that, from time to time, cross circuits to provide an unpredictable jolt within gay male cultural production. In a 1990 essay published in the pioneering lesbian and gay journal *Out/Look*—which appeared just as *Longtime Companion* first arrived on the nation's movie screens—Jacqueline Goldsby presciently interrogated why "the lesbian and gay male communities figure race in such disparate ways," as she urged the necessity for an engaged "queer of color" critique (a call that would be powerfully answered within academe in subsequent decades). But it is Goldsby's elegant distillation of the conventional tension— "Dykes politicize [race], gay men eroticize it"—that has most guided my own thinking and prompted my construction of this genealogy of the gay Latin/o lovers of the 1990s.[102] Indeed, these gay Latin/o lovers document a distinctive moment within gay male cultural production in which gay male performance-makers sought to exploit both the erotic and the political charge of racial difference to prompt needed apprehensions of LGBT diversity during the AIDS era.

Beginning with Alberto and continuing through Miguel, Ramon, and Angel, the 1990s stock character of the gay Latin/o lover animated dis-

Cha Cha Carlos (Photograph by Ayami Bassett)

courses of desire, difference, and disease in ways both celebratory and defiant. Indeed, as Goldsby notes, "[E]roticizing difference is a nose-thumbing gesture of sorts against racial ideologies of power," but as the brief and wondrous life of Carlos the doll starkly confirms, the strategic manipulation of the racial erotics of power also "depends on accepting racial hierarchies as legitimate truth."[103] Still, the emergence of this group of gay Latin/o lovers in the 1990s documents a particular historical moment when performance-makers scripted gay Latin/o characters to embody the sexiness of political awareness, to be fierce in the face of fear.

Bob

So where did this boomlet in gay Latino characters in mainstream film and theatre productions go?

In the decades after Carlos came out, a gay Latino presence continued to be found in print cultures (especially academic and young adult literatures), as well as in independent film and Latina/o drama and performance. But gay Latino men were not seen with similar frequency on the popular performance platforms after the 1990s, with the possible exception of reality television programs like *RuPaul's Drag Race* and *Project Runway*. In the mainstream, even the gay Latin/o lover was—depending on how you look at it—either abandoned as no longer expedient or incorporated into the back catalog of Latino stock character types right in between the lady with the tutti-frutti hat and the Latino gang member.

One of the ways we can understand the introduction, portrayal, and subsequent "retirement" of gay Latin/o characters in popular performance is to consider Bob. Also emerging in the 1990s, Bob was played by Cuban American actor Yul Vazquez in the iconic 1990s television sitcom *Seinfeld*. *Seinfeld* introduced Vazquez's Bob a couple of years before the Billy doll even "came out" (and Bob's final appearance aired the same spring in which Carlos arrived on the scene). Bob thus exists squarely inside the historical moment where gay Latin/o characters emerged as special devices to animate empathy for gay male relationships as a civil rights issue. Bob on *Seinfeld* maps the gay Latin/o lover's stock character status from its discovery to its familiarity to its disposal. At the same time, Bob confirms that by the time of Carlos's arrival in 1998 the gay Latin/o lover's moment in the pop culture sun had already begun to pass.

Yul Vazquez played Bob as a fast-talking, thickly-accented man in three separate episodes between the fall of 1995 and the spring of 1998. Over the course of these three brief appearances in the *Seinfeld* universe, Vazquez's Bob reveals himself to be a man of intense passions (especially when it comes to antiques, AIDS activism, and his Puerto Rican cultural heritage) who enjoys a committed relationship with his white male partner (who is known first as Ray, and then as Cedric, but is portrayed in each appearance by white actor John Paragon). Vazquez's Bob first appears in the seventh season's legendary "Soup Nazi" episode (November 2, 1995), when *Seinfeld* regular Kramer (Michael Richards) is tasked with guarding an armoire on the sidewalk until delivery can be arranged. Vazquez's Bob spies the armoire and decides to take it ("Ai, it's gorgeous. . . . Pick it up from the bottom over there"). When Kramer objects, Vazquez's Bob becomes an emphatically masculine spitfire, his rapid line delivery colliding with the thickness of his accent, as if *West Side Story*'s Bernardo was possessed by Googie Gomez. Later in the episode, when Kramer and Jerry spy Bob and his companion window-shopping ("Oh wow look, that one is gorgeous/ I would just kill for that one"), a still traumatized Kramer approaches the couple only to be met by spitfire Bob ("Was you talking to him? Because you was talking to one of us. So what is it? Who?! Who was you talking to?!"), which causes both Kramer and Jerry to flee in the opposite direction as the episode ends. Although the scene was not initially scripted to require either that the armoire thieves be gay or that Bob be Latino, the question emerged during casting and rehearsal of "what kind of people would steal an armoire?," to which the creative team answered "tough gay guys."[104] Once the gayness of the thieves was confirmed (and some scripted knife- and gunplay dropped), Vazquez's physical attitude and verbal dexterity became Bob's quite effective weapons against Kramer's diffident complacency, leading to the pair being immediately referred to in *Seinfeld* lore as "gay thugs."[105]

Vazquez's Bob and Paragon's Cedric would make two additional appearances as *Seinfeld*'s "gay thugs," just a month later in "The Sponge" episode (December 7, 1995) and in the series' penultimate and notorious "The Puerto Rican Day" episode (May 7, 1998). In these second and third appearances, the "gay thug" bit was refined. In "The Sponge," Kramer participates in the annual AIDS Walk but refuses to wear the requisite ribbon, causing a ruckus that leads Kramer to accuse the organizer of being a "ribbon bully," after which his obstinacy elicits the attention of Bob ("Who? Who does not want to wear the ribbon?").[106] Bob and Cedric, along with a small mob, guide Kramer to an alleyway, encased *West Side Story* style by a chain link fence, as Kramer protests ("This is

America! I don't have to wear anything I don't want to wear.") and Bob insists ("I guess—We're just—going to have to teach him—to wear—the ribbon—!!!"). In the scene's final instant, Kramer's hand reaches out from the encircling crowd as, in the words of episode writer Peter Mehlman, "he actually [gets] beat up by gay thugs."[107]

By the third appearance, nearly three years later, the mere appearance of Vazquez's Bob with Paragon's Cedric at his side was enough to cue the episode's culminating joke ("Who! Who is burning the flag?!") as the pair leads a mob in pursuit of Kramer, who has inadvertently set the Puerto Rican flag ablaze during New York's Puerto Rican Day parade ("Maybe we should stomp you like you stomp the flag! What you think of that?!").[108]

Seinfeld's deployment of Vazquez's Bob offers peculiar confirmation of the particular importance of the gay Latin/o characters in mainstream popular performance in the early 1990s. Just as the compositors of *Longtime Companion, Philadelphia, Love! Valour! Compassion!, Rent,* and other productions used the presence of characters like Alberto, Miguel, Ramon, and Angel to prompt greater political consciousness and empathy, the *Seinfeld* writers used Vazquez's Bob to cue politically inflected sentiment, albeit in the mode of cynical backlash. Vazquez's satiric surrogation of the spitfire stock character becomes both fierce and fearsome as it animates an incremental affective assault on Kramer's complacent entitlement (first on the general question of confronting queerness, then on encountering politicized queerness, and finally in a collision with Latino cultural pride). Indeed, with Vazquez's Bob, the *Seinfeld* writers ingeniously exploited the incrementally legible utility of the gay Latin/o character as a device to hail the imperatives of diversity within an acid parody of the particular peer pressures of the multicultural 1990s. With each fiercely fearsome appearance in the *Seinfeld* universe, Vazquez's Bob exacerbates such "politically correct" tensions, not to advocate empathy but to mock such advocacy as gay thuggery.

Seinfeld's Bob cues the ease with which the "fierce" gay Latin/o lover—as both stock character and plot device—might be deployed to animate particular pleasures in popular performance, with and without any gesture toward diversity, inclusion, or tolerance. In the 2001 courtroom comedy film *Legally Blonde,* for example, a crucial plot point pivots on the testimony of the hot pool boy Enrique (Greg Serrano), who claims to have been the lover of the defendant. When Enrique upbraids her for her footwear choices ("Don't stomp your little last season Prada shoes at me, honey"), plucky law student Elle Woods (Reese Wither-

spoon) discerns Enrique's fashion connoisseurship as proof of his decep-
tion. Her insights lead to a brisk scene in which Enrique inadvertently
reveals his boyfriend's name ("Chuck") and backpedals ("I thought you
said 'friend'—Chuck is just a friend"), which compels Chuck to rise and
exclaim "You bitch!" before storming from the courtroom as Enrique
calls after him "Chuck, wait!" This quick reversal joke relies on the
excessive gender performance (fierce and fearsome) typical of the gay
Latin/o lover, even as it toys with the idea that such fierceness is all for
show, easily unveiled as a scam.

Some have pointed to Ricky Martin's ascendance in the summer of
1999 as the moment when the fantasy of the gay Latin/o lover jumped
its particular shark,[109] thereby evacuating the promise of social, cultural, and political transformation that seemingly new forms of visibility
so tauntingly implies. Yet, as *Seinfeld*'s Bob and *Legally Blonde*'s Enrique
remind us, the formalization of the conventions of the gay Latin/o lover as a ready punch line also augured the end of the peculiar 1990s
moment when the presence of a gay Latino character cued new conversations about diversity.

Epilogue

⌒⌒

On June 14, 1999, the *New Yorker* published a cartoon by longtime magazine contributor Jack Ziegler. As a regular cartoonist for the *New Yorker* since the early 1970s, Ziegler had long enjoyed his well-earned reputation as an "absurd gagman . . . who reveled in pop culture."[1] Ziegler's cartoon—published a couple weeks after Ricky Martin went "pop" on the cover of *Time,* and barely a month prior to *Newsweek*'s "Latin U.S.A." theme week—also addressed the "Latin Explosion" of the summer of 1999, albeit in a different register.

In the Ziegler cartoon, a small combo of musicians appears smiling, instruments at the ready, as the group's ostensible (and maraca-bearing) leader introduces the ensemble to its unseen audience: "A lot of you used to know us as the L.A. Punksters," the bandleader says. "Then for a while we were the Rappin' Rapmen. Now we call ourselves Los Latinos del Momento."[2] The joke of the cartoon is both simple and complex. The band is currently decked out in ruffle-sleeved dress shirts, embroidered slacks, carefully combed black hair, and matching mustaches—a stylized appearance that is their "new" look. Moreover, such a drastic metamorphosis of both musical and visual style does not appear to jeopardize the group's core audience base, a group of "fans" who appear to have previously weathered comparable transformations of this little band.

Ziegler's comic conceit in this single-panel cartoon draws on the wealth of "gags" to be derived from the absurdities discernible within shifting cultural styles. Yet Ziegler's mockery does not seem to be

"A lot of you used to know us as the L.A. Punksters. Then for a while we were the Rappin' Rapmen. Now we call ourselves Los Latinos del Momento."

Robert Ziegler's *Latinos del Momento.* **"A lot of you used to know us as the L.A. Punksters . . ."** *New Yorker,* **June 1999. (Reprinted by permission of Condé Nast, Inc.)**

addressed through any special cruelty to either "Los Latinos del Momento" or their current fans. Rather, as the band members assemble, grinning, ready to play (an apparently "pan-Latino" musical set given their possession of instruments like maracas, acoustic guitar, conga drums, and an accordion, each deriving from a distinct regional tradition of "Latin" music), Ziegler's comic barbs seem mostly directed toward the incoherence and incongruity resulting from conspicuous shifts in popular taste. Moreover, even as Ziegler ribs both the band and its accommodating fans for their aesthetic whims, the cartoon seems also to admire this combo's creative dexterity, its capacity to "keep up" with the rapidly shifting literacies obliged by the contemporary cultural scene.

For my purposes, however, the Ziegler cartoon also distills the core questions that arise when any performance-maker opts to "play Latino." Ziegler's "Los Latinos del Momento" (literally translated as "The Latins of the Moment") embody the perpetual novelty status so frequently accorded Latinos in US pop culture. Ziegler's "Latins of the Moment" gag knowingly manipulates many cultural and racial genealogies embedded within the archive of US popular performance. Drawing (literally) on the utility of "type" (in contradistinction to "stereotype"), Ziegler scripts an astute laugh from the incongruous pleasures of the sophisticated manipulation of legible ethnoracial types in performance and the fetishization of the authentic in US popular entertainment. At the same time, Ziegler's cartoon tacitly underscores how the pleasures of performed Latin-ness in US popular performance are frequently at a distance from the lives and cultures of "actual" Latinos. Most especially, however, I find the putative, racially hybrid genealogy of "Los Latinos del Momento" themselves to be a provocative iteration of some of the core themes of this project. The particular visual and aural cues—including the outfits and musical instruments—of the performative Latin-ness of "Los Latinos del Momento" also expediently distinguish their "Latin" performance from more conventionalized tropes of racial distinction. Put another way, the "Latin-ness" of "Los Latinos del Momento" is always already all about performance. Indeed, even as "Los Latinos del Momento" reference ostensibly Latino culture and history, their "performance" helps to conventionalize the tropes cueing "Latin-ness" in the contemporary cultural context. This "Latin bandleader" introducing "Los Latinos del Momento" at century's end is not unlike the Californian "border daughters" of the early twentieth century or Broadway's midcentury "Latino gang member." All stand as racializing stock characters whose conventionalization animates "new" nodes in the cultural genealogy in which Latins have intermittently "exploded" within US popular performance.

The Ziegler cartoon also demonstrates an acute lucidity about the idiosyncratic location of Latinos within the layered histories of racialized performance. Indeed, Ziegler's "Los Latinos del Momento" are situated within—but also beyond—a legible genealogy of whiteness and blackness. Prior to their ruffled-sleeve present, Ziegler's "Los Latinos" were—we are amusedly to believe—first the "L.A. Punksters" and then the "Rappin' Rapmen." In a single panel of less than thirty words, Ziegler's cartoon thus efficiently stages an ironic narrative of ethnoracial accession and inclusion in which the arrival of "Los Latinos" on the cultural stage has (always) already been framed by an ostensive musical, cultural, and racial polarity of whiteness and blackness. Moreover, the heightened performance of "Los Latinos," in imaginative retrospect, underscores how the ostensibly "authentic" previous performances of whiteness ("L.A. Punksters") and blackness ("Rappin' Rapmen") were themselves performative constructions of both musical and racial identities. The comedic disruption of racial distinction mobilized in the cartoon panel—first "Los Latinos" were white, then they were black, now they are Latin—stages the absurdities of racial distinction while also enacting their purchase within US popular performance.

Ziegler's deft narrative of ethnoracial accession also tacitly underscores the most elusive aspect of each "Latin explosion" in US popular performance. In this way, "Los Latinos del Momento" cue the historical specificity of each "Latin explosion." Like "Los Latinos del Momento," each "Latin explosion" is fundamentally of its moment. Unlike the "L.A. Punksters" or "Rappin' Rapmen"—whose cultural, historical, and racial referents remain fairly secure, even as they have receded into the combo's past—"Los Latinos del Momento," with a giddy yet poignant clarity, bear within their new moniker the promise of their own obsolescence. The contemporary moment that cues "Los Latinos del Momento" to begin playing will soon pass, and they will almost certainly be playing something other than Latino shortly.

Latin Numbers has sought to reach beyond the discourse of stereotype to plumb the archive of popular performance and to chart the peculiar history of how the repertoires of "playing Latino" were conventionalized during the twentieth century. Whether enacted within a musical extravaganza or danced by Latino gang members or coming out with a gay Latin/o lover, each of the case studies in *Latin Numbers* confirms how the history of Latinos in US popular performance defies conventional explanations of historic exclusion and incremental inclusion, of inaccuracies and inauthenticities. Rather, these disparate modes of "playing Latino" cast the contours of Latina/o raciality in the United States in twentieth-century US popular performance. Whether entertaining or appalling, these seemingly idiosyncratic performances of "Latin-ness" in which US Latinos "pop" onto the mainstream scene are also pivotal cultural moments wherein US popular performance has relied on Latina/o performers and Latina/o characters to rehearse the restructuring of broader structures of racial distinction in the United States. Indeed, the "Latin numbers" may come and go with the cultural breezes, but the historical impact of "playing Latino" on the stages of US popular performance endures.

Notes

Prologue

1. The accompanying article is "It's Your Turn in the Sun," *Time*, October 16, 1978, 51–55.

2. "*¡Magnifico!* Hispanic Culture Breaks Out of the Barrio," *Time*, July 11, 1988, 49–66.

3. *Time*, May 24, 1999, 76.

4. The accompanying article is John Leland and Veronica Chambers, "Generation Ñ," *Newsweek*, July 12, 1999, 5, 52–61.

5. For a thoughtful assessment of De La Hoya's cultural significance, see Fernando Delgado, "Golden but Not Brown: Oscar De La Hoya and the Complications of Culture, Manhood, and Boxing," *International Journal of the History of Sport* 22 (March 2005): 196–211.

6. Diogenes Cespedes and Silvio Torres-Saillant, "Fiction Is the Poor Man's Cinema: An Interview with Junot Díaz," *Callaloo* 23 (Summer 2000): 892–907.

7. María Elena Cepeda offers a thorough assessment of Shakira in "Shakira as the Idealized, Transnational Citizen: A Case Study of Colombianidad in Transition," *Latino Studies* 1 (July 2003): 211–32.

8. Leland and Chambers, "Generation Ñ," 5.

9. Provocative scholarly assessments of Jennifer Lopez's star persona can be found in Isabel Molina-Guzmán and Angharad N. Valdivia, "Brain, Brow, and Booty: Latina Iconicity in U.S. Popular Culture," *Communication Review* 7 (April–June 2004): 205–21; as well as Frances Negrón-Mutaner, "Jennifer's Butt," *Aztlán: A Journal of Chicano Studies* 22 (Fall 1997): 182–95.

10. Juan Flores, "Nueva York, Diaspora City: Latinos between and Beyond," in *Bilingual Games: Some Literary Investigations*, ed. Doris Sommer (New York: Palgrave Macmillan, 2003), 69–75.

11. *Saturday Night Live*, episode 465, May 8, 1999, NBC, directed by Beth McCarthy Miller, written by Tina Fey (head writer).

12. For an especially critical view of what he calls 1999's "LatPop" moment, see Stephen W. Bender, "Will the World Survive: Latino/a Pop Music in the Cultural Mainstream," *Denver University Law Review* 78 (2000–2001): 719–52. See also Ed Morales, *The Latin Beat: The Rhythms and Roots of Latin Music, from Bossa Nova to Salsa and Beyond* (Cambridge, MA: Da Capo Press, 2003), especially 157–65.

13. Philip J. Deloria, *Playing Indian* (New Haven, CT: Yale University Press, 1998); Henry Bial, *Acting Jewish: Negotiating Ethnicity on the American Stage and Screen* (Ann Arbor: University of Michigan Press, 2005).

14. Deloria, *Playing Indian,* 7; Bial, *Acting Jewish,* 3.

15. Deloria, *Playing Indian,* 3.

16. Bial, *Acting Jewish,* 13–14.

17. Vicki Ruiz, "Nuestra América: Latino History as United States History," *Journal of American History* 93 (December 2006): 656.

18. As I began this work in earnest, David Román, José Esteban Muñoz, and Alberto Sandoval-Sánchez had each published monographs directly engaged with the queer complexities of Latina/o popular entertainment and performance. As I continued my work, Michelle Habell-Palan, Clara Rodriguez, Angharad N. Valdivia, and William Nericcio published volumes that each, in very different ways, proved indispensable to my own work. Then, as I was completing the first full iteration of my manuscript, Frances Negrón-Mutaner, David Román (again), and Deborah Paredez published exemplary inquiries that raised the methodological bar. Then, in the last handful of years, adventurous works by Ramón H. Rivera-Servera, Mary Beltrán, Priscilla Peña Ovalle, Lawrence La Fountain-Stokes, and Isabel Molina-Guzman, along with Michael Hames-Garcia and Ernesto Javier Martínez's" transformative anthology *Gay Latino Studies: A Critical Reader* (Durham, NC: Duke University Press, 2011), have stimulated and challenged my own intellectual purpose as I have listened for what my particular voice might add to the broader conversations about Latinas/os, popular culture, and the media.

19. This definition follows the one offered by pioneering cultural historian Lawrence W. Levine. See Lawrence W. Levine, *The Unpredictable Past: Explorations in American Cultural History* (New York: Oxford University Press, 1993), 296. See also Lawrence W. Levine, "The Folklore of Industrial Society: Popular Culture and Its Audiences," and the *American Historical Review* forum it led in *American Historical Review* 97 (December 1992): 1369–1430.

20. David Román discusses the "romance with the indigenous" in the introduction to his *Performance in America: Contemporary U.S. Culture and the Performing Arts* (Durham, NC: Duke University Press, 2005), 35–37.

21. Henry Jenkins offers a complementary critique of the scholarly predisposition to diminish the popular in monolithic terms when he observes, "Popular culture has enjoyed complexity and diversity throughout its history; it is simply that most intellectuals lack the knowledge and competency to consume it with any real appreciation." Henry Jenkins, *The Wow Climax: Tracing the Emotional Impact of Popular Culture* (New York: New York University Press, 2007), 3.

22. Performance studies, almost since its inception as an academic interdiscipline, has adopted the notion of "liveness" as a constitutive feature of its subject of study. The notion of the "live" configures performance as an engine ignited by the animating presence of a spectator and clarifies performance as a mode of cultural experience instead of an apparatus of representation. In the early 1990s, performance theorist Peggy Phelan influentially configured the live as fundamental to the very essence—or

ontology—of performance. Phelan argues that "performance's only life is in the present. Performance cannot be saved, recorded, documented, or otherwise participate in the circulation of representations of representations: once it does so, it becomes something other than performance." This view of liveness—distilled by Phelan but explicitly and implicitly embraced by a wide range of performance scholars—remains perhaps the constitutive feature of what makes a cultural expression "performance." Even performance theorists like Philip Auslander, who are critical of such notions of liveness, tend to frame the discussion in terms of the spectator's experience of the performance as an intrinsically representational event. Peggy Phelan, *Unmarked: The Politics of Performance* (New York: Routledge, 1993), 146. For criticism of Phelan's privileging of the live, see Philip Auslander, *Liveness* (New York: Routledge, 1999).

23. My interpretive strategies in approaching popular performance have been greatly influenced by the work of Richard Dyer, especially as anthologized in his *The Culture of Queers* (New York: Routledge, 2002); *The Matter of Images: Essays on Representation* (New York: Routledge, 1993); and *Only Entertainment* (New York: Routledge, 2002). Most recently, my intermedial approach has been fortified by the interdisciplinary approach to cinematic performance enacted by Cynthia Baron and Sharon Marie Carnicke in *Reframing Screen Performance* (Ann Arbor: University of Michigan Press, 2008); as well as the exuberantly humane strategies of Henry Jenkins in *The Wow Climax*. Baron, Carnicke, and Jenkins all build from the critical principles of dramatic and performance theory as they approach, with interdisciplinary grace, mostly mediated popular performances.

24. Here I am thinking especially of Henry Bial, Kirsten Pullen, and Nick Salvato, as well as Anthea Kraut, Ariel Osterweiss, and Judith Hamera.

25. Nicholas De Genova and Ana Y. Ramos-Zayas, "Latino Racial Formations in the United States: An Introduction," *Journal of Latin American Anthropology* 8, no. 2 (2003): 2.

26. For an instructively simple discussion of terminology issues in Latino studies, see John S. Christie and José B. Gonzalez, "Introduction," in *Latino Boom: An Anthology of U.S. Latino Literature*, ed. John S. Christie and José B. Gonzalez (New York: Longman and Pearson Education, 2006), 1–5.

27. Alberto Sandoval-Sánchez, *"José, Can You See?" Latinos On and Off Broadway* (Madison: University of Wisconsin Press, 1999), 14–15.

28. Frances R. Aparicio and Susana Chávez-Silverman, "Introduction," in *Tropicalizations: Transcultural Representations of Latinidad*, ed. Frances R. Aparicio and Susana Chávez-Silverman (Hanover, NH: Dartmouth College Press, 1997), 3.

29. "Newest Americans: A Second Spanish Invasion," *U.S. News and World Report*, July 8, 1974, 35.

30. For a history of Latinos in the US racial system of classification, see Clara Rodriguez, *Changing Race: Latinos, the Census, and the History of Ethnicity in the United States* (New York: New York University Press, 2000), especially 3–26.

31. My racial approach to immigration history is informed both by Matthew Frye Jacobson's foundational text *Whiteness of a Different Color: European Immigrants and the Alchemy of Race* (Cambridge, MA: Harvard University Press, 1998); and by Mae M. Ngai, *Impossible Subjects: Illegal Aliens and the Making of Modern America* (Princeton, NJ: Princeton University Press, 2004).

32. Michael Omi and Howard Winant, *Racial Formation in the United States: From the 1960s to the 1990s* (New York: Routledge, 1994), 55–56.

33. Ibid., 64.

34. Sarah Chinn, "Racialized Things," *American Quarterly* 64, no. 4 (December 2012): 874.

35. Jon McKenzie, *Perform or Else: From Discipline to Performance* (New York: Routledge, 2001), 18.

Chapter 1

1. Karin Adir, *The Great Clowns of American Television* (Jefferson, NC: McFarland, 1998), 146. Most versions of this narrative borrow from the one presented in Kaye's authorized biography, Kurt Singer, *The Danny Kaye Story* (New York: Thomas Nelson and Sons, 1958), 75–79.

2. Bruce D. McClurg, *Lady in the Dark: Biography of a Musical* (New York: Oxford University Press, 2006), 87.

3. "Vaudeville: Danny Kaye at $1,500 Plus % in N.Y. Nitery," *Variety*, March 19, 1941, 45.

4. John Storm Roberts, *The Latin Tinge: The Impact of Latin American Music on the United States* (New York: Oxford University Press, 1979), 82.

5. Roberts, *The Latin Tinge*, 86. Gustavo Pérez Firmat, "Latunes: An Introduction," *Latin American Research Review* 43, no. 2 (2008): 184; John Storm Roberts, *Latin Jazz: The First of the Fusions, 1880s to Today* (New York: Schirmer Books, 1999), 64.

6. As a general rule, with regard to my use of the term *Latin number,* I reserve the use of quotation marks for those instances describing the recurring historical phenomenon of cultural fascination with (and subsequent discard of) Latina/o presence within US popular performance.

7. Although my use of the term *disidentification* here clearly evokes Judith Butler's use of it to discuss the politics of misrecognition, my application is more fully consonant with José Esteban Muñoz's redeployment of it to describe how resistant cultural practice "scrambles and reconstructs the encoded message of a cultural text in a fashion that both exposes the encoded message's universalizing and exclusionary machinations and recircuits its workings to account for, include, and empower minority identities and identifications." Although my application of Muñozian disidentification does not precisely align with the project of queers of color critique, I apply it here to excavate the practice's complex antecedents within the archive of US popular performance. See Judith Butler, *Bodies That Matter: On the Discursive Limits of Sex* (New York: Routledge, 1993) especially 219; and José Esteban Muñoz, *Disidentifications: Queers of Color and the Performance of Politics* (Minneapolis: University of Minnesota Press, 1999), especially 31.

8. Bert O. States, *Irony and Drama: A Poetics* (Ithaca, NY: Cornell University Press, 1971), 111–38, especially 126–32.

9. Thanks go to Joseph Meissner, Cusi Cram, Tanya Dean, and Gregory S. Moss for confirmations of Vogel's pedagogy.

10. I am paraphrasing Bryce Wood, *Dismantling the Good Neighbor Policy* (Austin: University of Texas Press, 1985), ix.

11. My understanding of the Good Neighbor policy is guided by Fredrick B. Pike's comprehensive *FDR's Good Neighbor Policy: Sixty Years of Generally Gentle Chaos* (Austin: University of Texas Press, 1995). See also George Black, *The Good Neighbor: How the United States Wrote the History of Central America and the Caribbean* (New York: Pantheon, 1988).

12. For a summary of the range of activities encouraged on Pan-American Day, see

Harriet McCune Brown and Helen Miller Bailey, *Our Latin American Neighbors* (New York: Houghton Mifflin, 1944), especially 436–45, 456, and 461.

13. Adrián Pérez Melgosa, "Opening the Cabaret America Allegory: Hemispheric Politics, Performance, and Utopia in *Flying Down to Rio*," *American Quarterly* 64, no. 2 (June 2012): 253.

14. Pike, *FDR's Good Neighbor Policy*, 253. For a discussion of Nelson Rockefeller, see especially 252–54.

15. For an excellent recent summary of OCIAA activities and their legacy in providing a model for subsequent efforts toward cultural diplomacy, see Justin Hart, *Empire of Ideas: The Origins of Public Diplomacy and the Transformation of U.S. Foreign Policy* (New York: Oxford University Press, 2013), 14–40.

16. Michael Denning, *The Cultural Front: The Laboring of American Culture in the Twentieth Century* (New York: Verso, 1998), 296.

17. Glenn Collins, "Harold Rome, 85, Writer of Socially Pointed Songs," *New York Times*, October 27, 1993.

18. Stanford University Dramatists' Alliance, *Bulletin of the Dramatists' Alliance* (Palo Alto, CA: Stanford University, 1940): 29.

19. Harold Rome, interview with Llewellyn H. Hedgebeth, May 2, 1973, Biographical Materials, 1961–1968, Box 49, Folder 1, Miscellaneous Items, Harold Rome Collection, Sterling Music Library, Yale University, New Haven, Connecticut (hereafter, HRC).

20. Harold Rome, "Got an Idea, Mister?," undated manuscript, Biographical Materials, 1961–1968, Box 49, Folder 3, Miscellaneous Items, HRC.

21. Firmat, "Latunes," 191.

22. "News of the Stage," *New York Times*, May 15, 1941.

23. Though mostly remembered today as a novelist, Erskine Caldwell was also notable among the southern writers of the period for what one biographer terms his "leftist political activity, which grew out of his social concern." Wayne Mixon, *The People's Writer: Erskine Caldwell and the South* (Charlottesville: University of Virginia Press, 1995), 157. For an efficient index of the range of Caldwell's affiliations and activities on the American Left, see Michael Denning's multiple mentions of Caldwell in *The Cultural Front*, especially 212 and 263.

24. Harold Rome, "Be a Good Neighbor," undated typewritten lyric, Box 49, Folder 134, HRC.

25. For an apt discussion of the concept of the "prestige film" and how it might apply to the Welles project, see Chris Cagle, "Two Modes of Prestige Film," *Screen* 48 (Autumn 2007): 291–311.

26. My discussion of "Give a Viva" is drawn from the dozen or so typewritten lyrics noted as components of the piece, which are interspersed throughout Box 49, Folders 134–141, HRC.

27. Gerald Bordman, *American Theatre: A Chronicle of Comedy and Drama, 1930–1969* (New York: Oxford University Press, 1996), 206.

28. Brooks Atkinson, "*Viva O'Brien* Adds Swimming Pool to the Usual Comforts of Musical Comedy," *New York Times*, October 10, 1941. See also Bordman, *American Theatre*, 585.

29. Vesta Kelley, "New Broadway Show Has a Great Ballet with Odd Effects," *St. Petersburg Independent*, October 15, 1941, 7.

30. *New York Critic's Theatre Reviews* (New York: Critics Theatre Reviews, 1941), 271–73.

31. Quoted in Peter H. Smith, *Talons of the Eagle: Dynamics of U.S.–Latin American Relations* (New York: Oxford University Press, 2000), 82.

32. Quoted in Allen L. Woll, *The Latin Image in American Film* (Los Angeles: Latin American Center Publications, University of California, Los Angeles, 1980), 55.

33. For a thorough summary of Disney's work during these years, see J. B. Kauffman, *South of the Border with Disney: Walt Disney and the Good Neighbor Program, 1941–1948* (New York: Disney Editions, 2009); as well as the original 1942 documentary film *South of the Border with Disney* (dir. Norman Ferguson) and the more recent documentary *Walt and El Grupo* (2008; dir. Theodore Thomas). For the best critical excavation of Disney in this era, see the work of Eric L. Smoodin, including both *Animating Culture: Hollywood Cartoons from the Sound Era* (New Brunswick, NJ: Rutgers University Press, 1993); and his edited volume, *Disney Discourse: Producing the Magic Kingdom* (New York: Routledge, 2013).

34. "Let Freedom Sing—Music and Lyrics Mostly by Harold Rome," Box 83, Folder 17, HRC. See also Betty Garrett's account of the production in her *Betty Garrett and Other Songs: A Life on Stage and Screen* (Lanham, MD: Madison Books, 1999), 59–60.

35. Robert Kimball and Linda Emmett, *The Complete Lyrics of Irving Berlin* (New York: Hal Leonard Collection, 2005), 158.

36. Joshua Logan, *Movie Stars, Real People, and Me* (New York: Delacorte Press, 1978), 158–73.

37. For one indication of the ubiquity of drag Carmen Mirandas, see the many mentions of them in Allan Bérubé, *Coming Out under Fire* (New York: Simon & Schuster, 2000), 67, 85, and especially 89.

38. I draw my understanding of both *Skirts* and *Stars and Gripes* from the clippings and programs included in the Harold Rome Collection, Box 83, Folders 16 and 17, HRC.

39. Steven Suskin, *Show Tunes: The Songs, Shows, and Careers of Broadway Major Composers* (New York: Oxford University Press, 2000), 196.

40. Harold Rome, "Manuscript Playscript for Call Me Mister," Box 56, Folder 6, HRC. See also Betty Garrett's account in *Betty Garrett and Other Songs*, 77–80.

41. Following the song's commercial release, Rome confirmed in a variety of newspaper profiles—including ones in the *New Haven Register* and *Hartford Times*—that "he had written it three years before" and "included the number apologetically" and "with some misgiving." Clipping files (probably from a clipping service), Harold Rome Collection, Box 85, Folder 15, HRC.

42. See for example "Call Me Mister," *Life*, May 27, 1946, 131–37; "Top Song Hits," *Life*, October 21, 1946, 94; and "South America . . . Take It Away!," *Dance*, June 1946, 29.

43. Robert Francis, "Donaldson Awards Winners," *Billboard*, August 3, 1946, 1.

44. "Xavier Cugat–Buddy Clark," *Billboard*, July 20, 1946, 32.

45. "Billboard's First Annual Music Record Poll," *Billboard*, January 4, 1947.

46. Alberto Sandoval-Sánchez, *José, Can You See? Latinos On and Off Broadway* (Madison: University of Wisconsin Press, 1999), 43; Firmat, "Latunes," 191.

47. Martha Schmoyer LoMonaco, *Every Week, a Broadway Revue: The Tamiment Playhouse, 1921–1960* (Westport, CT: Greenwood Press, 1992), 88–90. See also Bordman, *American Theatre*, 569.

48. This archly cynical turn away from the purported pleasures of Latin styles also manifested in the United Kingdom around the same time. As but one example, consider Noël Coward's patter song "Nina" as originally introduced in the hit 1945 West

End revue *Sigh No More.* The song's titular "Nina" disidentifies from the Latin dance craze by both refusing to participate ("Señorita Nina, from Argentina, knew all the answers / Though her relatives and friends were perfect dancers / She swore she'd never dance a step until she died") and offering a critique of the craze for all things Latin in popular cinema ("She said, 'I've seen too many movies, and all they prove is too idiotic. / They all insist that South America's exotic / Whereas it couldn't be more boring if it tried'"). Noël Coward, *Noël Coward: The Complete Lyrics,* ed. Barry Day (Woodstock, NY: Overlook Press, 1998), 222–24.

49. For an account of Arnaz's parody, see Cy Wagner, "Chicago, Chicago," *Billboard,* June 28, 1947. My account of Rome's song comes from Harold Rome, "Up North American Way (South America Strikes Back)," undated typewritten lyric (two versions), Box 71, Folder 141, HRC.

50. Eileen McKenney's biographer, Marion Meade, notes, "While Ruth's humorous anecdotes could be called true, they were not necessarily accurate." Meade's book provides the narrative context for my own observations. Marion Meade, *Lonelyhearts: The Screwball World of Nathaniel West and Eileen McKenney* (New York: Houghton Mifflin, 2010), 232.

51. Ruth McKenney, "Beware the Brazilian Navy," *New Yorker,* July 10, 1937, 28, 30, 32–35.

52. Meade, *Lonelyhearts,* 223–35, especially 229.

53. The legal travails of the radio adaptation of *My Sister Eileen* began around 1947 and continued until 1953. "'Irma' Held No Steal on 'Sister Eileen,'" *Billboard,* January 31, 1948, 9; "CBS, Others Face $3 Million Damage Suit," *Billboard,* September 19, 1953, 3. The radio troubles also quashed an early attempt at a television pilot. "Schubert Preps 'Quick as Flash' for TV Peddle," *Billboard,* June 17, 1950, 6.

54. *Dramatics* magazine (a publication of the International Thespian Society, targeted to high school theatre directors and participants) regularly included features mentioning *My Sister Eileen* in the later 1940s and early 1950s, including a detailed 1949 feature on staging the play in a high school or college setting. Jack Palangio, "Staging *My Sister Eileen*," *Dramatics,* October 1949, 14–15. Identified as the head of drama-speech at Iowa Wesleyan College, Palangio notes that "since the naval cadets are Latins, it would be well to make the selection from the darker complexioned boys." *Dramatics* also lists *My Sister Eileen* as among the "most frequently produced full-length plays by Thespian affiliated schools" each year between 1958 and 1963. The play would also see extensive production in community theatres, including a black-cast production at Oak Bluffs on Martha's Vineyard in 1958. See "Gerri Major's Society," *Jet,* September 18, 1958, 38.

55. In interesting ways, McKenney's narrative in "Beware the Brazilian Navy" offers a grotesque burlesque of the conventional scene of a dance encounter staged in *Flying Down to Rio* (1933), as discussed by Adrián Pérez Melgosa in "Opening the Cabaret America Allegory," 249–75.

56. All quotes are from the *New Yorker* story (1937), which was reprinted nearly exactly in Ruth McKenney, *My Sister Eileen* (New York: Harcourt, Brace, 1938), 211–26.

57. For a brief account of the compositional process, see Charlotte Greenspan, *Pick Yourself Up: Dorothy Fields and the American Musical* (New York: Oxford University Press, 2010), 112.

58. All quotes are from the playscript by Joseph Fields and Jerome Chodorov, *My Sister Eileen* (New York: Random House, 1941), 122–32, 160–63.

59. Quotations were transcribed from the film *My Sister Eileen* (1942; dir. Alexander Hall, Twentieth Century Fox).

60. The idea for the musical version is widely acknowledged to have come from Russell herself. See, for example, Dennis McDougal, *The Last Wasserman, MCA, and the Hidden History of Hollywood* (New York: Da Capo Press, 2001), 198.

61. Lyrics and other quotations are from Joseph Fields and Jerome Chodorov, with Betty Comden and Adolph Green, *Wonderful Town: A New Musical Comedy* (New York: Random House, 1953).

62. References to the film are from *My Sister Eileen* (1955; dir. Richard Quine, Twentieth Century Fox).

63. "Town House, L.A.," *Variety*, November 27, 1946, 54.

64. Firmat, "Latunes," 180–81.

65. See David Van Leer's discussion of the conflation of gender and ethnicity in the musicals of the 1950s in *The Queening of America: Gay Culture in Straight Society* (New York: Routledge, 1995), 166–67.

66. Caryl Finn, *From Brass Diva: The Life and Legends of Ethel Merman* (Berkeley: University of California Press, 2007), 269.

67. The scene survives in *Hidden Hollywood: Treasures from the 20th Century Fox Vaults* (1997; dir. Kevin Burns, Chatsworth, CA, Image Entertainment), DVD.

Chapter 2

1. Richard Dyer MacCann, "Hollywood's Oscars Make Bow to Stage," *Christian Science Monitor*, March 30, 1951, 10; "Judy Holliday and Jose Ferrer Named on House Red-Front List," *New York Herald Tribune*, April 5, 1951, 1.

2. Unless otherwise noted, all data for my discussion of the Academy Awards derive from the Academy of Motion Picture Arts and Science's reference site, Academy Award Database, http://awardsdatabase.oscars.org/ampas_awards/Basic-SearchInput.jsp (accessed August 1, 2013). See also Mason Wiley and Damien Bona, *Inside Oscar: The Unofficial History of the Academy Awards,* 10th anniversary ed. (New York: Ballantine Books, 1996).

3. For broader discussions of race in the Academy Awards, see Rebecca Wanzo, "Beyond a 'Just' Syntax: Black Actresses, Hollywood, and Complex Personhood," *Women and Performance: A Journal of Feminist Theory* 16 (March 2006): 135–52; Mark Harris, *Pictures at a Revolution: Five Movies and the Birth of the New Hollywood* (New York: Penguin, 2008); and Emanuel Levy, *All About Oscar: The History and Politics of the Academy Awards* (New York: Continuum, 2003), especially 131–42.

4. For the latter interpretation, see Levy, *All About Oscar*, 138–39.

5. This summary is derived from my work in progress, *Casting: A History*, a scholarly account of the material practices of casting as they were consolidated across theatre, film, television, radio, and amateur performance in the twentieth century. For a history of casting in film, see Pamela Robertson Wojcik, "Typecasting," *Criticism* 45, no. 2 (Spring 2003): 223–49; and the documentary film *Casting By* (2013; dir. Tom Donahue, New York, Creative Chaos Ventures, 2013), DVD. For a recent history of racial casting in theatre, see Angela C. Pao, *No Safe Spaces: Re-casting Race, Ethnicity, and Nationality in American Theater* (Ann Arbor: University of Michigan Press, 2010); and Daniel Banks, "The Welcome Table: Casting for an Integrated Society," *Theatre Topics* 23, no. 1 (March 2013): 1–18. The line about the good, bad and inspired comes from Robert Cohen, *Theatre*, 5th Edition (New York: McGraw-Hill, 2005), 535.

6. Notably, the vocality used by Moreno in both roles is audibly similar, perhaps an example of what the actress later described as the "universal ethnic accent" she "invented" for use whenever she was cast to portray an exotic maiden character. See Rita Moreno, *Rita Moreno: A Memoir* (New York: Celebra Hardcover, 2013), 91.

7. See Elizabeth Ewen and Stuart Ewen, *Typecasting: On the Arts and Science of Human Inequality* (New York: Seven Stories Press, 2006); as well as Donald Bogle, *Toms, Coons, Mulattoes, Mammies, and Bucks: An Interpretive History of Blacks in American Films* (New York: Viking Press, 1973); Raymond William Stedman, *Shadows of the Indian: Stereotypes in American Culture* (Norman: University of Oklahoma Press, 1982); Molly Haskell, *From Reverence to Rape: The Treatment of Women in the Movies* (New York: Holt, Rinehart and Winston, 1974); Vito Russo, *The Celluloid Closet: Homosexuality in the Movies* (New York: Harper & Row, 1981); Charles Ramírez Berg, *Latino Images in Film: Stereotypes, Subversion, Resistance* (Austin: University of Texas Press, 2002); Allen L. Woll, *The Latin Image in American Film* (Los Angeles: Latin American Center Publications, University of California, Los Angeles, 1980); Robert G. Lee, *Orientals: Asian Americans in Popular Culture* (Philadelphia: Temple University Press, 1999); and Jack G. Shaheen, *Reel Bad Arabs: How Hollywood Vilifies a People* (New York: Olive Branch Press, 2001).

8. See Wojcik, "Typecasting," 223–49. For a discussion of "ghosting," see Marvin Carlson, *The Haunted Stage: The Theatre as Memory Machine* (Ann Arbor: University of Michigan Press, 2003).

9. My thinking on the surrogative powers of racial self-making is guided by the legion of scholars addressing the complexities of racial mimicry. For this period in particular, however, see especially Michael Rogin's pathbreaking work in *Blackface, White Noise: Jewish Immigrants in the Hollywood Melting Pot* (Berkeley: University of California Press, 1996).

10. This biographical summary is mostly culled from Montalban's own account, Ricardo Montalban, with Bob Thomas, *Reflections: A Life in Two Worlds* (New York: Doubleday, 1980), especially 52–60. For more on "soundies," see Amy Herzog, "Discordant Visions: The Peculiar Musical Images of the Soundies Jukebox Film," *American Music* 22, no. 1 (Spring 2004): 27–39.

11. *Variety*, June 18, 1947, 8.

12. "TV Changes Montalban," *Hutchinson New*, June 10, 1961, 6A.

13. On Fogler's coaching, see Montalban and Thomas, *Reflections*, 113.

14. "Ricardo Montalban Ends 7 Years at Metro Plant," *Variety*, September 23, 1953, 10. See also Montalban and Thomas, *Reflections*, 105–7.

15. "New 'Don Juan in Hell' Troupe Booking Tour," *Variety*, August 24, 1955, 67. See also Montalban and Thomas, *Reflections*, especially 107–9.

16. Bob Spielman, "'Broken Arrow' Shows Little in Showcasing," *Billboard*, May 12, 1956, 6. See also "TCF Showcasing via 'Fox Hour,'" *Billboard*, March 3, 1956, 10.

17. "Ricardo Stars in Role of Kabuki Dancer," *Oakland Tribune*, January 2, 1958, 16.

18. David M. Jampel, "Logan's Woes in Japan Increase re 'Sayonara,'" *Variety*, February 20, 1957, 11.

19. Mel Heimer, "My New York," *Kittanning Leader Times (Pennsylvania)*, January 30, 1958, 6. See also Montalban and Thomas, *Reflections*, 81–82.

20. Truman Capote, "The Duke in His Domain," in *The Dogs Bark* (New York: Random House, 1973), 308–53. See also *New Yorker*, http://www.newyorker.com/archive/1957/11/09/1957_11_09_053_TNY_CARDS_000252812 (accessed August 1, 2013).

21. Mel Heimer, "My New York," *Kittanning Leader Times (Pennsylvania)*, January 30, 1958, 6. See also Montalban and Thomas, *Reflections*, 81–82.

22. "Montalban Convincing as Top Nippon Dancer," *Chicago Defender*, December 17, 1957, 17; Mel Heimer, "My New York," *Kittanning Leader-Times*, January 30, 1958, 6; Al Ricketts, "On the Town," *Pacific Stars and Stripes*, February 7, 1957, 5.

23. Phillip K. Scheuer, "'Sayonara' Features Two Love Stories," *Los Angeles Times*, November 17, 1957, F1; Edwin Schallert, "'Sayonara' Exerts Spell for Viewers," *Los Angeles Times*, December 26, 1957, B14.

24. William K. Zinsser, "Reviews: 'Sayonara,'" *New York Herald Tribune*, December 6, 1957, 14; Bosley Crowther, "Screen: Brando Stars in 'Sayonara,'" *New York Times*, December 6, 1957.

25. Joshua Logan, *Movie Stars, Real People, and Me* (New York: Delacorte Press, 1978), 114. For more on the filming of *Sayonara*, see Capote, "Duke in His Domain."

26. Gina Marchetti, *Romance and the "Yellow Peril": Race, Sex, and Discursive Strategies in Hollywood* (Berkeley: University of California Press, 1993), 142. See also Karla Rae Fuller, *Hollywood Goes Oriental: CaucAsian Performance in American Film* (Detroit: Wayne State University Press, 2010), especially 200–210.

27. For the best scholarly assessment of *Jamaica*, see Shane Vogel, "Jamaica on Broadway: The Popular Caribbean and Mock Transnational Performance," *Theatre Journal* 62, no. 1 (March 2010): 1–21.

28. All the *Jamaica* reviews are reprinted in *New York Theatre Critics' Reviews*, vol. 18 (New York: Critics' Theatre Reviews, 1958), 196–99.

29. Ibid.

30. Montalban's presence in the cast of *Jamaica* seemed to stir a special interest among the *Variety* staff, and the example of the Montalban-Horne pairing came up throughout the musical's run, not only in discussions of the show but also in comments by different writers on other presentations (such as the Barry Gray radio program and Actor Equity's Integration Showcase). See, respectively, "Jamaica," *Variety*, November 6, 1957, 72; "Radio Review: Barry Gray," *Variety*, January 22, 1958, 54; "Orson Bean Rebuts on 'Integration,' Says Race Consciousness Is Brief," *Variety*, April 29, 1959, 69, 74.

31. Montalban and Thomas, *Reflections*, 146–47.

32. "Los Amantes del Desierto," *Variety*, February 12, 1958, 6.

33. "Ricardo Montalban Is Booster for TV," *Austin* (Minnesota) *Daily Herald*, February 1, 1958, 18.

34. Armando Zegri, "Spanish Americans Invade," *Américas* 10, no. 11 (November 1958): 27.

35. "Montalban Convincing as Top Nippon Dancer," *Chicago Defender*, December 17, 1957.

36. "TV Followup: Colgate Theatre," *Variety*, September 10, 1958, 117, 128; "NBC-TV Prepping Ginger Rogers Show," *Variety*, December 20, 1958, 52; "The Chevy Show" *Variety*, March 30, 1960, 39. See also Montalban and Thomas, *Reflections*, 115–18.

37. This account draws from both Regina K Fadiman, *Faulkner's "Intruder in the Dust": Novel into Film* (Knoxville: University of Tennessee Press, 1978), 26–43, especially 35–36; and Scott Eyman, *Lion of Hollywood: The Life and Legend of Louis B. Mayer* (New York: Simon and Schuster, 2005), especially 429–33.

38. Bosley Crowther, "The Screen in Review; 'Intruder in the Dust,' M-G-M's Drama of Lynching in the South, at the Mayfair," *New York Times*, November 23, 1949.

39. Biographical details of Juano Hernandez's early life remain somewhat sketchy, with most reference texts drawing on the narrative presented by Hernandez in a 1950 *New York Times* profile by Gladwin Hill, where the cited quote also first appears. Gladwin Hill, "Man of Character: 'Intruder in the Dust' Opened Up a Busy Screen Career for Juano Hernandez," *New York Times*, May 28, 1950. The obituary "Juan Hernandez, Actor, Dies at 74," *New York Times*, July 19, 1970, draws heavily on the 1950 profile and also contributes to summaries of the actor's life in an array of academic and popular texts.

40. "News of the Theaters," *New York Herald Tribune*, August 21, 1931.

41. Brooks Atkinson, "For Negro Performers," *New York Times*, February 3, 1932.

42. Richard France, *Orson Welles on Shakespeare: The W.P.A. and Mercury Theatre Playscripts* (New York: Routledge, 2013), 97.

43. Christopher H. Serling, *Encyclopedia of Radio*, vol. 1 (New York: Taylor and Francis, 2003), 43.

44. "Vaudeville: 'John Henry' with Juano Hernandez," *Billboard*, January 27, 1934, 10.

45. This much reduced list of Hernandez's radio work was distilled from a variety of sources, including John Dunning, *The Encyclopedia of Old Time Radio* (New York: Oxford University Press, 1998); Jim Cox, *The A to Z of American Radio Soap Operas* (Lanham, MD: Scarecrow Press, 2009); Robert C. Reinehr and Jon D. Swarts, *The A to Z of Old Time Radio* (Lanham, MD: Scarecrow Press, 2010); and Jeffrey Shandler, *Jews, God, and Videotape: Religion and Media in America* (New York: New York University Press, 2009). For a solid overview of race on the radio in the 1940s, see J. Fred MacDonald, "Wartime Radio and Racial Stereotyping," *Don't Touch That Dial* (blog), http://www.jfredmacdonald.com/stereotyping.htm (accessed August 1, 2013).

46. "Juano Hernandez is 'Hottest' Actor on Hollywood Scene," *New Journal and Guide*, July 22, 1950, 17.

47. It does seem clear that Hernandez was central to pioneering radio exchange work done between New York and Puerto Rico during and immediately after World War II, and it likewise appears that he was central to the translation and adaptation of works by US dramatists like Eugene O'Neill for Spanish-language radio plays to be performed and broadcast on Puerto Rican radio stations. Unfortunately, the information about these endeavors remains fragmented and scanty, especially in the English-language archive.

48. "Hernandez Will Take Puerto Rico, Thanks," *Cedar Rapids Gazette*, June 18, 1950.

49. "Negro Actor Is Honored by Puerto Rico University," *New York Times*, June 1, 1950.

50. Hill, "Man of Character."

51. "Variety Bills: Juano Hernandez," *Variety*, February 1, 1950, 47. See also "Self-Educated Hernandez Idolized by Students," *Ebony*, November 1952, 124–26; and "Juano Hernandez to Present 'Othello,'" *Oakland Tribune*, October 19, 1954, D25.

52. Harry Levette, "Actor Juano Hernandez Doubles as a Teacher," *Afro-American*, July 16, 1955, 7. A fascinating portrait of Hernandez's work at the University of Puerto Rico can be found in "Self-Educated Hernandez Idolized by Students."

53. Dorothy Kilgallen, "Ali Khan Becomes High-Brow," *Daily Reporter (Dover, OH)*, June 13, 1958.

54. *Variety* mentioned "differences of opinion re teaching methods and techniques." "Juano Hernandez Quits His Native Puerto Rico for Europe, Hollywood,"

Variety, June 4, 1958, 11. The same article noted his plans to relocate to Hollywood in the fall.

55. Early advertisements in the *Los Angeles Times* (see the classifieds in the December 14, 1958 issue) confirm this. Hernandez's early plans are also referenced in Edwin Schallert, "Grant, Tierney Ideal 'Prescott Affair' Duo; Lyceum Plan on Slate," *Los Angeles Times,* October 8, 1958.

56. "Actor also a Star in Academic Fields," *Santa Fe New Mexican,* July 7, 1960. In 1957, before leaving Puerto Rico, Hernandez described his disinclination to engage in "mass class work" and his "insist[ence] upon giving individual lessons to each student." Bill Ornstein, "Juano Hernandez's San Juan Lyceum Gets Govt. Aid," *Variety,* August 14, 1957, 2, 18.

57. Advertisements for Juano Hernandez's Lyceum for Dramatic Art can be found in the *Los Angeles Times* beginning in late 1958. For example, see the display ad that ran in the paper's classifieds on December 21–22, 1958. For additional information on alumni instruction, see "Bennington College Names Four," *North Adams Transcripts,* September 14, 1959. See also Jan Pippins, with Henry Darrow, *Henry Darrow: Lightning in a Bottle* (Duncan, OK: BearManor Media, 2013).

58. Rufus Blair, "Juano Hernandez Plays a Double Role All the Time," *Oakland Tribune,* April 20, 1958, 6B.

59. Miriam Jiménez Román, "Notes on Eusebia Cosme and Juano Hernández," in *The Afro-Latin@ Reader: History and Culture in the United States* (Durham, NC: Duke University Press, 2010), 320.

60. The United Press International item appears to have run around Halloween in 1959 in papers nationwide, ranging from the *Farmington Daily Times* in New Mexico (October 29, 1959) to the *Pulaski Southwest Times* in Virginia (November 1, 1959).

61. Bosley Crowther, "The Screen in Review," *New York Times,* October 7, 1950.

62. Bogle, *Toms, Coons, Mulattoes, Mammies, and Bucks,* 157.

63. Román, "Notes on Eusebia Cosme and Juano Hernández," 319.

64. "Ferrer's 'Awhile to Work' Captures $50 Given by Intime for Undergraduate Play," *Daily Princetonian,* February 23, 1937, 1; "Born on Dance Floor and Baptized with Zeal, Ferrer's 'Awhile to Work' Rounds into Shape," *Daily Princetonian,* March 4, 1937, 1; "Paens of Praise Won by Ferrer: 'Awhile to Work' Closes Tonight," *Daily Princetonian,* March 24, 1937, 1; "M. G. Ferrer Wins Prize Play Award," *New York Times,* March 3, 1937; "'Awhile to Work' Staged," *New York Times,* March 20, 1937.

65. Biographical details of Ferrer's early life draw on accounts in various Audrey Hepburn biographies, as well as the thoughtful, thorough, and anonymously authored website, "Mel Ferrer: A Fan Appreciation Site," http://melferrer.com/ (accessed August 1, 2013), which provides an invaluable aggregation of information regarding Ferrer's life, family, and work. Additional useful information can be found in Barry Paris, *Audrey Hepburn* (New York: Putnam, 1996); and Alexander Walker, *Audrey: Her Real Story* (New York: Macmillan, 1997).

66. For the best account of Ferrer's post-Princeton years, see Paris, *Audrey Hepburn.* See also Helen Colton, "Reluctant Star: Mel Ferrer, Noted for His Performance in 'Lost Boundaries,' Hates Acting," *New York Times,* September 4, 1949.

67. For a summary of *Strange Fruit*'s stage adaptation, see Judith Giblin James, "Carson McCullers, Lillian Smith, and the Politics of Broadway," in *Southern Women Playwrights: New Essays in Literary History and Criticism,* ed. Robert McDonald and Linda Rohrer Paige (Tuscaloosa: University of Alabama Press, 2002), 42–61.

68. Ken Johnstone, "Legitimate: Strange Fruit," *Billboard,* October 13, 1945, 41;

E. B. Rea, "'Strange Fruit' Lacking as Drama, Reeks with Epithets," *Afro-American*, November 24, 1945, 10.

69. Lewis Nichols, "The Play: Strange Fruit," *New York Times*, November 30, 1945; Miles M. Jeffers, "The Negro on Broadway, 1945–1946," *Phylon* 7, no. 2 (1946): 188.

70. In 1947 Ferrer (with friends Gregory Peck and Dorothy McGuire) founded a theatre company, originally called the Actors Company, which would stage a summer season of short-run productions featuring Hollywood actors. The company soon found a venue in a small community near San Diego and renamed itself La Jolla Playhouse, with Ferrer, Peck, and McGuire sharing on- and off-stage creative responsibilities. "Selznick Stars Form Hayloft Co," *Variety*, April 16, 1947, 50. See also *James Morrison – The Life of an Actor* (fansite) http://www.lifeofanactor.com/lajolla.htm (accessed August 1, 2013).

71. Robert Simonson, *On Broadway Men Still Wear Hats* (New York: Smith & Kraus, 2004), 197.

72. Judith Weisenfeld, *Hollywood Be Thy Name: African American Religion in American Film, 1929–1949* (Berkeley: University of California Press, 2007), especially 214–16 and 312; Gayle Wald, *Crossing the Line: Racial Passing in Twentieth Century U.S. Literature and Culture* (Durham, NC: Duke University Press, 2000), 91–93.

73. Al Weisman, "He Passed as a Negro," *Negro Digest*, October 1951, 18, 16–20.

74. David J. Skal, *Screams of Reason: Mad Science and Modern Culture* (New York: W. W. Norton, 1998), 191.

75. Adilifu Nama, *Black Space: Imagining Race in Science Fiction Film* (Austin: University of Texas Press, 2010), 47.

76. "Belafonte, Ferrer Vie for Girl," *Jet*, December 4, 1958, 58.

77. "Movie of the Week: The World, The Flesh and The Devil," *Jet*, June 4, 1959, 65.

78. "Montalban Heads Coast Group in Better Shake on Jobs for 'Latins,'" *Variety*, March 18, 1970, 17.

79. Ibid.

80. Ibid.

81. Pippins and Darrow, *Henry Darrow*.

82. Paul Hodgins, "One of La Jolla Playhouse's Founders Remembers Early Days on the Eve of Its 50th Anniversary," *Orange County Register*, May 18, 1997, F31.

83. "Myra/Raquel: The Predator of Hollywood," *Time*, November 28, 1969, 75.

84. John Hallowell, "Hollywood's Wonder Woman: Raquel Welch Movieland's Latest Sex Bomb," *Charleston Sunday Gazette-Mail (West Virginia)*, August 18, 1968, 8s, 12s.

85. Mireya Navarro, "Raquel Welch Is Reinvented as a Latina," *New York Times*, June 11, 2002, http://www.nytimes.com/2002/06/11/movies/raquel-welch-reinvented-latina-familiar-actress-now-boasts-her-heritage.html (accessed August 1, 2013).

86. Sandra Marquez, "Becoming Raquel," *Hispanic Online*, April 2003, http://www.hispaniconline.com/magazine/2003/april/CoverStory/ (accessed August 16, 2006).

87. "Myra/Raquel," 75.

88. Army Archerd, "No Such Thing as a 'New Raquel Welch,'" *Cuero Record* (Texas), May 20, 1969, 6.

89. Hallowell, "Hollywood's Wonder Woman."

90. "Myra/Raquel, 75.

91. Ibid.

92. Navarro, "Raquel Welch Is Reinvented as a Latina."
93. Ibid.

Chapter 3

1. Ronald Savery, "Echoes from Broadway: New York Plays Reviewed," *Theatre World*, November 1958.

2. Frances Negrón-Muntaner, *Boricua Pop: Puerto Ricans and the Latinization of American Culture* (New York: New York University Press, 2004), 61. For a discussion of how these two threads of discussion about *West Side Story*—the celebration and the critique—converged in interesting ways during a 2009 revival of the musical, see my earlier work, Brian Eugenio Herrera, "Compiling *West Side Story*'s Parahistories, 1949–2009," *Theatre Journal* 64, no. 2 (May 2012): 231–47.

3. My chronicle of the genesis of *West Side Story* synthesizes accounts provided by the many biographers of Robbins, Bernstein, and Sondheim, each of whom details the backstory of *West Side Story* with idiosyncratic flourishes and contradictions. Still, the basic contours of the narrative of *West Side Story*'s creation remain clear and consistent. I therefore approach *West Side Story*'s genesis story as a legend in the folkloric sense, as a narrative of human actions believed by both the teller and the listener to be factual and historical, in which the veracity of any particular account is less important than the generally shared belief in the actual narrative. For a discussion of folkloric definitions of *legend*, see Linda Dégh, *Legend and Belief: Dialectics of a Folklore Genre* (Bloomington: Indiana University Press, 2001), 23–25, 98. See also Barre Toelken, *The Dynamics of Folklore*, rev. and expanded ed. (Logan: Utah State University Press, 1996).

4. Leonard Bernstein, *Findings* (New York: Simon & Schuster, 1982), 144.

5. Joan Peyser, *Bernstein: A Biography*, rev. and updated ed. (New York: Billboard Books, 1998), 261; Keith Garebian, *The Making of West Side Story* (Toronto: ECW Press, 1995), 31.

6. Abe Laufe, *Broadway's Greatest Musicals*, rev. ed. (New York: Funk & Wagnalls, 1977), 222; Harley Erdman, *Staging the Jew: The Performance of an American Ethnicity, 1860–1920* (New Brunswick, NJ: Rutgers University Press, 1998), 159.

7. Arthur Laurents, *Original Story By: A Memoir of Broadway and Hollywood* (New York: Knopf, 2000), 337–38. See also Garebian, *The Making of West Side Story*, 35; and Peyser, *Bernstein*, 264.

8. Bernstein, *Findings*, 145; Laurents, *Original Story By*, 338. Robbins consistently attributes both the gang and the Puerto Rican idea to Bernstein and Laurents. See also "The Show's the Thing," *Newsweek*, October 7, 1957, 104.

9. Garebian, *The Making of West Side Story*, 31. *East Side Story* and *Gangway!* were only "working titles" for the show that would ultimately become *West Side Story*. Some confusion has emerged regarding an apocryphal 1949 play (*East Side Story*), which some recent scholarly accounts claim provided the dramatic basis for *West Side Story*. For one example of this argument, see Negrón-Muntaner, *Boricua Pop*, 63.

10. Ethan Mordden, *Coming Up Roses: The Broadway Musical in the 1950s* (New York: Oxford University Press, 1998), 240.

11. Historian Eric C. Schneider notes that "gangs were [understood to be] either the result of normal play activity or they belonged to the adult criminal world. No category existed in the gang boy studies for adolescent gangs whose playthings included firearms but who were not linked to organized crime." Eric C. Schneider, *Vampires,*

Dragons, and Egyptian Kings: Youth Gangs in Postwar New York (Princeton, NJ: Princeton University Press, 1999), 63, 51–77.

12. Lorrin Thomas, *Puerto Rican Citizen: History and Political Identity in Twentieth-Century New York City* (Chicago: University of Chicago Press, 2010), 135, 141.

13. Juan Gonzalez, *Harvest of Empire: A History of Latinos in America*, rev. ed. (New York: Penguin, 2011), 81.

14. Arthur Laurents, *West Side Story, a Musical* (New York: Random House, 1958).

15. Bernstein, *Findings*, 145.

16. Hollis Alpert, "'West Side Story': A Brilliant Stage Production Starts to Become a Film," *Dance*, October 1960, 39.

17. Emily Coleman, "The Story behind *West Side Story*," *Theatre Arts*, December 1957, 81.

18. Henry Hewes, "The Cool Generation," *Saturday Review*, October 5, 1957, 22.

19. Jack Smith and Barry Frank, "Found in the Drama Mailbag," *New York Times*, October 13, 1957.

20. Bruno Bettelheim and Morris Janowitz, *Social Change and Prejudice, Including the Dynamics of Prejudice* (New York: Free Press, 1975), 56–65.

21. Laufe, *Broadway's Greatest Musicals*, 226.

22. Brooks Atkinson, "The Jungles of the City," *New York Times*, September 27, 1957.

23. Walter Kerr, "West Side Story," *New York Herald Tribune*, September 27, 1957.

24. For a contemporary discussion of Puerto Ricans in 1950s New York, see Winifred Raushenbush, "New York and the Puerto Ricans," *Harper's*, May 1953, 79. For a similar analysis of the question of immigration versus migration, see Anzia Yezierska, "The Lower Depths of Upper Broadway," *The Reporter*, January 19, 1957, 26–29; and Peter Kihss, "Gains Made Here by Puerto Ricans," *New York Times*, May 31, 1957.

25. A full historical genealogy of the myriad local protests instigated by *West Side Story* awaits composition. However, media accounts of the 1999 student protest led by Camille Solá against her Massachusetts high school's production efficiently illuminate the constellation of concerns that have typically guided such protests. See "West Side Story," *All Things Considered*, National Public Radio, December 8, 1999, http://www.npr.org/templates/story/story.php?storyId=1067627 (accessed February 13, 2012); and Bruce Penniman, "When a School Decides There's No Place for 'West Side Story,'" *Christian Science Monitor*, December 14, 1999, http://www.csmonitor.com/1999/1214/p18s1.html (accessed February 13, 2012).

26. Roberto Marquez, "One Boricua's Baldwin: A Personal Remembrance," *American Quarterly* 42, no. 3 (September 1990): 465.

27. Jesús Colón, *A Puerto Rican in New York and Other Sketches* (New York: International Publishers, 1982), 9.

28. Alberto Sandoval-Sánchez, *José, Can You See? Latinos On and Off Broadway* (Madison: University of Wisconsin Press, 1999), 62.

29. See especially Judith Ortiz Cofer's widely anthologized prose piece "The Myth of the Latin Woman: I Just Met a Girl Named María," in *The Latin Deli: Prose and Poetry by Judith Ortiz Cofer* (Athens: University of Georgia Press, 1993), 148–54. See also Herrera, "Compiling *West Side Story*'s Parahistories," 241.

30. José Esteban Muñoz, *Disidentifications: Queers of Color and the Performance of Politics* (Minneapolis: University of Minnesota Press, 1999), 25.

31. For Miranda's comments on the influence of *West Side Story* on his creative aesthetic, see Maria Hinojosa's "Lin-Manuel Miranda," *One on One*, WGBH Boston,

http://www.wgbh.org/org/programs/Maria-Hinojosa-One-on-One-12/episodes/
Lin-Manuel-Miranda-15067 (accessed January 17, 2012). For her part, Jennifer Lopez
has often been quoted as wanting to play Anita. The most commonly cited quotation,
in which Lopez claims to have "never noticed that Natalie Wood wasn't really a Puerto
Rican girl," can be found in Negrón-Muntaner, *Boricua Pop*, 59. For a more recent
Lopez statement on *West Side Story*, see Mark Seliger, "'West Side Story' Revisited,"
Vanity Fair, March 17, 2009, http://www.vanityfair.com/culture/features/2009/03/
west-side-story-portfolio200903 (accessed February 13, 2012). In this Web-only feature, Lopez asserted, "I never wanted to be that wimpy Maria, who sits around pining
for the guy. I wanted to be Anita, who danced her way to the top."

32. For more on the disidentifying gestures made by those crafting subsequent
stage productions of the musical, see Herrera, "Compiling *West Side Story*'s Parahistories." For a measured critique of how Latina/o studies scholars have engaged the
film, see Ernesto R. Acevedo-Muñoz's comments in the final chapter of his *West Side
Story as Cinema: The Making and Impact of an American Masterpiece* (Lawrence: University
Press of Kansas, 2013), especially 150–69.

33. The Jets' triptych does not include its members' contribution to "Quintet"—
the construction of which gives further credence to the notion that they operate as
a collective character. Notably, "Quintet" is the only occasion on which the stage version gives The Sharks a musical voice, and even there it is embedded. But the basic
point is that "Quintet" is a piece for five characters: Maria, Tony, and Anita, as well
as The Jets and The Sharks. The piece is a quintet of five characters, performed by
twenty or so actual people.

34. In *Finishing the Hat*, Stephen Sondheim confirms that "America" was "intended to be an argument between Bernardo and Anita . . . but Jerry [Robbins] insisted
that the song be for the girls only, as it was the only chance for a full out all-female
dance number. The character of Rosalia was invented to take Bernardo's part. When
the movie was made four years later, Jerry agreed to revert to the original lyric." Stephen Sondheim, *Finishing the Hat: Collected Lyrics (1954–1981) with Attendant Comments, Principles, Heresies, Grudges, Whines, and Anecdotes* (New York: Knopf, 2010), 40–
42.

35. David Krasner offers this thumbnail sketch of the rehearsal process most typical of the American "method," noting that the performer "combines work on the
role, with an emphasis on researching and experiencing the character's life, and
work on the self, which stresses the actor's personal investment and commitment to
memory, experience and worldview." David Krasner, "I Hate Strasberg: Method Bashing in the Academy," in *Method Acting Reconsidered*, ed. David Krasner (New York: St.
Martin's, 2000), 4.

36. Keith Garebian, *The Making of West Side Story* (Toronto: ECW Press, 1995),
112.

37. Stephen Banfield, *Sondheim's Broadway Musicals* (Ann Arbor: University of
Michigan Press, 1993), 35.

38. John Chapman, "'West Side Story'—a Splendid and Super-modern Musical
Drama," *New York Daily News*, September 27, 1957.

39. Only the *New York Times*' Howard Taubman specifically commented on the
disparity, faulting Bernstein's music for not matching the acidity of Sondheim's lyric.

40. Brooks Atkinson, "West Side Story," *New York Times*, October 6, 1957. John
McClain, "Music Magnificent in Overwhelming Hit," *Journal American*, September 27,
1957.

41. Richard Watts, "Romeo and Juliet in a Gang War," *New York Post*, September 27, 1957. Frank Aston, "Love and Hate Make Beauty," *New York World-Telegram*, September 27, 1957.

42. Henry Hewes, "The Cool Generation," *Saturday Review*, October 5, 1957, 22.

43. James Gilbert, *A Cycle of Outrage: America's Reaction to the Juvenile Delinquent in the 1950s* (New York: Oxford University Press, 1986), 73.

44. Tim Shary, *Teen Movies: American Youth on Screen* (New York: Columbia University Press, 2005), 25–26.

45. "Sal Mineo Has New Teen-Age Tantrums," *Syracuse Herald-Journal*, September 12, 1957, 58.

46. In October 1958, *Dino* was listed as among the top five "most frequently produced three-act plays by Thespian affiliated schools during 1957–58" as "tabulated from the Annual Reports of 1419 Thespian affiliated schools" ("1957–58 Three-Act Plays," *Dramatics*, October 1958, 11). According to the published tabulations, *Dino* received 52 productions, the same as *Our Town*. *Dino* continued to rank among the most produced high school plays in the next decade. The play reliably appeared on *Dramatics* magazine's list for 1958–59 (22 productions, 1,610 troupes), 1959–60 (23 productions, 1,581 troupes), not ranked for 1960–61, 1961–62 (15 productions, 1,633 reporting troupes), 1962–63 (17 productions, 1,719 reporting troupes), 1963–64 (18 productions, 1,958 reporting troupes), and 1964–65 (13 productions, 1,845 reporting troupes). Returns after a one-year absence in 1966–67 list 12 productions out of 1,857 reporting troupes).

47. Frank Aston, "Love and Hate Make Beauty," *New York World Telegram*, September 27, 1957.

48. Sondheim confirms that the notion of flipping the placement of "Cool" and "Krupke" occurred during the last phase of rehearsals for the original Broadway production, but set requirements prevented experimentation. ("Cool" required the full stage for its choreography, while "Krupke" needed only the forestage, permitting a scene change to occur behind the curtain.) See Sondheim, *Finishing the Hat*, 40–42.

49. Henry Hewes, "The Cool Generation," *Saturday Review*, October 5, 1957, 22. Hewes's review saw The Jets' belief that "the growing proportion of Puerto Ricans in the block demands an all-out attempt to destroy them before they become too powerful" and their insistence on the "war council" as akin to the tense relations between the US and Soviet governments.

50. Throughout his early story notes on the "modern Romeo" project, Jerome Robbins consistently used the phrase "the gang" to refer to the characters who would become The Jets. Jerome Robbins Papers, (S) *MGZMD 130, Jerome Robbins Dance Division, New York Public Library for the Performing Arts, Box 85, Folders 3, 5, 7, and 11.

51. David Román, *Performance in America: Contemporary U.S. Culture and the Performing Arts* (Durham, NC: Duke University Press, 2005), 33.

52. Jerome Robbins Papers, (S) *MGZMD 130, Jerome Robbins Dance Division, New York Public Library for the Performing Arts. Box 85, Folder 11.

53. Murray Schumach, "Talent Dragnet: Casting for 'West Side Story' Caused Unusual Number of Headaches," *New York Times*, September 22, 1957.

54. Although Actors Equity was actively advocating diversity initiatives in casting actors on Broadway in this same period, most of its efforts (in, e.g., the highly publicized Integration Showcase of 1959) appear not to have considered Latina/o performers within the mandate of integration. So it remains unclear whether and how

Equity supported *West Side Story*'s search for Puerto Rican and other Latina/o actors for roles in the 1957 stage production.

55. This discussion derives from the call sheets contained in the Jerome Robbins Papers, (S) *MGZMD 130, Jerome Robbins Dance Division, New York Public Library for the Performing Arts, Box 85, Folder 12. For later castings, see also Folders 15–17.

56. See Jerome Robbins Papers, (S) *MGZMD 130, Jerome Robbins Dance Division, New York Public Library for the Performing Arts, Box 85, Folder 11.

57. BarBara Luna was of Spanish/Filipino/Hungarian heritage, but she was raised in "Nuyorican" New York neighborhoods. For confirmation of Robbins's preference for Moreno over Luna, see Jerome Robbins Papers, (S) *MGZMD 130, Jerome Robbins Dance Division, New York Public Library for the Performing Arts, Box 86, Folder 1.

58. See Deborah Paredez, "'Queer for Uncle Sam': Anita's Latina Diva Citizenship in 'West Side Story,'" *Latino Studies Journal* 12, no. 3 (2014): 332–52.

59. Emily Coleman, "The Story behind *West Side Story*," *Theatre Arts*, December 1957, 81.

60. Chapman, "West Side Story."

61. Euphemia Van Rensselaer Wyatt, "Theater," *Catholic World*, December 1957, 224–25.

62. Howard A. Rusk, "The Facts Don't Rhyme: An Analysis of Irony in Lyrics Linking Puerto Rico's Breezes to Tropical Diseases," *New York Times*, September 29, 1957.

63. Greg Lawrence, *Dancing with Demons: The Life of Jerome Robbins* (New York: Putnam, 2001), 250.

64. Deborah Jowitt, *Jerome Robbins: His Life, His Theater, His Dance* (New York: Simon & Shuster, 2004), 283–86, 288–91.

65. See Tomás Almaguer, *Racial Fault Lines: Historical Origins of White Supremacy in California* (Berkeley: University of California Press, 1994), especially 62–64.

66. Eric C. Schneider, *Vampires, Dragons, and Egyptian Kings: Youth Gangs in Postwar New York* (Princeton, NJ: Princeton University Press, 1999), 4.

67. The *New York Herald Tribune* ran regular reports on Puerto Rican youth criminality throughout the early fall of 1959. This quote comes from "'Cape Man's' Pal Guilty in Row with Policeman," *New York Herald Tribune*, September 11, 1959, 11.

68. Dan Wakefield, "The Other Puerto Ricans," *New York Times Magazine*, October 11, 1959, 24, 82–85.

69. "The Real West Side Story," *LOOK*, February 16, 1960, 22–27.

Chapter 4

1. "Latin Beauty Wonders Why Her Type Is Always Type Cast," *Newsday*, November 30 1960, 5C.

2. Rita Moreno, "West Side Story People," *Eureka Humboldt-Examiner*, July 14, 1961, 2.

3. Dick Kleiner's column appeared—with a variety of edits and under an array of headlines—in dozens of regional papers throughout October and November 1961. The quoted excerpts appear in most published versions of the column. The cited headlines are drawn from, respectively, the *Corpus Christi Caller-Times*, October 8, 1961, 3F; *Long Beach Independent Press-Telegram*, October 15, 1961, 9; and *Ogden Standard-Examiner*, November 15, 1961,10B.

4. William Laffler, "Rita Moreno Said to Steal Filmed 'West Side Story,'" *Boston Globe*, September 10, 1961, A25.

5. Mae Tinee, "'West Side Story' Is Savage Tale of Slums," *Chicago Daily Tribune*, February 21, 1962, B3; Marjory Adams, "'West Side Story' Great Musical Drama at Gary," *Boston Globe*, November 2, 1961, 18; Bosley Crowther, "Film at the Rivoli Is Called Masterpiece," *New York Times*, October 19, 1961, 39.

6. Don Alpert, "Spitfire! Don't Call Me That," *Los Angeles Times*, January 14, 1962, B8.

7. Rita Moreno, *Rita Moreno: A Memoir* (New York: Celebra Hardcover, 2013), 240–41.

8. Shaun Considine, "A Latin from Manhattan Stars at Last," *New York Times*, March 30, 1975.

9. Ibid.

10. Frances Negrón-Mutaner, *Boricua Pop: Puerto Ricans and the Latinization of American Culture* (New York: New York University Press, 2004), 80; Mary Beltrán, *Latina/o Stars in US Eyes: The Makings and Meanings of Film and TV Stardom* (Urbana: University of Illinois Press, 2009), 83.

11. Rachel Lee Rubin and Jeffrey Paul Melnick, *Immigration and American Popular Culture: An Introduction* (New York: New York University Press, 2007), 118; Priscilla Peña Ovalle, *Dance and the Hollywood Latina: Race, Sex, and Stardom* (New Brunswick, NJ: Rutgers University Press, 2011), 120–22.

12. Considine, "Latin from Manhattan."

13. David Dugas, "'The Ritz' Survives as Movie," *Salt Lake Tribune*, August 14, 1976, 6B; Joan E. Van De Bon Coeur, "'Ritz' Transfers Well," October 25, 1976, 17.

14. In 1977 Performer Q—the influential "show business personality popularity rating service"—confirmed that Charo was recognized by 57 percent of its national television audience sample. Joel Kotkin, "The Edsel Is Back! TV Talk Shows Need Help from Left Field and beyond the Television Talk Shows," *Washington Post*, July 14, 1977.

15. Bill Carter, "That Old Standby the Talk Show Shows No Sign of Fading," *Baltimore Sun*, June 18, 1978.

16. Angharad N. Valdivia observes, "Latina women in Hollywood film almost always have thick, unshakable, often humorous, and self-deprecating accents, most extremely portrayed by Charo, though dating back to Carmen Miranda and others." Angharad N. Valdivia, *"A Latina in the Land of Hollywood" and Other Essays on Media Culture* (Tucson: University of Arizona Press, 2000), 92.

17. Quoted in Nicole Trujillo-Pagán, "'Charo' (María Rosario Pilar Martínez Molina Baeza) (1942–)," in *Latinas in the United States: A Historical Encyclopedia*, ed. Vicki L. Ruíz and Virginia Sánchez Korrol (Bloomington: Indiana University Press, 2006), 144–45. Charo has offered variations of this statement in any number of media appearances, but I chose this source to underscore the point that most scholarly considerations of Charo appear in academic encyclopedias like this one or popular almanacs like Luis Reyes and Peter Rubie, *Hispanics in Hollywood* (Hollywood, CA: Lone Eagle Publishing, 2000), 442.

18. Tomás Rívera Policy Institute, *Missing in Action: Latinos In and Out of Hollywood* (Los Angeles: Screen Actors Guild, 1999). The quoted passage comes from Chon Noriega's historical preface. Because this document is intermittently paginated, all citations from it note page numbers only when they have been included by the publisher.

19. *Oxford English Dictionary Online*, s.v. "stereotype," OED Online (Oxford University Press, September 2014), http://www.oed.com/view/Entry/189957?rskey=syYJ6y &result=2&isAdvanced=false (accessed October 8, 2014).

20. Mireille Rosello notes that the term *stereotype* was used metaphorically prior to Lippman's *Public Opinion*, most notably in France, where *stéréotype* was utilized "as a synonym for cliché as early as 1869." Mireille Rosello, *Declining the Stereotype: Ethnicity and Representation in French Cultures* (Hanover, NH: University Press of New England, 1997), 177.

21. Elizabeth Ewen and Stuart Ewen, *Typecasting: On the Arts and Science of Human Inequality* (New York: Seven Stories Press, 2006), 4.

22. Walter Lippman, *Public Opinion* (New York: Free Press, 1997), 60–61.

23. Ibid.

24. Ibid., 53–62, especially 59.

25. Ibid., 60–61.

26. Ewen and Ewen, *Typecasting*, 8–9.

27. Gordon W. Allport, *ABC's of Scapegoating* (New York: Anti-Defamation League of B'Nai B'Rith, 1948), 33.

28. Gordon Allport, *The Nature of Prejudice*, 25th anniversary ed. (Reading, MA: Perseus Books, 1979), 191.

29. Allport, *ABC's of Scapegoating*, 35.

30. For a discussion of the role of social psychology in 1950s cultural controversies, see Graham Richards, *Race, Racism, and Psychology: Towards a Reflexive History* (New York: Routledge, 1997), 224–60, especially 232–33. See also John P. Jacobson Jr., *Science for Segregation: Race, Law, and the Case against Brown v. Board of Education* (New York: New York University Press, 2005), 103–18; and Waldo E. Martin, *Brown v. Board of Education: A Brief History with Documents* (New York: Macmillan, 1998), 28.

31. For an incisive and fresh assessment of this tradition, see Robin Bernstein, *Racial Innocence: Performing American Childhood from Slavery to Civil Rights* (New York: New York University Press, 2011), 235–43.

32. See David Buckingham, *Media Education: Literacy, Learning, and Contemporary Culture* (Malden, MA: Blackwell Publishing, 2003), 53–59.

33. Donald Bogle, *Toms, Coons, Mulattoes, Mammies, and Bucks: An Interpretive History of Blacks in American Films* (New York: Viking Press, 1973); Raymond William Stedman, *Shadows of the Indian: Stereotypes in American Culture* (Norman: University of Oklahoma Press, 1982); Molly Haskell, *From Reverence to Rape: The Treatment of Women in the Movies* (New York: Holt, Rinehart and Winston, 1974); Vito Russo, *The Celluloid Closet: Homosexuality in the Movies* (New York: Harper & Row, 1981).

34. As the titles of the following books indicate, each text adopts a transhistorical survey of the modes of representation conventionalized around specific ethnoracial groups within the United States. See Robert G. Lee, *Orientals: Asian Americans in Popular Culture* (Philadelphia: Temple University Press, 1999); Charles Ramírez Berg, *Latino Images in Film: Stereotypes, Subversion, Resistance* (Austin: University of Texas Press, 2002); Clara Rodriguez, *Heroes, Lovers, and Others: The Story of Latinos in Hollywood* (Washington, DC: Smithsonian Institution Press, 2004); and Jack G. Shaheen, *Reel Bad Arabs: How Hollywood Vilifies a People* (New York: Olive Branch Press, 2001).

35. Lee, *Orientals*, 11.

36. Chon A. Noriega, *Shot in America: Television, the State, and the Rise of Chicano Cinema* (Minneapolis: University of Minnesota Press, 2000). See especially "'The Stereotypes Must Die': Social Protest and the Frito Bandito," 28–50.

37. Frank Chin and Jeffery Paul Chan, "Racist Love," in *Seeing through Shuck*, ed. Richard Kostelanetz (New York: Ballantine Books, 1972), 65–79.

38. Ernst H. Gombrich, "The Visual Image," in *Media and Symbols: The Forms of Expression, Communication, and Education*, ed. David R Olson (Chicago: University of Chicago Press, 1974), 255–58.

39. Richard Dyer, *The Matter of Images: Essays on Representation* (New York: Routledge, 1993), 13.

40. Ibid., 13–15; see also Richard Dyer, "Homosexuality and Film Noir," *Jump Cut: A Review of Contemporary Media* 16 (November 1977): 18–21. A slightly revised version of Dyer's 1977 essay also appears in Dyer, *The Matter of Images*, 52–72.

41. In his 1997 textbook, *Representation: Cultural Representations and Signifying Practices* (Thousand Oaks, CA: Sage Publications, 1997), Stuart Hall nods to Dyer's work on stereotype as foundational to his own approach to the racial operation of stereotype (257–59). For Hall's own encoding/decoding paradigm, see Stuart Hall, "The Whites of Their Eyes: Racist Ideologies and the Media," in *Silver Linings: Some Strategies for the Eighties*, ed. George Bridges and Rosalind Brunt (London: Lawrence & Wishart, 1981); and "Encoding/Decoding," in *Media and Cultural Studies: Keyworks*, rev. ed., ed. Meenakshi Gigi Durham and Douglas Kellner (New York: Blackwell Publishing, 2006).

42. Hall, *Representation*, 225–28.

43. Ibid., 226.

44. Homi Bhabha, *The Location of Culture* (New York: Routledge, 1994), 81, 66–67.

45. For Gilman, writing in 1985, stereotype is a cognitive device ("dynamic in its ability to alter itself"), useful for drawing the "imaginary line" separating "self and Other." Noting that "the most negative stereotype has an overtly positive counterweight," Gilman argued that stereotypes are "protean rather than rigid," capable of shifting their valence to accommodate the exigencies of the psyche. Sander L. Gilman, *Difference and Pathology: Stereotypes of Sexuality, Race, and Madness* (Ithaca, NY: Cornell University Press, 1985): 16–20.

46. Bhabha, *Location of Culture*, 77–78, 81. As the cultural critic and performance artist Coco Fusco affirms in her explication of Bhabha's argument, the ubiquity of the stereotype suggests how imbricated discourses of modernity are with discourses of colonialism. Summarizing Bhabha's analysis, Fusco writes, "[R]acial classification through stereotyping is a necessary component of colonialist discourse, as it justifies domination and masks the colonizer's fear of the inability to always already know the Other." Coco Fusco, "The Other History of Intercultural Performance," *TDR: The Drama Review* 38 (Spring 1994): 153.

47. Dyer, *Matter of Images*, 11.

48. Ramírez Berg, *Latino Images in Film*, 41.

49. Rosello, *Declining the Stereotype*, 33.

50. Joseph Roach, *Cities of the Dead: Circum-Atlantic Performance* (New York: Columbia University Press, 1996), 36.

51. Ibid.

52. Jorge Huerta, "Luis Valdez's *Zoot Suit*: A New Direction for Chicano Theatre?" *Latin American Theatre Review* (Summer 1980): 69–76, especially 69–70.

53. Luis Valdez and El Teatro Campesino, *Actos* (San Juan Batista, CA: Menyah Productions, 1971), 36.

54. Ibid., 44–49.

55. Harry Justin Elam, *Taking It to the Streets: The Social Protest Theater of Luis Valdez and Amiri Baraka* (Ann Arbor: University of Michigan Press, 2001), 60.

56. Here my reading is both informed by and shares affinity with—even as it also departs emphatically from—Yolanda Broyles-Gonzáles's influential interpretation of Reyna and Pachuco as two parts of a whole. See Yolanda Broyles-Gonzáles, *El Teatro Campesino: Theater in the Chicano Movement* (Austin: University of Texas Press, 1994), 197–99.

57. Kathy Peiss, *Zoot Suit: The Enigmatic Career of an Extreme Style* (Philadelphia: University of Pennsylvania Press, 2011), 187.

58. Roach, *Cities of the Dead*, 36.

59. The influential *teatrista* Diane Rodriguez offers but one example of how the encounter with stereotype instigated independent Latina/o theatre-making in the 1980s when she reflects on why she (along with cofounders Rick Nájera, Luisa Leschin, and Armando Molina) founded the performance ensemble Latins Anonymous: "[We] founded Latins Anonymous [because we] felt strapped because in Los Angeles and especially in the 1980s, you were slotted into . . . a stereotype, and that's what you did. . . . [W]e all felt that way." Chantal Rodríguez, "Living the Politics of Teatro in Los Angeles: An Interview with Diane Rodriguez," *Latin American Theatre Review* 43 (Fall 2009): 144–45.

60. See Jorge Huerta, "Looking for the Magic: Chicanos in the Mainstream," in *Negotiating Performance: Gender, Sexuality, and Theatricality in Latin/o America*, eds. Diana Taylor and Juan Villegas Morales (Durham, NC: Duke University Press, 1994), 43. John Leguizamo, "Introduction," in *Mambo Mouth: A Savage Comedy* (New York: Bantam Books, 1993), 16.

61. The section of *Still Missing* detailing the results of TRPI's survey of SAG's Latino membership is titled "Obstacles to Latino Actors." See Harry Pachon et al., *Still Missing in Action: Latinos In and Out of Hollywood* (Los Angeles: Tomás Rívera Policy Institute and Screen Actors Guild, 2000), 4–8.

62. This sentence by Alberto Sandoval-Sánchez conveys both the compositional impulse toward negative prefixing and the affirmative instinct inspiring such an intervention: "My interest in decentering, demythifying, and deconstructing ethnic and racial stereotypes of Latinas/os inscribed in the musical was the result of witnessing the reaction of an Anglo-American audience that applauded euphorically after witnessing the number 'America' [in *West Side Story*]." Alberto Sandoval-Sánchez, *José, Can You See? Latinos On and Off Broadway* (Madison: University of Wisconsin Press, 1999), 63. A cursory database search for the word *stereotype* in conjunction with any negatively prefixed action verb will likely elicit an array of examples of this observation.

63. William Anthony Nericcio, *Tex[t]-Mex: Seductive Hallucinations of the "Mexican" in America* (Austin: University of Texas Press, 2007), 143.

64. Jon D. Rossini, *Contemporary Latina/o Theater: Wrighting Ethnicity* (Carbondale: Southern Illinois University Press, 2008), 25.

65. Jerry Parker, "Chita Rivera Advertises Herself," *Newsday*, September 9, 1977.

66. See, for example, Claude M. Steele, *Whistling Vivaldi and Other Clues as to How Stereotypes Affect Us* (New York: W. W. Norton, 2010); and Mahzarin Banaji and Anthony G. Greenwald, *Blind Spot: Hidden Biases of Good People* (New York: Delacorte Press, 2013).

67. Here I use *effigy* in the sense rehearsed by Joseph Roach. See Roach, *Cities of the Dead*, 36–41.

68. Anne Bogart, *A Director Prepares: Seven Essays on Art and Theatre* (New York: Routledge, 2000), 95–96.

69. Bernstein, *Racial Innocence*, 71.

70. Chin and Chan, "Racist Love," 66.

71. Roach, *Cities of the Dead*, 90. Roach also demonstrates how the performance of Native Americans by non-Natives in the theatre of the early republic utilized Native characters as effigies in the performative construction of an emergent "American" national identity. Though not drawing on Roach's terms, Philip J. Deloria's work, especially *Playing Indian* (New Haven, CT: Yale University Press, 1998), provides numerous illustrations of how the performance "of" Indians by non-Indians privileges the aesthetic and cultural significance of the effigy of the Indian over the historical contributions, creations, and perspectives of Native peoples.

72. Fred Moten, *In the Break: The Aesthetics of the Black Radical Tradition* (Minneapolis: University of Minnesota Press, 2003), 235.

73. Dolores Prida, *'Beautiful Señoritas' and Other Plays* (Houston: Arte Público Press, 1991), 20–21.

74. Ibid., 21–22.

75. Ibid., 36–39.

76. Ibid., 42.

77. Ibid., 42–45.

78. Ibid., 44.

79. Luz María Umpierre, "Interview with Dolores Prida," *Latin American Theatre Review* 22 (Fall 1998): 82.

80. Shawn Michelle Smith, *Photography on the Color Line: W. E. B. DuBois, Race, and Visual Culture* (Durham, NC: Duke University Press, 2004), 42.

81. The foundational text of intersectional feminist analysis is Kimberlé Crenshaw's "Demarginalizing the Intersection of Race and Sex: A Black Feminist Critique of Antidiscrimination Doctrine, Feminist Theory, and Antiracist Politics," *University of Chicago Legal Forum* (1989): 139–67. For more contemporary analyses of intersectional feminism, see also Patricia Hill Collins, "It's All in the Family: Intersections of Gender, Race, and Nation," in *Decentering the Center: Philosophy for a Multicultural, Post-colonial, and Feminist World*, ed. Uma Narayan and Sandra Harding (Bloomington: Indiana University Press, 2000), 156–76; as well as a very helpful essay by Leslie McCall, "The Complexity of Intersectionality," *Signs: Journal of Women in Culture and Society* 30 (Spring 2005): 1771–1800.

82. Cherríe Moraga and Gloria Anzaldúa, *This Bridge Called My Back: Writings by Radical Women of Color* (Boston: South End Press, 1983); Beah E. Richards, *Black Woman Speaks* (1950), in *9 Plays by Black Women*, ed. and introduced by Margaret B. Wilkerson (New York: New American Library, 1986), 29–39; Ntozake Shange, *For Colored Girls Who Have Considered Suicide When the Rainbow Is Enuf: A Choreopoem* (New York: Macmillan, 1977).

Chapter 5

1. Nicola Barbour, "Size Matters, Particularly if You're Only 13 Inches Tall," *Observer*, August 31, 1997, 59.

2. Corey Sabourin, "Billy's Got the Beat," *H/X*, June 5, 1998, 18.

3. Ernie Glam, "Boy Toy," *Latina*, July 1998, 20.

4. Max Harrold, "*Hola*, Gorgeous!," *Genre*, March 1998, 32.

5. Angela Tribelli, "Put Your Tiny Hand in Mine," *New York Times*, April 26, 1998, 4.

6. Donald Suggs, "Valley of the Dolls," *TimeOut New York*, March 12–19, 1998, 105.

7. Judd Winick, *Pedro and Me: Friendship, Loss, and What I Learned* (New York: Henry Holt, 2000), 112.

8. José Esteban Muñoz's account of Pedro Zamora's life and work remains definitive in "'Pedro Zamora's Real World of Counterpublicity: Performing an Ethics of the Self," in *Disidentifications: Queers of Color and the Performance of Politics* (Minneapolis: University of Minnesota Press,, 1999), 143–61. For an instructively close reading of how Zamora intervened in the emerging conventions of reality television, see Erika Suderburg, "Real/Young/TV Queer," in *Between the Sheets, in the Streets*, ed. Chris Holmlund and Cynthia Fuchs (Minneapolis: University of Minnesota Press, 1997), 46–70, especially 52–58.

9. Betsy Israel, "HIV, and Positive," *People*, November 28, 1996, 185–86. "Tribute to Pedro Zamora," aired on the MTV network on December 1, 1994. For a contemporary review of the special, see James Martin, "Free Your Mind: A Tribute to Pedro Zamora," *America*, December 31, 1994, 21; and William J. Clinton, "Statement on the Death of Pedro Zamora" (November 11, 1994), in Gerhard Peters and John T. Woolley, *The American Presidency Project*, http://www.presidency.ucsb.edu/ws/?pid=49482 (accessed August 2, 2013).

10. Jeffrey Schmalz, "As Gay Marchers Gather, Mood Is Serious and Festive," *New York Times*, April 25, 1993.

11. "José Zuniga, 28, AIDS Activist," *The Advocate*, August 19, 1997, 62.

12. José Zuniga, *Soldier of the Year: The Story of a Gay American Patriot* (New York: Pocket Books, 1994).

13. Sue Fulton, "In Honor of Specialist José Zuniga," *OutServe*, September 2011, http://outservemag.com/2011/09/682/ (accessed August 2, 2013).

14. José Quiroga, *Tropics of Desire: Interventions from Queer Latino America* (New York: New York University Press, 2000), 176.

15. Ann Pellegrini, "Women on Top, Boys on the Side, but Some of Us Are Brave: Blackness, Lesbianism, and the Visible," *College Literature* 59 (February 1997): 88.

16. As Lisa Duggan has influentially argued, *homonormativity* describes the "neoliberal privatization of affective as well as economic and public life," wherein ostensibly activist claims orient away from actions of resistance and critique and toward the "freedom" and "equality" of access to state-aligned institutions like marriage and the military. Lisa Duggan, "The New Homonormativity: The Sexual Politics of Neoliberalism," in *Materializing Democracy: Toward a Revitalized Cultural Politics*, edited by Russ Castronovo and Dana D. Nelson (Durham, NC: Duke University Press, 2002), 175–94.

17. Nan Alamilla Boyd, *Wide Open Town: A History of Queer San Francisco* (Berkeley: University of California Press, 2003), 20–24. For a narrative summary of Sarria's early organizing, see Randy Shilts, *The Mayor of Castro Street* (New York: St. Martin's, 1982), 51–54. See also Michael Robert Gorman, *The Empress Is a Man: Stories from the Life of José Sarria* (London: Haworth Press, 1998).

18. For a summary of Montez's early career, see Daniel Kauffman, *Ridiculous: The Theatrical Life and Times of Charles Ludlam* (New York: Applause Books, 2005), especially 48–63. For an incisive historiographic assessment of how Montez has been interpreted within queer studies, see Lawrence La Fountain-Stokes, "Gay Shame, Latina- and Latino-Style: A Critique of White Queer Performativity," in *Gay Latino Studies: A Critical Reader*, ed. Michael Hames-Garcia and Ernest Javier Martínez (Durham, NC: Duke University Press, 2011), 55–80.

19. Juan Bruce-Novoa's work on Rechy's persona remains some of the most instructive. See especially "Rechy and Rodriguez: Double Crossing the Public Private

Line," in *Double Crossings/Entrecruzamientos*, ed. Mario Martin Flores and Carlos Von Son (Ediciones Nuevo Espacio, 2001), 15–34. See also John Rechy, *Sexual Outlaw: A Documentary* (New York: Grove Press, 1984).

20. For a thorough reassessment of Sylvia Rivera's activist work and legacy, see the dossier devoted to her in *Centro Journal: Puerto Rican Queer Sexualities* 19, no. 1 (Spring 2007): 116–61. See especially Tim Retzloff, "Eliding Trans Latino/a Queer Experience in U.S. LGBT History: José Sarria and Sylvia Rivera Reexamined" (141–61); and Jessi Gan, "'Still at the Back of the Bus': Sylvia Rivera's Struggle" (125–39).

21. Darrel Enck-Wanzer, "Introduction: Toward Understanding the Young Lords," in *The Young Lords: A Reader*, ed. Darrel Enck-Wanzer (New York: New York University Press, 2010), 1.

22. Douglas Brode, *Multiculturalism and the Mouse: Race and Sex in Disney Entertainment* (Austin: University of Texas Press, 2006), 240. For a fuller discussion of gender play in variants of the Zorro story, see Catherine Williamson, "'Draped Crusaders': Disrobing Gender in the 'Mark of Zorro,'" *Cinema Journal* 36, no. 2 (Winter 1997): 3–16; and David William Foster, "Of Gay Caballeros and Other Noble Heroes," *Bilingual Review/La Revista Bilingüe* (May–December 2008–9): 23–44.

23. Gabriel S. Estrada, "Indian Icon, Gay Macho: Felipe Rose of Village People," in *Performing the US Latina and Latino Borderlands*, ed. Arturo J. Aldama, Chela Sandoval, and Peter J. Garcia (Bloomington: Indiana University Press, 2012), 344–62.

24. Ed Anger [Rafe Klinger], "Watch Out, Barbie!," *Weekly World News*, October 23, 1997, 17. For more about Rafe Klinger, see "Tabloid Eaten Alive by Aliens! Fake Columnist Loses His Job!," *New York Times*, July 30, 2007.

25. For discussion of Antonio Fargas, See Charles I. Nero's essay "Why Are Gay Ghettoes White?," in *Black Queer Studies: A Critical Anthology*, ed. E. Patrick Johnson and Mae G. Henderson (Durham, NC: Duke University Press, 2005), 236.

26. An evocative summary of *Short Eyes*'s original production can be found in Mel Gussow's *New York Times* review of January 7, 1974, reprinted in Ben Brantley, ed., *The New York Times Book of Broadway: On the Aisle for the Unforgettable Plays* (New York: Macmillan, 2001), 193–94. Jon Rossini and Michael Hames-Garcia offer especially apt readings of the play in Jon D. Rossini, *Contemporary Latina/o Theater: Wrighting Ethnicity* (Carbondale: Southern Illinois University Press, 2008), 32–43; and Michael Hames-Garcia, *Fugitive Thought: Prison Riots, Race, and the Meaning of Justice* (Minneapolis: University of Minnesota Press, 2004), 165–89.

27. See Alberto Sandoval-Sánchez, "'A Chorus Line': Not Such a 'One Singular Sensation,'" in *José, Can You See? Latinos On and Off Broadway* (Madison: University of Wisconsin Press, 1999), 83–99.

28. The fullest assessment of the "clone" as style, practice, and identity remains Martin P. Levine, *Gay Macho: The Life and Death of the Homosexual Clone*, ed. and introduced by Michael S. Kimmel (New York: New York University Press, 1998). These quotations, though, come from John Preston's impassioned 1981 defense of the clone in "Goodbye to Sally Gearhart," reprinted in *The Christopher Street Reader*, ed. Michael Denneny, Charles Ortleb, and Thomas Steele (New York: Perigree Books, 1983), 368–80, especially 369.

29. "Michael Carmine, 30, Stage and Film Actor," *New York Times*, October 18, 1989, D29.

30. Lynn Geller and Leon Ichaso, "Leon Ichaso," *BOMB* 78 (Winter 2001–2): 39.

31. E. Creger, "Michael Carmie's [*sic*] Doing It All," *New Pittsburgh Courier*, April 30, 1988, 7.

32. For the most efficient summary of the production of the film, see Margot Dougherty, "Moving Pictures," *Entertainment Weekly*, May 18, 1990. See also Craig Lucas, "Longtime Companion," *The Advocate*, November 12, 2002, 37.

33. David Denby, "Tender Mercy," *New York*, May 21, 1990, 68–69.

34. Vincent Canby, "Manhattan's Privileged and the Plague of AIDS," *New York Times*, May 11, 1990.

35. Greg Merritt, *Celluloid Mavericks: The History of American Independent Film* (New York: Basic Books, 2000), 390.

36. As Vito Russo presciently observed on the film's commercial release, "*Longtime Companion* will be criticized on many counts by the same people who always want films like this one to cover all bases and be all things to all people. . . . Virtually all the characters in *Longtime Companion* are white, handsome and upscale professionals— and rightly so, because this is exactly the population first identified with this disease in exactly the setting in which it happened." Vito Russo, Review of *Longtime Companion*, *The Advocate*, May 8, 1990, 53. Craig Lucas later reflected on "the real dismay and anger" among viewers "who had waited to see their experience of the epidemic on screen (including I.V. drug users, activists as well as gay people from all walks of life, many without health insurance and what they perceived to be the social advantages of the characters in *Longtime Companion*)." Quoted in Steven Drunkman, "Craig Lucas on 'Movie-Land': An Interview by Steven Drunkman," in Craig Lucas, "*The Dying Gaul" and Other Screenplays* (New York: Alyson Books, 2008), x. For one example of such a review, which faults the film for both its form and its content, see Elayne Rapping, "'My Own Private Idaho' and 'Longtime Companion,'" in *Media-Thons: Forays into the Gender and Culture Wars* (Boston: South End Press, 1994), 131–34.

37. Not infrequently, such references also anonymize Carmine's death, in the manner of *Entertainment Weekly*'s Margot Dougherty, who wrote, "One actor died of AIDS before filming began. Another, with a small role, has died since." Dougherty, "Moving Pictures," 48.

38. For a valuable historical theorization of buddy work as a mode of activism, see Tom Roach, *Friendship as a Way of Life: Foucault, AIDS, and the Politics of Shared Estrangement* (Albany, NY: State University of New York Press, 2012), 110–13.

39. For Lucas this dramatic arc was intended. The characters of *Longtime Companion* were intended to represent those "initially so hard hit by the AIDS virus [who were] also some of the first people to organize, which meant coming out of their shells, confronting their privilege and ignorance." Quoted in Drunkman, "Craig Lucas on 'Movie-Land,'" x.

40. Canby, "Manhattan's Privileged and the Plague of AIDS."

41. Farrah Anwar, "*Longtime Companion*," *Monthly Film Bulletin*, November 1, 1990, 326–27.

42. David Elliott, "Companion Is Realistic about AIDS," *San Diego Union*, May 25, 1990, D1.

43. David Román, "Tropical Fruit," in *Tropicalizations: Transcultural Representations of Latinidad*, ed. Frances R. Aparicio and Susana Chávez-Silverman (Hanover, NH: Dartmouth College Press, 1997), 122.

44. Janet Maslin, "*Philadelphia*: Tom Hanks as an AIDS Victim Who Fights the Establishment," *New York Times*, December 22, 1993.

45. Roger Ebert, Review of *Philadelphia*, January 14, 1994, http://www.rogerebert.com/reviews/philadelphia-1994 (accessed July 29, 2013); Owen Gleiberman, *Enter-*

tainment Weekly, December 24, 1993, http://www.ew.com/ew/article/0,,309047,00. html (accessed July 29, 2013).

46. "Playing the Part: Straight Tom Hanks Gives a Lesson on Being Gay," *Newsweek*, February 14, 1994, 46.

47. Wolf Schneider, "Dead Serious: It's No Laughing Matter When Hanks Takes on AIDS," *Kokomo Tribune*, December 30, 1993, 2.

48. Ronald Mark Kraft, "Fearless in Philadelphia: Antonio Banderas Plays Gay with Gusto," *The Advocate*, February 8, 1994, 51.

49. Ibid.

50. Vincent Canby, "McNally, True, but Vaguely Neo-Chekhovian," *New York Times*, November 6, 1994; Michael Musto, "Some Straight Dope on a Gay Heartthrob," *New York*, June 2, 1997, 13.

51. David Román, *Acts of Intervention: Performance, Gay Culture, and AIDS* (Bloomington: Indiana University Press, 1998), 253.

52. Santiago Castillanos, "Hauntings by the Latin Lover: The Ambiguities of Eroticized Latino Male Bodies in Contemporary U.S. Queer Commercial Narrative Cinema" (PhD diss., University of California, Davis, 2008), 29. Particularly note Castillanos's extensive discussion of *Love! Valour! Compassion!* in "The Eroticized Latino Body and the Policing of (Homo)Normativities," 38–55.

53. José Esteban Muñoz, "Dead White: Notes on the Whiteness of the New Queer Cinema," *GLQ: A Journal of Lesbian and Gay Studies* 4, no. 1 (1998): 127–38. In this same essay, Muñoz also briefly assesses Becker's role in the 1995 film *Lay Down with Dogs*, a gay independent feature filmed before Becker took the role of Ramon but released during the play's Broadway run. Muñoz describes Becker's role as "a shifty, brainless, oversexed Latino whose character reinscribes every toxic stigma attached to Latino bodies by white-supremacist culture" (129). Becker's appearance in this role made the young actor the subject of a number of profiles, in the *New York Times*, *New York*, and *The Advocate*, all of which used his hunkiness as a hook, commenting on the novelty of his straightness while leaving unaddressed the fact that he was a non-Latino playing a series of Latino roles. In addition to Musto, "Some Straight Dope on a Gay Heartthrob," see Mike Ford, "Randy Becker's Nude Scene in *Love! Valour! Compassion!* Catapults Him out of Obscurity and into a New Film Role," *The Advocate*, July 25, 1995, 56–59; and Anita Gates, "Up and Coming: Randy Becker, A Broadway Baby at 24," *New York Times*, February 12, 1995. Becker's prior experience playing queer Latino characters is also unmentioned: Becker played Cupcakes in a college production of *Short Eyes* five years before playing Ramon in *Love! Valour! Compassion!* on Broadway. (I played the character of "Juan" in the same college production: *Short Eyes*, by Miguel Piñero, dir. Michael Silver, Production Workshop, Brown University, Providence, Rhode Island, November 1989.)

54. In not dissimilar ways, John Leguizamo's various "little Latin boy in a dress" roles of the early 1990s—as Manny in his 1990 solo play *Mambo Mouth*, as Ruby in the 1995 short film *Time Expired*, and as ChiChi Rodriguez in the 1995 Hollywood road comedy *To Wong Foo*—also inhabit the gendered duality of dragged desire, with each character's story line an aspirational plaint for the possibility of queer couplehood.

55. David Van Leer, "Visible Silence: Spectatorship in Black Gay and Lesbian Film," in *Representing Blackness: Issues in Film and Video*, ed. Valerie Smith (New Brunswick, N.J.: Rutgers University Press, 1997), 160.

56. Barbour, "Size Matters," 59.

57. "When G.I. Joe Just Won't Do," *Newsweek*, February 17, 1997, 6.

58. This language is taken from the now defunct BillyWorld.com website, www. BillyWorld.com/billysez/mystory. All quotations from the website draw on a nearly complete printout of the text and graphics produced in April 1998, which remains in the author's possession (hereafter BillyWorld.com). At the time the printout was made, there were no references to Carlos.

59. "When G.I. Joe Just Won't Do."

60. Eddie Dominguez, "New Billy Doll Not after Barbie," *Daily Herald*, June 11, 1997.

61. "Billy the Gay Doll Is Out, Proud," *Cedar Rapids Gazette*, March 15, 1997, 2A.

62. Anger, "Watch Out, Barbie!"

63. Jan Moir, "Who's a Big Boy-Toy, Then?," *The Guardian*, November 25, 1994.

64. "Nancy Toy, Ken's Longtime Companion?," *Details*, April 1995, n.p.

65. Copyright was registered initially in the United Kingdom, with John McKitterick credited as "designer" and Juan Andres credited as "collaborator." See http://eprints.kingston.ac.uk/4700/ (accessed August 2, 2013).

66. Barbour, "Size Matters."

67. BillyWorld.com.

68. Levine, *Gay Macho*, 65, 67.

69. BillyWorld.com.

70. "Tzabaco, Your Out Source," Winter 1998, catalog in author's possession.

71. Ibid.

72. "Billy's Friend Carlos a Doll," *NewsPlanet*, February 25, 1998. Printout circa April 1998 in author's possession.

73. Little is known about Juan Antonio Andres, whose name and profession (Spanish entrepreneur) came up in only a handful of Web articles in the mid-2000s, mostly originating in the Spanish-speaking world. As an example, see "Billy, el mejor regalo de Reyes para los mitómanos juguetones," http://www.ragap.es/actualidad/fashion/billy-el-mejor-regalo-de-reyes-para-los-mitomanos-juguetones/570590 (accessed July 29, 2013). See also the copyright information at http://eprints.kingston.ac.uk/4700/ (accessed August 2, 2013).

74. Quiroga, *Tropics of Desire*, 180.

75. Daniel Harris, *The Rise and Fall of Gay Culture* (New York: Hyperion Books, 1997), 102.

76. *Hombres Latinos* was a glossy gay erotic magazine, featuring both pictorials and fiction, which was published among a suite of gay erotic "fetish" magazines by BrushCreek Media beginning in 1995. Most of BrushCreek's magazines abruptly ceased publication in 2001. *Hombres Latinos* published a total of nineteen issues between 1995 and 2000. This quote comes from "Hombres Letters," *Hombres Latinos,* January 1998, 12.

77. "Ohhhh . . . CARLOS!!!," *QV*, March–April 1998, 7.

78. Suggs, "Valley of the Dolls," 105.

79. Jamoo, *The Films of Kristen Bjorn* (Laguna Hills, CA: Companion Press, 1997), 37.

80. Ibid.

81. Joe A. Thomas, "Gay Male Pornography since Stonewall," in *Sex for Sale: Prostitution, Pornography, and the Sex Industry,* ed. Ronald Weitzer (New York: Routledge, 2009), 72.

82. Steve Jensen, "Review: The Games We Play," *Unzipped*, May 26, 1998, 37.

83. Eduardo Contreras, "'Ricanlicious," *ñ* 1, no. 1 (Spring–Summer 1998): 14–15.

84. Quiroga, *Tropics of Desire*, 176.

85. Suggs, "Valley of the Dolls," 105.

86. This language is drawn from a direct mail flyer announcing the products newly available in spring 1999, copy in author's possession.

87. Erica Rand, *Barbie's Queer Accessories* (Durham, NC: Duke University Press, 1995), 84. Frances Negrón-Muntaner briefly comments on Carlos in her broader discussion of the 1998 release of Puerto Rican Barbie in "Selling Out Puerto Rican Identity in the Global Market," in *Contested Images: Women of Color in Popular Culture* (Lanham, MD: AltaMira Press, 2012), 137–56, especially 152.

88. Ann DuCille, *Skin Trade* (Cambridge, MA: Harvard University Press, 1996), 56–57.

89. Review of *Billy 2000: Billy Goes to Hollywood*.

90. Ibid.

91. Dianora Niccolini, with David Leddick, *Big Fun with Billy* (New York: Universe Publishing, 2001).

92. Ibid.

93. Billy had worn blackface at a 1998 LifeBEAT event as part of designer Nicole Miller's "funked up" contribution to the benefit. See "Out of the Dollhouse and onto the Runway," *Newsweek*, May 4, 1998, 6.

94. George Rush and Joanna Molloy, "One Tyson Could Be a Real Doll," *New York Daily News*, November 29, 1999.

95. Ibid.

96. Niccolini and Leddick, *Big Fun with Billy*.

97. Patricia M. LeMay, "UPS Keeps Brown-Uniformed 'Billy Doll' Off Shelves," *Aiken Standard*, January 25, 2002, 3C.

98. Beauregard Houston-Montgomery, "Guys and Dolls," *The Advocate*, November 9, 1999, 54.

99. John Medeiros, "Tom of Finland 001 Rebel Action Figure," *Doll Digest*, September 30, 2003, http://www.mastercollector.com/articles/dolls/dollnews093003.shtml (accessed July 30 2013); Norm Lloyd, "Art in Action," Tom of Finland Foundation, Autumn 2003, http://tomoffinlandfoundation.org/foundation/Dispatch/2003-Autumn/ArtInAction.htm (accessed July 30, 2013).

100. Confirmation of McKitterick's active employment as head of the Department of Fashion at Kingston University can be found in "Fashion Ace Swaps Centre Court for Catwalk," *Bridge: The Kingston University Magazine*, June 2004, 8. Dennis Milam Bensie offers his account of searching for John McKitterick in "In Search of Gay Bob and Billy," February 12, 2012, in his blog http://shorn.coffeetownpress.com/?p=773 (accessed March 28, 2014). McKitterick's copyright information is summarized in Kingston University's research repository, http://eprints.kingston.ac.uk/4700/ (accessed July 29, 2013).

101. To confirm this timeline, see cached snapshots of BillyWorld.com at archive.org's "Way Back Machine," https://web.archive.org/web/*/http://billyworld.com (accessed July 29, 2013).

102. Jackie Goldsby, "What It Means to Be Colored Me," *Out/Look: The National Lesbian and Gay Quarterly* 2, no. 1 (Summer 1990): 11.

103. Ibid., 12.

104. Jerry Seinfeld, with Andy Ackerman (director) and Spike Feresten (writer),

"Soup Nazi," "Soup Nazi—Commentary," and "Soup Nazi—Notes on Nothing," *Seinfeld*, season 7, episode 6, November 2, 1995. NBC-TV, DVD.

105. The term *gay thugs*, as used to describe Bob and his companion, emerges in a variety of Seinfeld literatures, including scholarly treatments of the series. See, as examples, Margo Miller, "Masculinity and Male Intimacy in Nineties Sitcoms: 'Seinfeld and the Ironic Dismissal," in *The New Queer Aesthetic on Television: Essays on Recent Programming*, ed. James R. Keller and Leslie Tratyner (Jefferson, NC: McFarland, 2006), 151; and Ron Becker, "Prime-Time TV in the Gay Nineties: Network Television, Quality Audiences, and Gay Politics," in *The Television Studies Reader*, edited by Robert C. Allen and Annette Hill (New York: Routledge, 2004), 392.

106. For a compelling reading of this episode, see Sander L. Gilman, *Diseases and Diagnoses: The Second Age of Biology* (New Brunswick, NJ: Transaction Publishers, 2011), 61–62.

107. Jerry Seinfeld, with Andy Ackerman (director) and Peter Mehlman (writer), "The Sponge," "The Sponge—Commentary," and "The Sponge—Notes on Nothing," *Seinfeld*, season 7, episode 9, December 7, 1995, NBC-TV, DVD.

108. Jerry Seinfeld, with Andy Ackerman (director) and David Mandel and Steve Koren (writers), "The Puerto Rican Day," "The Puerto Rican Day—Commentary," and "The Puerto Rican Day—Notes on Nothing," *Seinfeld*, season 9, episode 20, May 7, 1998, NBC-TV, DVD.

109. See, for example, Frances Negrón-Mutaner, *Boricua Pop: Puerto Ricans and the Latinization of American Culture* (New York: New York University Press, 2004), 247–71; or Quiroga, *Tropics of Desire*, 181–90.

Epilogue

1. Ben Yagoda, *About Town: The New Yorker and the World It Made* (New York: Scribner, 2000), 376.

2. Jack Ziegler, "A Lot of You Used to Know Us as the L.A. Punksters . . ." *New Yorker*, June 14, 1999, 29.

Selected Bibliography

For a list of cited films, plays, television programs, and other performances, along with other supplementary content, see this volume's website, http://latin-numbers.com/.

Acevedo-Muñoz, Ernesto R. *West Side Story as Cinema: The Making and Impact of an American Masterpiece.* Lawrence: University Press of Kansas, 2013.

Adir, Karin. *The Great Clowns of American Television.* Jefferson, NC: McFarland, 1998.

Allen, Irving Lewis. *Unkind Words: Ethnic Labeling from Redskin to WASP.* New York: Bergin & Garvey, 1990.

Allport, Gordon W. *ABC's of Scapegoating.* New York: Anti-Defamation League of B'Nai B'Rith, 1948.

Allport, Gordon W. *The Nature of Prejudice.* 25th anniversary ed. Reading, MA: Perseus Books, 1979.

Almaguer, Tomás. *Racial Fault Lines: Historical Origins of White Supremacy in California.* Berkeley: University of California Press, 1994.

Aparicio, Frances R. "Jennifer as Selena: Rethinking Latinidad in Media and Popular Culture." *Latino Studies* 1 (March 2003): 90–105.

Aparicio, Frances R., and Susana Chávez-Silverman, eds. *Tropicalizations: Transcultural Representations of Latinidad.* Hanover, NH: Dartmouth College Press, 1997.

Arrizón, Alicia. *Queering Mestizaje: Transculturation and Performance.* Ann Arbor: University of Michigan Press, 2006.

Auslander, Philip. *From Acting to Performance: Essays in Modernism and Postmodernism.* New York: Routledge, 1997.

Auslander, Philip. *Liveness: Performance in a Mediatized Culture.* New York: Routledge, 1999.

Auslander, Philip. "Musical Personae." *TDR: The Drama Review* 50 (Spring 2006): 100–119.

Auslander, Philip. "The Performativity of Performance Documentation." *PAJ: A Journal of Performance and Art* 28 (September 2006): 1–10.

Banaji, Mahzarin, and Anthony G. Greenwald. *Blind Spot: Hidden Biases of Good People.* New York: Delacorte Press, 2013.

Banfield, Stephen. *Sondheim's Broadway Musicals.* Ann Arbor: University of Michigan Press, 1993.

Banks, Daniel. "The Welcome Table: Casting for an Integrated Society." *Theatre Topics* 23, no. 1 (March 2013): 1–18.

Barajas, Frank P. "The Defense Committees of Sleepy Lagoon: A Convergent Struggle against Fascism, 1942–1944." *Aztlán: A Journal of Chicano Studies* 31 (Spring 2006): 33–62.

Baron, Cynthia, and Sharon Marie Carnicke. *Reframing Screen Performance.* Ann Arbor: University of Michigan Press, 2008.

Barton, Ruth. *Acting Irish in Hollywood: From Fitzgerald to Farrell.* Dublin: Irish Academic Press, 2006.

Beard, Belle Boone. "Puerto Rico—The Forty-Ninth State?" *Phylon* 6 (Second Quarter 1945): 105–17.

Becker, Ron. "Prime-Time TV in the Gay Nineties: Network Television, Quality Audiences, and Gay Politics." In *The Television Studies Reader,* edited by Robert C. Allen and Annette Hill, 389–403. New York: Routledge, 2004.

Beltrán, Mary. "Dolores Del Rio, the First 'Latin Invasion,' and Hollywood's Transition to Sound." *Aztlán: A Journal of Chicano Studies* 30 (Spring 2005): 55–85.

Beltrán, Mary. *Latina/o Stars in US Eyes: The Makings and Meanings of Film and TV Stardom.* Urbana: University of Illinois Press, 2009.

Bender, Steven. *Greasers and Gringos: Latinos, Law, and the American Imagination.* New York: New York University Press, 2005.

Bender, Stephen W. "Will the World Survive: Latino/a Pop Music in the Cultural Mainstream." *Denver University Law Review* 78 (2000–2001): 719–52.

Bergquist, Kathy. *Ricky Martin.* New York: Billboard Books, 1999.

Bernstein, Leonard. *Findings.* New York: Simon & Schuster, 1982.

Bernstein, Robin. *Racial Innocence: Performing American Childhood from Slavery to Civil Rights.* New York: New York University Press, 2011.

Bérubé, Allan. *Coming Out under Fire.* New York: Simon & Schuster, 2000.

Berumen, Frank Javier Garcia. *Brown Celluloid: Latino/a Film Icons and Images in the Hollywood Film Industry.* New York: Vantage Press, 2003.

Bettelheim, Bruno, and Morris Janowitz. *Social Change and Prejudice, Including the Dynamics of Prejudice.* New York: Free Press, 1975.

Bhabha, Homi. *The Location of Culture.* New York: Routledge, 1994.

Bial, Henry. *Acting Jewish: Negotiating Ethnicity on the American Stage and Screen.* Ann Arbor: University of Michigan Press, 2005.

Bial, Henry. "In America, There Are No Cats: Identity, Utopia, and the Giant Mouse of Minsk." Paper presented at the annual meeting of the American Society of Theatre Research, Phoenix, Arizona, November 15–18, 2007.

Bird, Elizabeth S., ed. *Dressing in Feathers: The Construction of the Indian in American Popular Culture.* Boulder, CO: Westview Press, 1996.

Birringer, Johannes. "La Melancolía de la Jaula (The Melancholy of the Cage)." *Performing Arts Journal* 52 (January 1996): 103–28.

Black, Fredrick B. *FDR's Good Neighbor Policy: Sixty Years of Generally Gentle Chaos.* Austin: University of Texas Press, 1995.

Black, George. *The Good Neighbor: How the United States Wrote the History of Central America and the Caribbean.* New York: Pantheon, 1988.

Bogart, Anne. *A Director Prepares: Seven Essays on Art and Theatre.* New York: Routledge, 2000.

Bogle, Donald. *Toms, Coons, Mulattoes, Mammies, and Bucks: An Interpretive History of Blacks in American Films.* New York: Viking Press, 1973.

Bona, Damien. *Starring John Wayne as Genghis Khan: Hollywood's All-Time Worst Casting Blunders.* Secaucus, NJ: Citadel Press, 1996.

Bordman, Gerald. *American Theatre: A Chronicle of Comedy and Drama, 1930–1969.* New York: Oxford University Press, 1996.

Boyd, Nan Alamilla. *Wide Open Town: A History of Queer San Francisco.* Berkeley: University of California Press, 2003.

Bramen, Carrie Tirado. "Speaking in Typeface: Characterizing Stereotypes in Gayl Jones's 'Mosquito.'" *MFS: Modern Fiction Studies* 49 (Spring 2003): 124–54.

Brode, Douglas. *Multiculturalism and the Mouse: Race and Sex in Disney Entertainment.* Austin: University of Texas Press, 2006.

Brown, Harriet McCune, and Helen Miller Bailey. *Our Latin American Neighbors.* New York: Houghton Mifflin, 1944.

Broyles-Gonzáles, Yolanda. *El Teatro Campesino: Theater in the Chicano Movement.* Austin: University of Texas Press, 1994.

Bruce-Novoa, Juan. "Rechy and Rodriguez: Double Crossing the Public Private Line." In *Double Crossings/Entrecruzamientos,* edited by Mario Martin Flores and Carlos Von Son, 5–34. Ediciones Nuevo Espacio, 2001.

Buckingham, David. *Media Education: Literacy, Learning, and Contemporary Culture.* Malden, MA: Blackwell Publishing, 2003.

Burke, Kenneth. *On Symbols and Society.* Chicago: University of Chicago Press, 1989.

Butler, Judith. *Bodies That Matter: On the Discursive Limits of Sex.* New York: Routledge, 1993.

Cagle, Chris. "Two Modes of Prestige Film." *Screen* 48 (Autumn 2007): 291–311.

Cameron, Kenneth M., with Patti P. Gillespie, Jim Hunter, and Jim A. Patterson. *The Enjoyment of Theatre.* 7th ed. New York: Allyn & Bacon, 2008.

Capote, Truman. *The Dogs Bark.* New York: Random House, 1973.

Carlson, Marvin. *The Haunted Stage: The Theatre as Memory Machine.* Ann Arbor: University of Michigan Press, 2003.

Carlson, Marvin. *Performance: A Critical Introduction.* 2nd ed. New York: Routledge, 2003.

Castillanos, Santiago. "Hauntings by the Latin Lover: The Ambiguities of Eroticized Latino Male Bodies in Contemporary U.S. Queer Commercial Narrative Cinema." PhD diss., University of California, Davis, 2008.

Cepeda, María Elena. "Shakira as the Idealized, Transnational Citizen: A Case Study of Colombianidad in Transition." *Latino Studies* 1 (July 2003): 211–32.

Cespedes, Diogenes, and Silvio Torres-Saillant. "Fiction Is the Poor Man's Cinema: An Interview with Junot Díaz." *Callaloo* 23 (Summer 2000): 892–907.

Chansky, Dorothy. *Composing Ourselves: The Little Theatre Movement and the American Audience.* Carbondale: Southern Illinois University Press, 2004.

Chin, Frank, and Jeffery Paul Chan. "Racist Love." In *Seeing through Shuck,* edited by Richard Kostelanetz, 65–79. New York: Ballantine Books, 1972.

Chinn, Sarah. "Racialized Things." *American Quarterly* 64, no. 4 (December 2012): 873–83.

Cho, Margaret. *I'm the One That I Want.* Chicago: Ballantine Books, 2002.

Christie, John S., and José B. Gonzalez. *Latino Boom: An Anthology of U.S. Latino Literature.* New York: Longman and Pearson Education, 2006.

Clarke, Cheryl. *After Mecca: Women Poets and the Black Arts Movement*. New Brunswick, NJ: Rutgers University Press, 2005.

Cohen, Robert. *Theatre*. 3rd ed. Mountain View, CA: Mayfield Publishing, 1994.

Collins, Patricia Hill. "It's All in the Family: Intersections of Gender, Race, and Nation." In *Decentering the Center: Philosophy for a Multicultural, Post-colonial, and Feminist World*, edited by Uma Narayan and Sandra Harding, 156–76. Bloomington: Indiana University Press, 2000.

Colón, Jesús. *A Puerto Rican in New York and Other Sketches*. New York: International Publishers, 1982.

Contreras, Eduardo. "'Ricanlicious," *ñ* 1, no. 1 (Spring–Summer 1998): 14–15.

Coward, Noël. *Noël Coward: The Complete Lyrics*. Edited by Barry Day. Woodstock, NY: Overlook Press, 1998.

Cox, Jim. *The A to Z of American Radio Soap Operas*. Lanham, MD: Scarecrow Press, 2009.

Crenshaw, Kimberlé. "Demarginalizing the Intersection of Race and Sex: A Black Feminist Critique of Antidiscrimination Doctrine, Feminist Theory, and Antiracist Politics." *University of Chicago Legal Forum* (1989): 139–67.

Crenshaw, Kimberlé. "Mapping the Margins: Intersectionality, Identity Politics, and Violence against Women of Color." *Stanford Law Review* 43 (July 1991): 1241–99.

Davis, Natalie Zemon. *Slaves on Screen: Film and Historical Vision*. Cambridge, MA: Harvard University Press, 2002.

Dawson, Anthony A. P. "Hollywood's Labor Troubles." *Industrial and Labor Relations Review* 1 (July 1948): 638–47.

Deboo, Ana. "The Non-Traditional Casting Project Continues into the '90s." *TDR: The Drama Review* 34 (Winter 1990): 188–91.

Deburg, William L. Van. *New Day in Babylon: The Black Power Movement and American Culture, 1965–1975*. Chicago: University of Chicago Press, 1993.

De Genova, Nicholas, and Ana Y. Ramos-Zayas. "Latino Racial Formations in the United States: An Introduction." *Journal of Latin American Anthropology* 8, no. 2 (2003): 2–16.

Dégh, Linda. *Legend and Belief: Dialectics of a Folkloric Genre*. Bloomington: University of Indiana Press, 2001.

Delgado, Fernando. "Golden but Not Brown: Oscar De La Hoya and the Complications of Culture, Manhood, and Boxing." *International Journal of the History of Sport* 22 (March 2005): 196–211.

Deloria, Philip J. *Playing Indian*. New Haven, CT: Yale University Press, 1998.

Demastes, William W., and Iris Smith Fischer, eds. *Interrogating America through Theatre and Performance*. New York: Palgrave Macmillan, 2006.

Denning, Michael. *The Cultural Front: The Laboring of American Culture in the Twentieth Century*. New York: Verso, 1998.

Deuchert, Eva, with Kossi Adjamah and Florian Pauly. "For Oscar Glory or Oscar Money? Academy Awards and Movie Success." *Journal of Cultural Economics* 29 (August 2005): 159–76.

Dolan, Jill. *Utopia in Performance: Finding Hope at the Theater*. Ann Arbor: University of Michigan Press, 2005.

Dougherty, Margot. "Moving Pictures." *Entertainment Weekly*, May 18 1990, 46–50.

Duany, Jorge. "Nation, Migration, Identity: The Case of Puerto Ricans." *Latino Studies* 1 (November 2003): 424–28.

Du Bois, W. E. B. *The Souls of Black Folk*. New York: Library of America, 1990. Originally published in 1903.

DuCille, Ann. "The Color of Class: Classifying Race in the Popular Imagination." *Social Identities* 7 (Fall 2001): 409–419.

DuCille, Ann. *Skin Trade*. Cambridge, MA: Harvard University Press, 1996.

Duggan, Lisa. "The New Homonormativity: The Sexual Politics of Neoliberalism." In *Materializing Democracy: Toward a Revitalized Cultural Politics*, edited by Russ Castronovo and Dana D. Nelson, 175–94. Durham, NC: Duke University Press, 2002.

Drunkman, Steven. "Craig Lucas on 'Movie-Land': An Interview by Steven Drunkman." In Craig Lucas, *"The Dying Gaul" and Other Screenplays*, ix–xvii. New York: Alyson Books, 2008.

Dunning, John. *The Encyclopedia of Old Time Radio*. New York: Oxford University Press, 1998.

Dyer, Richard. *The Culture of Queers*. New York: Routledge, 2002.

Dyer, Richard. "Homosexuality and Film Noir." *Jump Cut: A Review of Contemporary Media* 16 (November 1977): 18–21.

Dyer, Richard. *The Matter of Images: Essays on Representation*. New York: Routledge, 1993.

Dyer, Richard. *Only Entertainment*. New York: Routledge, 2002.

Dyer, Richard. *White*. New York: Routledge, 1997.

Elam, Harry, Jr. *Taking It to the Streets: The Social Protest Theater of Luis Valdez and Amiri Baraka*. Ann Arbor: University of Michigan Press, 2001.

Ely, Melvin Patrick. *The Adventures of Amos 'n' Andy: A Social History of an American Phenomenon*. New York: Simon & Schuster, 1992.

Enck-Wanzer, Darrel. "Introduction: Toward Understanding the Young Lords." In *The Young Lords: A Reader*, edited by Darrel Enck-Wanzer, 1–8. New York: New York University Press, 2010.

Erdman, Harley. *Staging the Jew: The Performance of an American Ethnicity, 1860–1920*. New Brunswick, NJ: Rutgers University Press, 1998.

Estrada, Gabriel S. "Indian Icon, Gay Macho: Felipe Rose of Village People." In *Performing the US Latina and Latino Borderlands*, edited by Arturo J. Aldama, Chela Sandoval, and Peter J. Garcia, 344–62. Bloomington: Indiana University Press, 2012.

Ewen, Elizabeth, and Stuart Ewen. *Typecasting: On the Arts and Science of Human Inequality*. New York: Seven Stories Press, 2006.

Fadiman, Regina K. *Faulkner's "Intruder in the Dust": Novel into Film*. Knoxville: University of Tennessee Press, 1978.

Fernandez, Ronald. *The Disenchanted Island: Puerto Rico and the United States in the Twentieth Century*. 2nd ed. Westport, CT: Praeger, 1996.

Fields, Joseph, and Jerome Chodorov. *My Sister Eileen*. New York: Random House, 1941.

Fields, Joseph, and Jerome Chodorov, with Betty Comden and Adolph Green. *Wonderful Town: A New Musical Comedy*. New York: Random House, 1953.

Finn, Caryl. *From Brass Diva: The Life and Legends of Ethel Merman*. Berkeley: University of California Press, 2007.

Firmat, Gustavo Pérez. "Latunes: An Introduction." *Latin American Research Review* 43, no. 2 (2008): 180–203.

Flores, Juan. "Nueva York, Diaspora City: Latinos between and Beyond." In *Bilingual Games: Some Literary Investigations*, ed. Doris Sommer, 69–75. New York: Palgrave Macmillan, 2003.

Foster, David William. "Of Gay Caballeros and Other Noble Heroes." *Bilingual Review/ La Revista Bilingüe* (May–December 2008–9): 23–44.

France, Richard. *Orson Welles on Shakespeare: The W.P.A. and Mercury Theatre Playscripts.* New York: Routledge, 2013.

Fregoso, Rosa Linda. *The Bronze Screen: Chicana and Chicano Film Culture.* Minneapolis: University of Minnesota Press, 1993.

Fuller, Karla Rae. *Hollywood Goes Oriental: CaucAsian Performance in American Film.* Detroit: Wayne State University Press, 2010.

Fusco, Coco. *English Is Broken Here: Notes on Cultural Fusion in the Americas.* New York: New Press, 1995.

Fusco, Coco. "The Other History of Intercultural Performance." *TDR: The Drama Review* 38 (Spring 1994): 143–67.

Fusco, Coco, and Brian Wallis, eds. *Only Skin Deep: Changing Visions of the American Self.* New York: International Center of Photography and Harry N. Abrams, 2003.

Gan, Jessi. "'Still at the Back of the Bus': Sylvia Rivera's Struggle." *Centro Journal: Puerto Rican Queer Sexualities* 19 (Spring 2007): 125–39.

Garebian, Keith. *The Making of "West Side Story."* Toronto: ECW Press, 1995.

Garrett, Betty. *Betty Garrett and Other Songs: A Life on Stage and Screen.* Lanham, MD: Madison Books, 1999.

Geller, Lynn, and Leon Ichaso. "Leon Ichaso." *BOMB* 78 (Winter 2001–2): 36–41.

George, Nelson. *Blackface: Reflections on African-Americans and the Movies.* New York: Cooper Square Press, 2002.

Gilbert, James. *A Cycle of Outrage: America's Reaction to the Juvenile Delinquent in the 1950s.* New York: Oxford University Press, 1986.

Gilman, Sander L. *Difference and Pathology: Stereotypes of Sexuality, Race, and Madness.* Ithaca, NY: Cornell University Press, 1985.

Gilman, Sander L. *Diseases and Diagnoses: The Second Age of Biology.* New Brunswick, NJ: Transaction Publishers, 2011.

Gilroy, Paul. "Cruciality and the Frog's Perspective: An Agenda of Difficulties for the Black Arts Movement in Britain." *Third Text* 2 (Winter 1988): 33–44.

Ginsburgh, Victor, and Sheila Weyers. "On the Perceived Quality of Movies." *Journal of Cultural Economics* 23 (November 1999): 269–83.

Goldsby, Jackie. "What It Means to Be Colored Me." *Out/Look: The National Lesbian and Gay Quarterly* 2 (Summer 1990): 8–17.

Gomez, Laura. *Manifest Destinies: The Making of the Mexican American Race.* New York: New York University Press, 2007.

Gonzalez, Juan. *Harvest of Empire: A History of Latinos in America.* Rev. ed. New York: Penguin, 2011.

Gorman, Michael Robert. *The Empress Is a Man: Stories from the Life of José Sarria.* London: Haworth Press, 1998.

Greenspan, Charlotte. *Pick Yourself Up: Dorothy Fields and the American Musical.* New York: Oxford University Press, 2010.

Gutiérrez, David. *Walls and Mirrors: Mexican Americans, Mexican Immigrants, and the Politics of Ethnicity.* Berkeley: University of California Press, 1995.

Habell-Palan, Michelle. *Loca Motion: The Travels of Chicana and Latina Popular Culture.* New York: New York University Press, 2005.

Habell-Palan, Michelle, and Mary Romero, eds. *Latina/o Popular Culture.* New York: New York University Press, 2001.

Hadley-Garcia, George. *Hispanic Hollywood: The Latins in Hollywood.* Secaucus, NJ: Carol Publishing Group, 1990.

Hall, Stuart. "Encoding/Decoding." In *Media and Cultural Studies: Keyworks.* Rev. ed., edited by Meenakshi Gigi Durham and Douglas Kellner, 164–73. New York: Blackwell Publishing, 2006.

Hall, Stuart. *Representation: Cultural Representation and Signifying Practice.* Thousand Oaks, CA: Sage Publications, 1997.

Hall, Stuart. "The Whites of Their Eyes: Racist Ideologies and the Media." In *Silver Linings: Some Strategies for the Eighties,* edited by George Bridges and Rosalind Brunt, 28–52. London: Lawrence & Wishart, 1981.

Hames-Garcia, Michael. *Fugitive Thought: Prison Riots, Race, and the Meaning of Justice.* Minneapolis: University of Minnesota Press, 2004.

Hames-Garcia, Michael, and Ernesto Javier Martínez, eds. *Gay Latino Studies: A Critical Reader.* Durham, NC: Duke University Press, 2011.

Hardwick, Leon H. "Negro Stereotypes on the Screen." *Hollywood Quarterly* 1 (January 1946): 234–36.

Harris, Daniel. *The Rise and Fall of Gay Culture.* New York: Hyperion Books, 1997.

Harris, Mark. *Pictures at a Revolution: Five Movies and the Birth of the New Hollywood.* New York: Penguin, 2008.

Hart, Justin. *Empire of Ideas: The Origins of Public Diplomacy and the Transformation of U.S. Foreign Policy.* New York: Oxford University Press, 2013.

Haskell, Molly. *From Reverence to Rape: The Treatment of Women in the Movies.* New York: Holt, Rinehart and Winston, 1974.

Herrera, Brian Eugenio. "Compiling *West Side Story*'s Parahistories, 1949–2009." *Theatre Journal* 64, no. 2 (May 2012): 231–47.

Herrera, Brian Eugenio. "Toying with Desire." *TDR: The Drama Review* 58 (Winter 2014): 32–45.

Herzog, Amy. "Discordant Visions: The Peculiar Musical Images of the Soundies Jukebox Film." *American Music* 22, no. 1 (Spring 2004): 27–39.

Hinojosa, Maria. "Lin-Manuel Miranda." *One on One,* WGBH Boston. http://www.wgbh.org/org/programs/Maria-Hinojosa-One-on-One-12/episodes/Lin-Manuel-Miranda-15067. Accessed January 17, 2012.

Huerta, Jorge. *Chicano Drama: Performance, Society, and Myth.* New York: Cambridge University Press, 2000.

Huerta, Jorge. *Chicano Theatre: Themes and Forms.* Ypsilanti, MI: Bilingual Press, 1982.

Huerta, Jorge. "Looking for the Magic: Chicanos in the Mainstream." In *Negotiating Performance: Gender, Sexuality, and Theatricality in Latin/o America,* edited by Diana Taylor and Juan Villegas Morales, 37–48. Durham, NC: Duke University Press, 1994.

Jackson, Shannon. *Professing Performance: Theatre in the Academy from Philology to Performativity.* New York: Cambridge University Press, 2004.

Jacobson, John P., Jr. *Science for Segregation: Race, Law, and the Case against Brown v. Board of Education.* New York: New York University Press, 2005.

Jacobson, Matthew Frye. *Barbarian Virtues: The United States Encounters Foreign Peoples at Home and Abroad, 1876–1917.* New York: Hill And Wang, 2001.

Jacobson, Matthew Frye. *Roots Too: White Ethnic Revival in Post–Civil Rights America.* Cambridge, MA: Harvard University Press, 2006.

Jacobson, Matthew Frye. *Whiteness of a Different Color: European Immigrants and the Alchemy of Race.* Cambridge, MA: Harvard University Press, 1998.

James, Judith Giblin. "Carson McCullers, Lillian Smith, and the Politics of Broadway." In *Southern Women Playwrights: New Essays in Literary History and Criticism*, edited by Robert McDonald and Linda Rohrer Paige, 42–61. Tuscaloosa: University of Alabama Press, 2002.

Jamoo. *The Films of Kristen Bjorn*. Laguna Hills, CA: Companion Press, 1997.

Jeffers, Miles M. "The Negro on Broadway, 1945–1946." *Phylon* 7, no. 2 (1946): 185–96.

Jeffords, Susan, and Lauren Rabinowitz, eds. *Seeing through the Media: The Persian Gulf War*. New Brunswick, NJ: Rutgers University Press, 1994.

Jenkins, Henry. *The Wow Climax: Tracing the Emotional Impact of Popular Culture*. New York: New York University Press, 2007.

Jones, John Bush. *Our Musicals, Ourselves: A Social History of the American Musical Theatre*. Hanover, NH: Brandeis University Press and University Press of New England, 2003.

Jowitt, Deborah. *Jerome Robbins: His Life, His Theater, His Dance*. New York: Simon & Shuster, 2004.

Kamilipour, Yahya R., and Theresa Carilli, eds. *Cultural Diversity and the U.S. Media*. Albany: State University of New York Press, 1998.

Kanellos, Nicolás. *A History of Hispanic Theatre in the United States: Origins to 1940*. Austin: University of Texas Press, 1990.

Kanellos, Nicolás. *Mexican American Theatre: Legacy and Reality*. Pittsburgh: Latin American Literary Review, 1987.

Kanellos, Nicolás, ed. *Mexican American Theatre: Then and Now*. Houston: Arte Público Press, 1983.

Kanellos, Nicolás. *Nuevos Pasos: Chicano and Puerto Rican Drama*. Houston: Arte Público Press, 1989.

Kanellos, Nicolás. *Two Centuries of Hispanic Theatre in the Southwest*. New York: Players Press, 1982.

Kauffman, Daniel. *Ridiculous: The Theatrical Life and Times of Charles Ludlam*. New York: Applause Books, 2005.

Kauffman, J. B. *South of the Border with Disney: Walt Disney and the Good Neighbor Program, 1941–1948*. New York: Disney Editions, 2009.

Kenaga, Heidi. "Making the 'Studio Girl': The Hollywood Studio Club and Industry Regulation of Female Labour." *Film History* 18 (June 2006): 129–39.

Kimball, Robert, and Linda Emmett. *The Complete Lyrics of Irving Berlin*. New York: Hal Leonard Collection, 2005.

Kinn, Gail. *The Academy Awards: The Complete History of Oscar*. New York: Black Dog and Leventhal Publishing, 2002.

Knight, Arthur. *Disintegrating the Musical: Black Performance and American Musical Film*. Durham, NC: Duke University Press, 2002.

Knopf, Robert, ed. *Theater and Film: A Comparative Anthology*. New Haven, CT: Yale University Press, 2004.

Krasner, David. "I Hate Strasberg: Method Bashing in the Academy." In *Method Acting Reconsidered*, edited by David Krasner, 3–39. New York: St. Martin's, 2000.

Krasner, David. *Resistance, Parody, and Double Consciousness in African American Theatre, 1895–1910*. New York: St. Martin's, 1997.

La Fountain-Stokes, Lawrence. "Gay Shame, Latina- and Latino-Style: A Critique of White Queer Performativity." In *Gay Latino Studies: A Critical Reader*, edited by Michael Hames-Garcia and Ernest Javier Martínez, 55–80. Durham, NC: Duke University Press, 2011.

La Fountain-Stokes, Lawrence. *Queer Ricans: Cultures and Sexualities in the Diaspora.* Minneapolis: University of Minnesota Press, 2009.

Laufe, Abe. *Broadway's Greatest Musicals.* Rev. ed. New York: Funk & Wagnalls, 1977.

Laurents, Arthur. *Original Story By: A Memoir of Broadway and Hollywood.* New York: Knopf, 2000.

Laurents, Arthur. *West Side Story, a Musical.* New York: Random House, 1958.

Lawrence, Greg. *Dancing with Demons: The Life of Jerome Robbins.* New York: Putnam, 2001.

Lee, Robert G. *Orientals: Asian Americans in Popular Culture.* Philadelphia: Temple University Press, 1999.

Leguizamo, John. *Mambo Mouth: A Savage Comedy.* New York: Bantam Books, 1993.

Lemert, Charles, and Ann Branaman, eds. *The Goffman Reader.* Malden, MA: Blackwell, 1997.

Leval, Susana Torruella. "Recapturing History: The (Un)Official Story in Contemporary Latin American Art." *Art Journal* 51 (Winter 1992): 69–80.

Levine, Lawrence W. "The Folklore of Industrial Society: Popular Culture and Its Audiences." *American Historical Review* 97 (December 1992): 1369–1430.

Levine, Lawrence W. *The Unpredictable Past: Explorations in American Cultural History.* New York: Oxford University Press, 1993.

Levine, Martin P. *Gay Macho: The Life and Death of the Homosexual Clone.* Edited and introduced by Michael S. Kimmel. New York: New York University Press, 1998.

Levy, Emmanuel. *All About Oscar: The History and Politics of the Academy Awards, Updated Edition.* New York: Continuum, 2003.

Levy, Emmanuel. *Oscar Fever: The History and Politics of the Academy Awards.* New York: Continuum Books, 2002.

Lippman, Walter. *Public Opinion.* New York: Free Press, 1997. Originally published in 1922.

Lockhart, Tara. "Jennifer Lopez: The New Wave of Border Crossing." In *From Bananas to Buttocks: The Latina Body in Popular Film and Culture,* ed. Myra Mendible, 149–66. Austin: University of Texas Press, 2007.

Logan, Joshua. *Movie Stars, Real People, and Me.* New York: Delacorte Press, 1978.

LoMonaco, Martha Schmoyer. *Every Week, a Broadway Revue: The Tamiment Playhouse, 1921–1960.* Westport, CT: Greenwood Press, 1992.

López, Ian Haney. "Race on the 2010 Census: Hispanics and the Shrinking White Majority." *Daedalus* 134 (Winter 2005): 42–52.

Mapp, Edward. *African Americans and the Oscar: Decades of Struggle and Achievement.* 2nd ed. Lanham, MD: Scarecrow Press, 2008.

Marchetti, Gina. *Romance and the "Yellow Peril": Race, Sex, and Discursive Strategies in Hollywood Fiction.* Berkeley: University of California Press, 1993.

Markson, Elizabeth W., and Carol A. Taylor. "Real versus Reel World: Older Women and the Academy Awards." *Women and Therapy* 14 (June 1993): 157–72.

Marquez, Roberto. "One Boricua's Baldwin: A Personal Remembrance." *American Quarterly* 42, no. 3 (September 1990): 456–77.

Marron, Maggie. *Ricky Martin.* New York: Michael Friedman Publishing, 1999.

Martin, Waldo E. *Brown v. Board of Education: A Brief History with Documents.* New York: Macmillan, 1998.

Marubbio, M. Elise. *Killing the Indian Maiden: Images of Native American Women in Film.* Lexington: University Press of Kentucky, 2006.

Mazón, Mauricio. *The Zoot-Suit Riots: The Psychology of Symbolic Annihilation.* Austin: University of Texas Press. 1984.

McCall, Leslie. "The Complexity of Intersectionality." *Signs: Journal of Women in Culture and Society* 30 (Spring 2005): 1771–1800.

McClurg, Bruce D. *Lady in the Dark: Biography of a Musical.* New York: Oxford University Press, 2006.

McConachie, Bruce. *Melodramatic Formations: American Theatre and Society, 1820–1870.* Iowa City: University of Iowa Press, 1992.

McDougal, Dennis. *The Last Wasserman, MCA, and the Hidden History of Hollywood.* New York: Da Capo Press, 2001.

McKenney, Ruth. "Beware the Brazilian Navy." *New Yorker,* July 10, 1937, 28–35.

McKenney, Ruth. *My Sister Eileen.* New York: Harcourt, Brace, 1938.

McKenzie, Jon. *Perform or Else: From Discipline to Performance.* New York: Routledge, 2001.

McLean, Adrienne L. *Being Rita Hayworth: Labor, Identity, and Hollywood Stardom.* New Brunswick, NJ: Rutgers University Press, 2004.

McMains, Juliet. "Brownface: Representations of Latin-ness in Dancesport." *Dance Research Journal* 33 (Winter 2001): 54–71.

Meade, Marion. *Lonelyhearts: The Screwball World of Nathaniel West and Eileen McKenney.* New York: Houghton Mifflin, 2010.

Melgosa, Adrián Pérez. "Opening the Cabaret America Allegory: Hemispheric Politics, Performance, and Utopia in *Flying Down to Rio*." *American Quarterly* 64, no. 2 (June 2012): 249–75.

Melnick, Jeffrey, and Rachel Rubin. *Immigration and American Popular Culture: An Introduction.* New York: New York University Press, 2006.

Mercer, Kobena. *Welcome to the Jungle: New Positions in Black Cultural Studies.* New York: Routledge, 1994.

Merritt, Greg. *Celluloid Mavericks: The History of American Independent Film.* New York: Basic Books, 2000.

Michael, Paul. *The Academy Awards: A Pictorial History.* New York: Bonanza Books, 1974.

Miller, Margo. "Masculinity and Male Intimacy in Nineties Sitcoms: *Seinfeld* and the Ironic Dismissal." In *The New Queer Aesthetic on Television: Essays on Recent Programming,* edited by James R. Keller and Leslie Tratyner, 147–59. Jefferson, NC: McFarland, 2006.

Mixon, Wayne. *The People's Writer: Erskine Caldwell and the South.* Charlottesville: University of Virginia Press, 1995.

Molina-Guzmán, Isabel. *Dangerous Curves: Latina Bodies in the Media.* New York: New York University Press, 2010.

Molina-Guzmán, Isabel. "Mediating Frida: Negotiating Discourses of Latina/o Authenticity in Global Media Representations of Ethnic Identity." *Critical Studies in Media Communication* 23 (August 2006): 232–51.

Molina-Guzmán, Isabel, and Angharad N. Valdivia. "Brain, Brow, and Booty: Latina Iconicity in U.S. Popular Culture." *Communication Review* 7 (April–June 2004): 205–21.

Montalban, Ricardo, with Bob Thomas. *Reflections: A Life in Two Worlds.* New York: Doubleday, 1980.

Moraga, Cherríe, and Gloria Anzaldúa. *This Bridge Called My Back: Writings by Radical Women of Color.* Boston: South End Press, 1983.

Morales, Ed. *The Latin Beat: The Rhythms and Roots of Latin Music, from Bossa Nova to Salsa and Beyond.* Cambridge, MA: Da Capo Press, 2003.

Mordden, Ethan. *Broadway Babies: The People Who Made the Broadway Musical.* New York: Oxford University Press, 1986.

Mordden, Ethan. *Coming Up Roses: The Broadway Musical in the 1950s.* New York: Oxford University Press, 1998.

Moreno, Rita. *Rita Moreno: A Memoir.* New York: Celebra Hardcover, 2013.

Most, Andrea. "Re-imagining the Jew's Body." In *You Should See Yourself: Jewish Identity in Postmodern American Culture,* ed. Vincent Brook, 19–36. New Brunswick, NJ: Rutgers University Press, 2006.

Moten, Fred. *In the Break: The Aesthetics of the Black Radical Tradition.* Minneapolis: University of Minnesota Press, 2003.

Muñoz, José Esteban. "Dead White: Notes on the Whiteness of the New Queer Cinema." *GLQ: A Journal of Lesbian and Gay Studies* 4, no. 1 (1998): 127–38.

Muñoz, José Esteban. *Disidentifications: Queers of Color and the Performance of Politics.* Minneapolis: University of Minnesota Press, 1999.

Nama, Adilifu. *Black Space: Imagining Race in Science Fiction Film.* Austin: University of Texas Press, 2010.

Naremore, James. *Acting in the Cinema.* Berkeley: University of California Press, 1990.

Negrón-Muntaner, Frances. *Boricua Pop: Puerto Ricans and the Latinization of American Culture.* New York: New York University Press, 2004.

Negrón-Muntaner, Frances. "Feeling Pretty: 'West Side Story' and Puerto Rican Identity Discourses." *Social Text* 18 (Summer 2000): 83–106.

Negrón-Muntaner, Frances. "Jennifer's Butt." *Aztlán: A Journal of Chicano Studies* 22 (Fall 1997): 182–95.

Negrón-Muntaner, Frances. "Selling Out Puerto Rican Identity in the Global Market." In *Contested Images: Women of Color in Popular Culture,* edited by Alma M. Garcia, 137–56. Lanham, MD: AltaMira Press, 2012.

Nelson, Randy A., with Michael R. Donihue, Donald M. Waldman, and Calbraith Wheaton. "What's an Oscar Worth?" *Economic Inquiry* 39 (January 2001): 1–16.

Nericcio, William Anthony. "Autopsy of a Rat: Odd, Sundry Parables of Freddy Lopez, Speedy Gonzales, and Other Chicano/Latino Marionettes Prancing around Our First World Emporium." *Camera Obscura* 37 (January 1996): 189–237.

Nericcio, William Anthony. *Tex[t]-Mex: Seductive Hallucinations of the "Mexican" in America.* Austin: University of Texas Press, 2007.

Nero, Charles I. "Why Are Gay Ghettoes White?" In *Black Queer Studies: A Critical Anthology,* edited by E. Patrick Johnson and Mae G. Henderson, 228–49. Durham, NC: Duke University Press, 2005.

Newman, Harry. "Holding Back: The Theatre's Resistance to Non-Traditional Casting." *TDR: The Drama Review* 33 (Autumn 1989): 22–36.

Newman, Louise. *White Women's Rights: The Racial Origins of Feminism in the United States.* New York: Oxford University Press, 1999.

Ngai, Mae M. "The Architecture of Race in American Immigration Law: A Reexamination of the Immigration Act of 1924." *Journal of American History* 86 (June 1999): 67–92.

Ngai, Mae M. *Impossible Subjects: Illegal Aliens and the Making of Modern America.* Princeton, NJ: Princeton University Press, 2004.

Ngai, Mae M. "The Strange Career of the Illegal Alien: Immigration Restriction and Deportation Policy in the United States, 1921–1965." *Law and History Review* 21 (Spring 2003): 69–107.

Ngai, Sianne. "'A Foul Lump Started Making Promises in My Voice': Race, Affect, and the Animated Subject." *American Literature* 74 (September 2002): 571–601.

Niccolini, Dianora, with David Leddick. *Big Fun with Billy.* New York: Universe Publishing, 2001.

Noriega, Chon A. "Birth of the Southwest: Social Protest, Tourism, and D. W. Griffith's Ramona." In *The Birth of Whiteness: Race and the Emergence of U.S. Cinema,* edited by Daniel Bernardi, 203–26. New Brunswick, NJ: Rutgers University Press, 1996.

Noriega, Chon A., ed. *Chicanos and Film.* Minneapolis: University of Minnesota Press, 1992.

Noriega, Chon A. *Shot in America: Television, the State, and the Rise of Chicano Cinema.* Minneapolis: University of Minnesota Press, 2000.

Nyong'o, Tavia. "Racial Kitsch and Black Performance." *Yale Journal of Criticism* 12 (Fall 2002): 371–91.

Olivier, Laurence. *On Acting.* New York: Simon & Schuster, 1986.

Omi, Michael, and Howard Winant. *Racial Formation in the United States: From the 1960s to the 1980s.* New York: Routledge, 1994.

Orenstein, Dara. "Void for Vagueness: Mexicans and the Collapse of Miscegenation Law in California." *Pacific Historical Review* 74 (August 2005): 367–407.

Ortiz Cofer, Judith. "The Myth of the Latin Woman: I Just Met a Girl Named María." In *The Latin Deli: Prose and Poetry by Judith Ortiz Cofer,* 148–54. Athens: University of Georgia Press, 1993.

Osborne, Robert. *Academy Awards Illustrated.* Hollywood: Marvin Miller Enterprises, 1965.

Osborne, Robert. *85 Years of the Oscar: The Official History of the Academy Awards.* New York: Abbeville Press, 2013.

Ovalle, Priscilla Peña. *Dance and the Hollywood Latina: Race, Sex, and Stardom.* New Brunswick, NJ: Rutgers University Press, 2011.

Pachon, Harry, Louis DiSipio, Rodolfo O. de la Garza, and Chon A. Noriega. *Missing in Action: Latinos In and Out of Hollywood.* Los Angeles: Tomás Rívera Policy Institute and Screen Actors Guild, 1999.

Pachon, Harry, Louis DiSipio, Rodolfo O. de la Garza, and Chon A. Noriega. *Still Missing in Action: Latinos In and Out of Hollywood.* Los Angeles: Tomás Rívera Policy Institute and Screen Actors Guild, 2000.

Pao, Angelo Chia-yi. "False Accents: Embodied Dialects and the Characterization of Ethnicity and Nationality." *Theatre Topics* 14 (March 2004): 353–72.

Pao, Angelo C. *No Safe Spaces. Re-casting Race, Ethnicity, and Nationality in American Theater.* Ann Arbor: University of Michigan Press, 2010.

Paredez, Deborah. "'Queer for Uncle Sam': Anita's Diva Citizenship in 'West Side Story.'" *Latino Studies Journal* 12, no. 3 (2014): 332–52.

Paredez, Deborah. *Selenidad: Selena, Latinos, and the Performance of Memory.* Durham, NC: Duke University Press, 2009.

Paris, Barry. *Audrey Hepburn.* New York: Putnam, 1996.

Peiss, Kathy. *Zoot Suit: The Enigmatic Career of an Extreme Style.* Philadelphia: University of Pennsylvania Press, 2011.

Pellegrini, Ann. "Women on Top, Boys on the Side, but Some of Us Are Brave: Blackness, Lesbianism, and the Visible. *College Literature* 59 (February 1997): 83–97.

Perez, Hiram. "Two or Three Spectacular Mulatas and the Queer Pleasures of Overidentification." *Camera Obscura* 23 (July 2008): 112–43.

Perez, Louis A. *On Becoming Cuban: Identity, Nationality, and Culture.* New York: Harper Perennial, 2001.

Peyser, Joan. *Bernstein: A Biography.* Rev. and updated ed. New York: Billboard Books, 1998.

Phelan, Peggy. *Unmarked: The Politics of Performance.* New York: Routledge, 1993.

Pike, Fredrick B. *FDR's Good Neighbor Policy: Sixty Years of Generally Gentle Chaos.* Austin: University of Texas Press, 1995.

Pippins, Jan, with Henry Darrow. *Henry Darrow: Lightning in a Bottle.* Duncan, OK: BearManor Media, 2013.

Pond, Steve. *Big Show: High Times and Dirty Dealings Backstage at the Academy Awards.* Boston: Faber and Faber, 2006.

Pratt, George C. *Spellbound in Darkness: A History of the Silent Film.* Boston: Little Brown, 1973.

Preston, John. "Goodbye to Sally Gearhart." In *The Christopher Street Reader,* edited by Michael Denneny, Charles Ortleb, and Thomas Steele, 368–80. New York: Perigree Books, 1983.

Prida, Dolores. *"Beautiful Señoritas" and Other Plays.* Houston: Arte Público Press, 1991.

Pullen, Kirsten. *Actresses and Whores: On Stage and in Society.* Cambridge: Cambridge University Press, 2005.

Pullen, William A. "The Ramona Pageant: A Historical and Analytical Study" (PhD diss., University of Southern California, 1973).

Quinn, Anthony. *The Original Sin: A Self-Portrait.* New York: Little Brown, 1972.

Quiroga, José. *Tropics of Desire: Interventions from Queer Latino America.* New York: New York University Press, 2000.

Ramírez, Elizabeth C. *Chicanas/Latinas in American Theatre: A History of Performance.* Bloomington: Indiana University Press, 2000.

Ramírez, Jason. "The Case of The Capeman: Appropriation of the 'Authentic.'" *Aztlán: A Journal of Chicano Studies* 30 (Spring 2005): 179–92.

Ramírez Berg, Charles. *Latino Images in Film: Stereotypes, Subversion, Resistance.* Austin: University of Texas Press, 2002.

Rand, Erica. *Barbie's Queer Accessories.* Durham, NC: Duke University Press, 1995.

Rapping, Elayne. "'My Own Private Idaho' and 'Longtime Companion.'" In *MediaThons: Forays into the Gender and Culture Wars,* 131–34. Boston: South End Press, 1994.

Ravid, S. Abraham. "Information, Blockbusters, and Stars: A Study of the Film Industry." *Journal of Business* 72 (October 1999): 463–92.

Real, Michael R. *Exploring Media Culture: A Guide.* Thousand Oaks, CA: Sage Publications, 1996.

Rechy, John. *Sexual Outlaw: A Documentary.* New York: Grove Press, 1984.

Reinehr, Robert C., and Jon D. Swarts. *The A to Z of Old Time Radio.* Lanham, MD: Scarecrow Press, 2010.

Retzloff, Tim. "Eliding Trans Latino/a Queer Experience in U.S. LGBT History: José Sarria and Sylvia Rivera Reexamined." *Centro Journal: Puerto Rican Queer Sexualities* 19, no. 1 (Spring 2007): 141–61.

Reyes, Luis, and Peter Rubie. *Hispanics in Hollywood.* Hollywood, CA: Lone Eagle Publishing, 2000.

Richards, Beah E. *Black Woman Speaks.* In *9 Plays by Black Women,* edited and introduced by Margaret B. Wilkerson, 29–39. New York: New American Library, 1986.

Richards, Graham. *Race, Racism, and Psychology: Towards a Reflexive History.* New York: Routledge, 1997.

Rivera, Geraldo. *His Panic: Why Americans Fear Hispanics in the U.S.* New York: Penguin, 2008.

Rivera-Servera, Ramón H. *Performing Queer Latinidad: Dance, Sexuality, Politics.* Ann Arbor: University of Michigan Press, 2012.

Roach, Joseph. *Cities of the Dead: Circum-Atlantic Performance.* New York: Columbia University Press, 1996.

Roach, Joseph. *It.* Ann Arbor: University of Michigan Press, 2007.

Roach, Joseph. *The Player's Passion: Studies in the Science of Acting.* Ann Arbor: University of Michigan Press, 1993.

Roach, Tom. *Friendship as a Way of Life: Foucault, AIDS, and the Politics of Shared Estrangement.* Albany: State University of New York Press, 2012.

Roberts, John Storm. *Latin Jazz: The First of the Fusions, 1880s to Today.* New York: Schirmer Books, 1999.

Roberts, John Storm. *The Latin Tinge: The Impact of Latin American Music on the United States.* New York: Oxford University Press, 1979.

Rodríguez, Chantal. "Living the Politics of *Teatro* in Los Angeles: An Interview with Diane Rodriguez." *Latin American Theatre Review* 43 (Fall 2009): 143–49.

Rodriguez, Clara. *Changing Race: Latinos, the Census, and the History of Ethnicity in the United States.* New York: New York University Press, 2000.

Rodriguez, Clara. *Heroes, Lovers, and Others: The Story of Latinos in Hollywood.* Washington, DC: Smithsonian Institution Press, 2004.

Rodriguez, Clara, ed. *Latin Looks: Latino Images in the Media.* Boulder, CO: Westview Press, 1997.

Rogin, Michael. *Blackface, White Noise: Jewish Immigrants in the Hollywood Melting Pot.* Berkeley: University of California Press, 1996.

Román, David. *Acts of Intervention: Performance, Gay Culture, and AIDS.* Bloomington: Indiana University Press, 1998.

Román, David. "Latino Performance and Identity." *Aztlán: A Journal of Chicano Studies* 22 (Fall 1997): 151–67.

Román, David. *Performance in America: Contemporary U.S. Culture and the Performing Arts.* Durham, NC: Duke University Press, 2005.

Román, David. "A Streetcar Named *Deseo.*" Paper presented at the annual meeting of the American Society of Theatre Research, Chicago, Illinois, August 3–6, 2006.

Román, David. "Tropical Fruit." In *Tropicalizations: Transcultural Representations of Latinidad,* edited by Frances R. Aparicio and Susana Chávez-Silverman, 119–35. Hanover, NH: Dartmouth College Press, 1997.

Román, Miriam Jiménez. "Notes on Eusebia Cosme and Juano Hernández." In *The Afro-Latin@ Reader: History and Culture in the United States,* edited by Miriam Jiménez Román and Juan Flores, 319–22. Durham, NC: Duke University Press, 2010.

Rosello, Mireille. *Declining the Stereotype: Ethnicity and Representation in French Cultures.* Hanover, NH: University Press of New England, 1997.

Ross, Murray. "Labor Relations in Hollywood." *Annals of the American Academy of Political and Social Science* 254 (November 1947): 58–64.

Rossini, Jon D. *Contemporary Latina/o Theatre: Wrighting Ethnicity.* Carbondale: Southern Illinois University Press, 2008.

Rubin, Rachel Lee, and Jeffrey Paul Melnick. *Immigration and American Popular Culture: An Introduction.* New York: New York University Press, 2007.

Ruiz, Vicki. "Nuestra América: Latino History as United States History." *Journal of American History* 93 (December 2006): 655–72.

Russo, Vito. *The Celluloid Closet: Homosexuality in the Movies.* New York: Harper & Row, 1981.

Saldívar, José David. "Nuestra America's Borders: Remapping American Cultural Studies." In *José Martí's "Our America,"* edited by Jeffrey Belnap and Raúl Fernandez, 145–78. Durham, NC: Duke University Press, 1998.

Salisbury, Harrison E. *The Shook-Up Generation.* New York: Harper & Brothers, 1958.

Sandoval-Sánchez, Alberto. *"José, Can You See?" Latinos On and Off Broadway.* Madison: University of Wisconsin Press, 1999.

Savran, David. "Choices Made and Unmade." *Theater* 31 (Summer 2001): 89–95.

Schechner, Richard. "Race Free, Gender Free, Body-Type Free, Age Free Casting." *TDR: The Drama Review* 33 (Spring 1989): 4–12.

Schneider, Eric C. *Vampires, Dragons, and Egyptian Kings: Youth Gangs in Postwar New York.* Princeton, NJ: Princeton University Press, 1999.

Sebesta, Judith. "Just 'Another Puerto Rican with a Knife'? Racism and Reception on the 'Great White Way.'" *Studies in Musical Theatre* 1 (August 2007): 183–97.

Serling, Christopher H. *Encyclopedia of Radio.* Vol. 1. New York: Taylor and Francis, 2003.

Shah, Nayan. *Contagious Divides: Epidemics and Race in San Francisco's Chinatown.* Berkeley: University of California Press, 2001.

Shaheen, Jack G. *Reel Bad Arabs: How Hollywood Vilifies a People.* New York: Olive Branch Press, 2001.

Shandler, Jeffrey. *Jews, God, and Videotape: Religion and Media in America.* New York: New York University Press, 2009.

Shange, Ntozake. *For Colored Girls Who Have Considered Suicide When the Rainbow Is Enuf: A Choreopoem.* New York: Macmillan, 1977.

Shary, Tim. *Teen Movies: American Youth on Screen.* New York: Columbia University Press, 2005.

Sheridan, Clare, and Steven H. Wilson, with Ariela J. Gross. "Forum—Whiteness and Others: Mexican Americans and American Law." *Law and History Review* 23 (Spring 2003): 109–213.

Shilts, Randy. *The Mayor of Castro Street.* New York: St. Martin's, 1982.

Shohat, Ella, and Robert Stam. *Unthinking Eurocentrism: Multiculturalism and the Media.* New York: Routledge, 1994.

Simonson, Robert. *On Broadway Men Still Wear Hats.* New York: Smith & Kraus, 2004.

Singer, Kurt. *The Danny Kaye Story.* New York: Thomas Nelson and Sons, 1958.

Skal, David J. *Screams of Reason: Mad Science and Modern Culture.* New York: W. W. Norton, 1998.

Smith, David Lionel. "The Black Arts Movement and Its Critics." *American Literary History* 3 (Spring 1991): 93–110.

Smith, Peter H. *Talons of the Eagle: Dynamics of U.S.–Latin American Relations.* New York: Oxford University Press, 2000.

Smith, Shawn Michelle. *Photography on the Color Line: W. E. B. Du Bois, Race, and Visual Culture.* Durham, NC: Duke University Press, 2004.

Smoodin, Eric L. *Animating Culture: Hollywood Cartoons from the Sound Era.* New Brunswick, NJ: Rutgers University Press, 1993.

Smoodin, Eric L., ed. *Disney Discourse: Producing the Magic Kingdom.* New York: Routledge, 2013.

Sondheim, Stephen. *Finishing the Hat: Collected Lyrics (1954–1981) with Attendant Comments, Principles, Heresies, Grudges, Whines, and Anecdotes*. New York: Knopf, 2010.

Sondheim, Stephen. *Look, I Made a Hat: Collected Lyrics (1981–2011) with Attendant Comments, Amplifications, Dogmas, Harangues, Digressions, Anecdotes, and Miscellany*. New York: Knopf, 2011.

States, Bert O. *Irony and Drama: A Poetics*. Ithaca, NY: Cornell University Press, 1971.

Stavans, Ilan. *The Hispanic Condition: Reflections on Culture and Identity in America*. New York: HarperCollins, 1996.

Stedman, Raymond William. *Shadows of the Indian: Stereotypes in American Culture*. Norman: University of Oklahoma Press, 1982.

Steele, Claude M. *Whistling Vivaldi and Other Clues as to How Stereotypes Affect Us*. New York: W. W. Norton, 2010.

Suderburg, Erika. "Real/Young/TV Queer." In *Between the Sheets, in the Streets*, edited by Chris Holmlund and Cynthia Fuchs, 46–70. Minneapolis: University of Minnesota Press, 1997.

Sun, William H. "Power and Problems of Performance across Ethnic Lines: An Alternative Approach to Nontraditional Casting." *TDR: The Drama Review* 44 (Winter 2000): 86–95.

Suskin, Steven. *Show Tunes: The Songs, Shows, and Careers of Broadway Major Composers*. New York: Oxford University Press, 2000.

Taylor, Diana. *The Archive and the Repertoire: Performing Cultural Memory in the Americas*. Durham, NC: Duke University Press, 2003.

Taylor, Diana. "Remapping Genre through Performance: From 'American' to 'Hemispheric' Studies." *PMLA* 122 (October 2007): 1416–30.

Tchen, John Kuo Wei. *New York before Chinatown: Orientalism and the Shaping of American Culture, 1776–1882*. Baltimore: Johns Hopkins University Press, 2001.

Thomas, Joe A. "Gay Male Pornography since Stonewall." In *Sex for Sale: Prostitution, Pornography, and the Sex Industry*, edited by Ronald Weitzer, 67–90. New York: Routledge, 2009.

Thomas, Lorrin. *Puerto Rican Citizen: History and Political Identity in Twentieth-Century New York City*. Chicago: University of Chicago Press, 2010.

Toelken, Barre. *Dynamics of Folklore*. Rev. and expanded ed. Logan: Utah State University Press, 1996.

Traber, Daniel S. "L.A.'s 'White Minority': Punk and the Contradictions of Self-Marginalization." *Cultural Critique* 48 (Spring 2001): 30–64.

Trujillo-Pagán, Nicole. "'Charo' (María Rosario Pilar Martínez Molina Baeza) (1942–)." In *Latinas in the United States: A Historical Encyclopedia*, edited by Vicki L. Ruíz and Virginia Sánchez Korrol, 144–45. Bloomington: Indiana University Press, 2006.

Turner, Patricia. *I Heard It through the Grapevine: Rumor in African American Culture*. Berkeley: University of California Press, 1994.

Umpierre, Luz María. "Interview with Dolores Prida," *Latin American Theatre Review* 22 (Fall 1998): 81–85.

Valdez, Luis, and El Teatro Campesino. *Actos*. San Juan Batista, CA: Menyah Productions, 1971.

Valdivia, Angharad N. *"A Latina in the Land of Hollywood" and Other Essays on Media Culture*. Tucson: University of Arizona Press, 2000.

Valdivia, Angharad N. "Stereotype or Transgression? Rosie Perez in Hollywood Film." *Sociological Quarterly* 39 (June 1998): 393–408.

Van Leer, David. *The Queening of America: Gay Culture in Straight Society*. New York: Routledge, 1995.

Van Leer, David. "Visible Silence: Spectatorship in Black Gay and Lesbian Film." In *Representing Blackness: Issues in Film and Video,* edited by Valerie Smith, 157–181. New Brunswick, NJ: Rutgers University Press, 1997.

Vazquez, Alexandra T. *Listening in Detail: Performances of Cuban Music.* Durham, NC: Duke University Press, 2013.

Vertrees, May. "Some Ingredients of a First-Year Puchero." *Hispania* 6 (March 1923): 93–101.

Vogel, Shane. "Jamaica on Broadway: The Popular Caribbean and Mock Transnational Performance." *Theatre Journal* 62, no. 1 (March 2010): 1–21.

Wainscott, Ronald Harold. *The Emergence of the Modern American Theater, 1914–1929.* New Haven, CT: Yale University Press, 1997.

Wald, Gayle. *Crossing the Line: Racial Passing in Twentieth Century U.S. Literature and Culture.* Durham, NC: Duke University Press, 2000.

Walker, Alexander. *Audrey: Her Real Story.* New York: Macmillan, 1997.

Wanzo, Rebecca. "Beyond a 'Just' Syntax: Black Actresses, Hollywood, and Complex Personhood." *Women and Performance: A Journal of Feminist Theory* 16 (March 2006): 135–52.

Watts, Jill. *Hattie McDaniel: Black Ambition, White Hollywood.* New York: HarperCollins, 2005.

Weisenfeld, Judith. *Hollywood Be Thy Name: African American Religion in American Film, 1929–1949.* Berkeley: University of California Press, 2007.

Wiley, Mason, and Damien Bona. *Inside Oscar: The Unofficial History of the Academy Awards.* 10th anniversary ed. New York: Ballantine Books, 1996.

Williams, Raymond. *Drama in Performance.* New York: Basic Books, 1968.

Williams, Raymond. *Keywords: A Vocabulary of Culture and Society.* London: Oxford University Press, 1992.

Williamson, Catherine. "'Draped Crusaders': Disrobing Gender in the 'Mark of Zorro.'" *Cinema Journal* 36, no. 2 (Winter 1997): 3–16.

Wilson, Clint C., with Félix Gutiérrez and Lena M. Chao, eds. *Racism, Sexism, and the Media: The Rise of Class Communication in Multicultural America.* Thousand Oaks, CA: Sage Publications, 2003.

Winick, Judd. *Pedro and Me: Friendship, Loss, and What I Learned.* New York: Henry Holt, 2000.

Wojcik, Pamela Roberston. "Typecasting." *Criticism* 45 (Spring 2003): 223–49.

Wolf, Stacy. *Changed for Good: A Feminist History of the Broadway Musical.* New York: Oxford University Press, 2011.

Wolf, Stacy. *A Problem Like Maria: Gender and Sexuality in the American Musical.* Ann Arbor: University of Michigan Press, 2002.

Woll, Allen L. *The Latin Image in American Film.* Los Angeles: Latin American Center Publications, University of California, Los Angeles, 1980.

Wood, Bryce. *Dismantling the Good Neighbor Policy.* Austin: University of Texas Press, 1985.

Yagoda, Ben. *About Town: The New Yorker and the World It Made.* New York: Scribner, 2000.

Yoakem, Lola G. "Casting." *Film Quarterly* 12 (Winter 1958): 36–42.

Zegri, Armando. "Spanish Americans Invade Broadway." *Americas* 10, no. 11 (November 1958): 26–30.

Zuniga, José. *Soldier of the Year: The Story of a Gay American Patriot.* New York: Pocket Books, 1994.

Index